Virginia
REAL ESTATE
Practice & Law

TENTH EDITION

Doris Barrell, GRI, DREI, CDEI, Consulting Editor

Dearborn™
Real Estate Education

This publication is designed to provide accurate and authoritative information in regard to the subject matter covered. It is sold with the understanding that the publisher is not engaged in rendering legal, accounting, or other professional advice. If legal advice or other expert assistance is required, the services of a competent professional should be sought.

President: Dr. Andrew Temte
Chief Learning Officer: Dr. Tim Smaby
Executive Director, Real Estate Education: Melissa Kleeman-Moy
Development Editor: Christopher Kugler

VIRGINIA REAL ESTATE PRACTICE & LAW TENTH EDITION
©2015 Kaplan, Inc.
Published by DF Institute, Inc., d/b/a Dearborn Real Estate Education
332 Front St. S., Suite 501
La Crosse, WI 54601

Printed in the United States of America

ISBN: 978-1-4754-2539-0 / 1-4754-2539-2
PPN: 1510-3510

Contents

CHAPTER 9
Leasing Real Estate in Virginia   158

CHAPTER 10
Virginia Fair Housing Law   178

APPENDIX A
Exclusive Right to Sell Listing Agreement   190

APPENDIX B
Exclusive Right to Represent Purchaser Agreement   201

APPENDIX C
Information Sources   206

Introduction

Although real estate activity in Virginia is subject to federal laws and regulations, it is controlled primarily by Virginia's laws, rules, and regulations and by state customs that prevail where no law covers a particular practice.

Virginia Real Estate Practice & Law offers real estate professionals a practical handbook of Virginia's real estate law and rules, along with the most current developments. Every effort has been made to ensure that the information contained in this book is both relevant and current. There are numerous references to Virginia statutes and the Real Estate Board's Rules and Regulations, enabling readers to look up the law themselves online or in most public and university libraries.

Virginia Real Estate Practice & Law is a component of Dearborn™ Real Estate Education's Complete Learning System. It may be used effectively with other Dearborn products:

- *Modern Real Estate Practice*
- *Real Estate Fundamentals*
- *Mastering Real Estate Principles*
- *Virginia Real Estate Principles online course*

The conversion chart on the inside front cover indicates which chapter or chapters in some of the national products correspond with your Virginia-specific text. We hope the conversion chart will be helpful as you study for your real estate exam.

Each chapter in this book is followed by a quiz. These quizzes serve as both learning and teaching devices. As you finish each chapter, and before going on to the next, be sure that you can answer each question and that you understand all the material covered. When you have completed the course, take the 75-question practice examination. An answer key for all questions is included before the Appendices.

ABOUT THE CONSULTING EDITOR

Doris Barrell, GRI, DREI, CDEI, has been in the real estate business for over 30 years, working first for a builder-developer, then as a general brokerage agent, and for nine years as managing broker for a 60-agent office in Alexandria, Virginia. She has brought this wealth of real-life experience into the classroom and in her writing on the subjects of real estate finance, agency, fair housing, ethics, diversity, and legal and legislative issues.

Doris is author of *Real Estate Finance Today*, *Know the Code: Real Estate Ethics*, *Everyday Ethics in Real Estate*, and *Essentials of Real Estate Finance, 14th Edition*, all published by Dearborn Real Estate Education. She is also a teaching consultant for the International Real Property Foundation, bringing real estate education to countries in Eastern Europe and Southeast Asia. Additionally, Doris has served as a senior instructor for NeighborWorks® America training institutes held in cities throughout the United States and as a Master Trainer for the National Association of REALTORS®.

■ ACKNOWLEDGMENTS

This new edition owes much to its reviewer, JoAnn Kokindo, associate broker, Long and Foster Real Estate.

Earlier editions of *Virginia Real Estate Practice & Law* were made possible with the assistance of F.A. Dan Daniels, ABR, principal broker of Governmental Employees Realty Associates, Alexandria, Virginia, and Florence L. Daniels, GRI, Associate Broker of Governmental Employees Realty Associates, Alexandria, Virginia.

CHAPTER 1

Virginia Real Estate Law

LEARNING OBJECTIVES *After successfully completing this chapter, you will be able to*

- **review** definitions included in Title 54.1 of the Code of Virginia;
- **state** the purpose and responsibilities of the Real Estate Board (REB) and the Common Interest Community (CIC) Board;
- **list** requirements and exemptions for licensing in Virginia;
- **describe** the use of the Virginia Real Estate Transaction Fund;
- **explain** the changes to the Virginia Residential Property Disclosure Act; and
- **identify** other state and federal legislation affecting real estate practice.

KEY TERMS

associate broker	Fair and Accurate	principal broker
broker	Credit Transaction Act	salesperson
CAN-SPAM Act	(FACTA)	sole proprietor
Do Not Call Registry	firm	stigmatized property
	licensee	subrogate
	managing broker	

The practice of real estate in the Commonwealth of Virginia is governed under the Code of Virginia in Title 54.1 – Professions and Occupations, and Title 55 – Property and Conveyances. The Virginia General Assembly is solely responsible for creating and amending the Code of Virginia. The General Assembly meets in January/February each year and any changes to the Code generally take place as of July 1 of the current year although some exceptions may be made. For example, changes to agency law usually require a longer period of time before enactment to allow time for the Virginia Real Estate Board to prepare new rules and regulations and required forms.

■ TITLE 54.1 – PROFESSIONS AND OCCUPATIONS

Chapter 3

Chapter 3 of Title 54.1 covers the Department of Professional and Occupational Regulation (DPOR). The Board for Professional and Occupational Regulation consists of nine members appointed by the Governor for staggered four-year terms. The Board meets at least four times a year.

Real Estate Board (REB)   As part of the DPOR, the Real Estate Board (REB) is charged with issuing regulations that further describe what will be expected of both salespersons and brokers. All regulations must be consistent with the Code of Virginia. The agency rules and regulations of the Real Estate Board can be found in the Virginia Administrative Code (VAC), Title 18 – Professional and Occupational Licensing. The Real Estate Board is Agency 135. A detailed discussion of Virginia Real Estate License Law can be found in Chapter 8 of this book.

Common Interest Community (CIC) Board   The Common Interest Community Board is a separate agency within the DPOR (agency 48). The Board was established to regulate Common Interest Community Managers by means of a licensure program. Also included under the CIC Board are four acts that were formerly regulated by the Real Estate Board:

- Condominium Act
- Real Estate Time-Share Act
- Real Estate Cooperative Act
- Property Owners' Association Act

The licensure program for Common Interest Community Managers (CIC Managers) requires licensing for firms providing management services. Permanent regulations for CIC Managers became effective on April 1, 2010. Each CIC Manager must have at least one qualifying supervisory employee with five years of experience in providing management services, and each must complete a comprehensive 80-hour CIC Manager Training Program, approved by the CIC Board. In addition, 50% of persons who have principal responsibility for management services will have to meet specific experience requirements, hold a specified designation, or complete an introductory 16-hour CIC Manager Training Program approved by the CIC Board.

Agency Rules and Regulations for the Common Interest Community Board are found in the Virginia Administrative Code (VAC) in Title 18, Agency 48.

References may be made throughout this text to either the Code of Virginia, Title 54.1 (Chapter 21, Professions and Occupations) (§54.1 et seq.) and Title 55 – Property and Conveyances or to VAC, Title 18 (18 VAC 135-10 et seq.) or (18 VAC 48-10 et seq.).

The most recent issue of the Rules and Regulations for both the Real Estate Board and the Common Interest Community Board are available from the Department of Professional and Occupational Regulation, 9960 Mayland Drive, Suite 400, Richmond, VA 23233. All licensees, real estate brokers, and real estate salespersons are responsible for staying informed about licensing laws, regulations, and current changes.

The REB can be contacted with questions about the laws or regulations governing the practice of real estate in Virginia via email (reboard@dpor.virginia.gov) or phone (804-367-8526).

Information is also available on the internet. Search Code of Virginia or Virginia Administrative Code on the Virginia General Assembly Legislative Information System (LIS) at http://leg1.state.va.us/lis.htm. This website also provides information on historical and current actions taken by the General Assembly.

Chapter 21

Chapter 21 of Title 54.1 covers Real Estate Brokers and Salespersons in Articles 54.1-2100 (Definitions) through the most recent Article 54.1-2146 that allows licensees to maintain required documents electronically in accordance with the Uniform Electronic Transaction Act.

Brokerage Definitions   In Virginia, a real estate **broker** is defined by statute as

> any person or business entity, including, but not limited to, a partnership, association, corporation, or limited liability corporation, who, for compensation or valuable consideration (i) sells or offers for sale, buys or offers to buy, or negotiates the purchase or sale or exchange of real estate, including units or interest in condominiums, cooperative interest . . . or time-shares in a time-share program . . . or (ii) leases or offers to lease, or rents or offers for rent, any real estate or the improvements thereon for others. (§54.1-2100)

In practice, the word *broker* may refer to a firm, a sole proprietor who transacts real estate business, a managing broker for a branch office of a larger firm, or a person who holds a broker's license but practices under the supervision of a principal broker (i.e., an associate broker). It is important to note that the brokerage relationship is established between the *broker* (principal broker or sole proprietor) as the *agent* and the *client* as the *principal*. All supervising brokers, managing brokers, associate brokers, and salespersons are general agents of the principal broker. There can only be one principal broker of a brokerage.

The statutory definition of a real estate **salesperson** is

> any person, or business entity of not more than two persons unless related by blood or marriage, who for compensation or valuable consideration is employed either directly or indirectly by, or affiliated as an independent contractor with, a real estate broker, to sell or offer to sell, or to buy or offer to buy, or to negotiate the purchase, sale, or exchange of real estate, or to lease, rent or offer for rent any real estate, or to negotiate leases thereof, or of the improvements thereon. (§54.1-2101)

Although a salesperson may generally perform the same functions as a broker, the salesperson must be employed by or affiliated with a licensed real estate broker. Brokers are expected to supervise all activities of the salespersons affiliated with their company and are responsible for the actions of every salesperson.

Brokers and salespersons can be further defined according to their specific roles within a brokerage firm. Any licensed broker or salesperson may prepare written contracts for the sale, purchase, option, exchange, or rental of real estate provided the preparation of such contracts is incidental to a real estate transaction in which the licensee is involved and does not charge a separate fee for preparing the contract (§54.1-2101.1).

Other definitions to be familiar with:

- **Firm**—any sole proprietorship (broker-owned or non-broker-owned) partnership, association, limited liability company, or corporation, other than a sole proprietorship (principal-broker-owned) that is required by regulation to obtain a separate brokerage firm license.
- **Sole proprietor**—an individual, not a corporation, who is doing business under either his or her own name or under a legally registered fictitious name. A licensed broker who is a sole proprietor shall have the same responsibilities as a principal broker. A sole proprietor who is not licensed must designate a licensed broker to perform the duties of a principal broker.
- **Licensee**—any person, partnership, association, limited liability company, or corporation that holds a license issued by the Virginia Real Estate Board (REB) to act as a real estate broker or salesperson.
- **Principal broker**—the individual broker designated by each firm to ensure compliance with Chapter 21 of Title 54.1 of the Code of Virginia and to receive all communications and notices from the REB that may affect the firm and/or its licensees. In the case of a sole proprietorship, the licensed broker who is the sole proprietor has the responsibilities of the principal broker. The principal broker shall have responsibility for the activities of the firm and all of its licensees.
- **Managing broker** (or *supervising broker*)—an individual associate broker who shall be designated by the firm to supervise the activities of a branch office.
- **Associate broker**—any individual licensed as a broker who practices within a brokerage firm as a sales associate. An associate broker is required to meet the same educational, experience, and testing requirements as a principal broker but is subject to the same restrictions of brokerage activity as a salesperson.
- **Standard agent**—a licensee, either broker or salesperson, who acts for or represents a client in an agency relationship according to the statutory duties later described in Chapter 2 – Brokerage Relationships and Agency.
- **Limited service agent**—performs only specific duties of a standard agent as agreed upon between agent and client.
- **Independent contractor**—a licensee who acts for or represents a client according to a written contract between the licensee and the client. This is a specific distinction pertaining to agency law and is not related to the definition of independent contractor as used for tax purposes by the Internal Revenue Service (IRS).

- **Common source information company**—any person or entity that compiles or provides information regarding real estate for sale or lease and other data and includes, but is not limited to, a multiple-listing service (MLS). No broker or salesperson license is required.
- **Distance learning**—instruction delivered by an approved provider through a medium other than a classroom setting.

Licensing Requirements   Any person or business entity that performs or advertises brokerage services must be licensed by the Real Estate Board (REB) as established in Chapter 21, §54.1-2104 (the general powers of the REB and all specific licensing requirements are described in Chapter 8). Licenses are issued for individuals, partnerships, limited liability companies (LLCs), associations, corporations, and non-broker-owned sole proprietorships. The license may be granted in a fictitious name, that is, a name other than that of the principal broker.

IN PRACTICE   A principal broker who wishes to operate and be called ABC Realty must obtain a broker's license as a principal broker, and ABC Realty must obtain a separate firm license.

A salesperson whose name is difficult to say and wishes to be known by a pseudonym must obtain a license in her real name with a "dba" (doing business as) for the pseudonym endorsement.

A salesperson who heads a team of licensees within a brokerage and wishes to advertise under the team name must obtain a business entity license for the team.

Every principal broker shall have the following readily available to the public: the business entity or firm license, the managing broker's license, and a roster of every salesperson and broker assigned to the office. If a firm has more than one physical location (e.g., branch offices), then all actual licenses are to be held at the firm's main office, with the exception of the entity's branch office license, which shall be available at the branch office. Every resident real estate broker must maintain a place of business in Virginia.

An individual with a broker's license may operate as a sole proprietor (sole proprietorship—broker-owned) without further licensure unless the sole proprietorship operates under a fictitious name, in which case a separate brokerage firm license is required.

Additional regulations for a firm license include the following:

- Every member or officer who actively participates in brokerage business must hold a license as a broker.
- Every employee or independent contractor who acts as a salesperson must hold a license as either salesperson or broker.
- A salesperson and a broker may not be principals in a firm together. By law, all salespersons come under the *supervision* of a principal broker.

A separate branch office license must be issued for each branch office of a brokerage firm, including the name of the supervising broker. The branch office license and a roster of every salesperson and broker assigned to the branch office shall be available to the public in each branch office.

Any person or firm engaging in unlicensed real estate activity will be subject to action by the REB and a civil penalty not to exceed $1,000 for any real estate transaction or the compensation received (§54-1.2105.2).

The requirements for license stated here pertain only to the practice of real estate in the Commonwealth of Virginia as governed by Title 54.1, Chapter 21 of the Code of Virginia and Title 18 of the Virginia Administrative Code. Further licensing or authority to conduct a brokerage business at a specific physical location is usually required by local jurisdictions.

Exemptions   Not everyone who performs an act of real estate brokerage or related real estate activities is required to hold a Virginia real estate license. The following are a few examples of persons exempt from the state licensing requirement:

- Any individual persons or firms or their employees who are selling or renting their own property
- Any person acting without compensation as attorney-in-fact under a power of attorney issued by a property owner
- Attorneys involved in real estate transactions in their normal role as attorneys
- Any person acting as a receiver, trustee, administrator, or executor
- Licensed auctioneers selling real estate at public auction

Virginia Real Estate Transaction Recovery Fund   The Virginia Real Estate Transaction Recovery Fund (§54.1-2112 et seq.) was established for the purpose of reimbursing parties who suffer monetary loss due to a licensee's improper or dishonest conduct.

Maintenance of the Fund   The establishment and maintenance of the fund is the duty of the Director of the DPOR. The cost of administering the fund is paid out of interest earned on deposits. The REB may, at its discretion, use part of the interest earned by the fund for research and education for the benefit of licensees.

Each new licensee, whether salesperson or broker, must pay $20 into the fund. The fund's minimum balance is $400,000. If the balance of the fund falls below $400,000, the REB may assess each active and inactive licensee a proportionate amount to bring the balance to the statutory minimum. No licensee may be assessed more than $20 during any two-year period ending on June 30 of even-numbered years. Licensees who fail to pay the assessment within 45 days of receiving the first notice are given a second notice. Failure to pay the assessment within 30 days of the second notice results in automatic suspension of the licensee's license. The licensee will be suspended until such time as the director receives the amount due. The REB has the power to assess all licensees at one time or on individual licensees' renewals.

At the close of each fiscal year, if the balance of the fund is more than $2 million, the excess amount over $2 million is transferred to the Virginia Housing Trust Fund (see Virginia Housing Development Authority [VHDA] in Chapter 6).

Claims Procedure   A person who files a claim for payment from the fund must first obtain a judgment against the licensee from a Virginia court of competent authority. After a licensee has been found guilty of misconduct, the injured party must take appropriate legal action against the licensee. Appropriate legal action includes

- forcing the sale of the licensee's assets to satisfy all or part of the claim;
- investigating any listings held by the licensee and determining any commissions that may be due;
- filing a claim in bankruptcy court, if the licensee has filed bankruptcy; and
- requiring the licensee to submit to interrogatories, if necessary.

If any portion of the claim remains unsatisfied, the individual may file a claim with the REB requesting payment from the fund for the unsatisfied portion of the claim within 12 months from the date of the final judgment.

A claimant must have pursued all legal means for possible recovery before a claim can be filed with the REB. On receipt of a claim, the REB will promptly consider the request and notify the claimant, in writing, of its findings.

Limitation on Recovery   The amount of the claim is limited to actual monetary damages suffered in the transaction, court costs, and attorney's fees. The claim cannot include interest, punitive, or exemplary damages, even though these amounts may have been included in the judgment awarded by the court.

If at any time the amount of claims to be paid from the fund would deplete the fund to an amount below the statutory minimum of $400,000, the processing of all claims will be suspended. The REB will assess licensees as previously outlined. As funds become available to satisfy the pending claims, the claims will be paid in the order in which they were originally received.

In all cases, the REB may withhold payment of any claim for 12 months if it has reason to believe that additional claims may be filed. In the event that there are multiple claims against a licensee that exceed the maximum allowable payment from the fund, each claimant will receive a proportionate share of the total payment.

Single transaction: In a single transaction, the maximum payment from the fund to all injured parties is $50,000. The maximum amount any single claimant may recover from the fund based on a single transaction is $20,000, regardless of the number of claimants.

Multiple transactions: If the same licensee is involved in multiple fraudulent transactions during any two-year period ending June 30 of even-numbered years, the maximum payment to all claimants combined is $100,000.

If a payment is made from the fund, the claimant must **subrogate** the rights to the REB. Subrogation permits the REB to take action against the licensee to recover the amount of claims paid due to the licensee's misconduct.

Penalty   Payment from the fund causes the licensee's license to be immediately revoked. The respondent may also be subject to other disciplinary action by the REB. The licensee may not apply for a new license until the fund has been repaid in full, plus interest at the judgment rate of interest from the date of payment from the fund.

Repayment to the fund does not guarantee that the license will be reissued. The REB may take disciplinary action against a licensee for a disciplinable violation whether or not the licensee has reimbursed the fund.

Law of Agency   The Virginia Law of Agency is covered in articles §54.1-2130 through §54.1-2144 and will be discussed in detail in Chapter 2.

■ TITLE 55 – PROPERTY AND CONVEYANCES

The Chapters from Title 55 – Property and Conveyances that have significant impact on the practice of real estate in Virginia are the following:

- Chapter 1 – Creation and Limitation of Estates
- Chapter 4.2 – Condominium Act
- Chapter 21 – Virginia Real Estate Time-Share Act
- Chapter 24 – Virginia Real Estate Cooperative Act
- Chapter 26 – Property Owners' Association Act

These five chapters will be covered in Chapter 3:

- Chapter 13 – Landlord and Tenant is covered in detail in Chapter 9.

- Chapter 27 – The Virginia Residential Property Disclosure Act is covered in detail in this chapter.

- Chapter 27.3 – Consumer Real Estate Settlement Protection Act is covered in detail in Chapter 7.

- Chapter 36 – Fair Housing is covered in detail in Chapter 10.

■ VIRGINIA RESIDENTIAL PROPERTY DISCLOSURE ACT

The Virginia Residential Property Disclosure Act has undergone significant changes since first enacted in 1992. The act has always applied to transfers by sale, exchange, installment land sales contract, or lease with option to buy for residential property of one to four dwelling units. The act applies whether or not the transaction is with the assistance of a licensed real estate broker or salesperson (§55-517). Most property owners attempting to sell a property on their own are not aware that they are also subject to this act.

Exemptions

There are exemptions to the provisions of the act, which include the following:

- Transfers pursuant to court order
- Transfers pursuant to a foreclosure sale
- Transfers made in the course of administration of an estate guardianship, conservatorship, or trust
- Transfers from one or more co-owners solely to one or more other co-owners
- Transfers made between spouses resulting from divorce or property settlement

- Transfers made by virtue of the owner's failure to pay federal, state, or local taxes
- Transfers to or from any governmental entity
- Transfers involving the first sale of a dwelling; the builder is still responsible to disclose all known material defects which would constitute a violation of applicable building code.

Disclosure Forms

In 2007, the General Assembly implemented a new law eliminating the old disclosure and disclaimer forms. The new form contained only disclosures mandated by the General Assembly. The Real Estate Board was charged with developing a Residential Property Disclosure Form by January 1, 2008. This form was subject to frequent changes over the years and created a concern that a wrong form could be used, putting the contract in jeopardy.

As of July 1, 2011, the REB form directs the purchaser to a website maintained by the REB for a list of seller's representations (see Figures 1.1 and 1.2). Although the responsibility for receiving disclosure information has been shifted to the purchaser, a licensee can print out the site's contents and provide it to the purchaser at the seller's discretion or if required by contract.

FIGURE 1.1

Residential Property Disclosure Statement

RESIDENTIAL PROPERTY DISCLOSURE STATEMENT
NOTICE TO SELLER AND PURCHASER

> The Virginia Residential Property Disclosure Act (§ 55-517 et seq. of the Code of Virginia) requires the owner of certain residential real property, whenever the property is to be sold or leased with an option to buy, to furnish this form to the purchaser and to refer the purchaser to a Virginia Real Estate Board website for additional information.
>
> Certain transfers of residential property are excluded from this requirement (see § 55-518).

Property Address/
Legal Description: _____

The owner makes no representations with respect to the matters set forth and described at the RESIDENTIAL PROPERTY DISCLOSURES web page. The purchaser is advised to consult the website (http://www.dpor.virginia.gov/dporweb/reb_consumer._cfm) for important information about the real property.

The undersigned owner(s) represents that there are no pending enforcement actions pursuant to the Uniform Statewide Building Code (§ 36-97 et seq.) that affect the safe, decent, and sanitary living conditions of the real property described above of which the owner has been notified in writing by the locality, nor any pending violation of the local zoning ordinance which the violator has not abated or remedied under the zoning ordinance, within a time period set out in the written notice of violation from the locality or established by a court of competent jurisdiction, except as disclosed on this statement.

_____

_____

_____

_____

_____

_____

The owner(s) acknowledge having carefully examined this statement and further acknowledge that they have been informed of rights and obligations under the Virginia Residential Property Disclosure Act.

_____ _____   _____ _____
       Owner   Date   Owner   Date

The purchaser(s) acknowledge receipt of a copy of this disclosure statement and further acknowledge that they have been informed of their rights and obligations under the Virginia Residential Property Disclosure Act.

_____ _____   _____ _____
      Purchaser   Date   Purchaser   Date

DPOR 7/11

Residential Property Disclosures

RESIDENTIAL PROPERTY DISCLOSURES

NOTICE TO SELLER AND PURCHASER

> The Virginia Residential Property Disclosure Act (§ 55-517 et seq. of the *Code of Virginia*) governs the information owners must disclose to prospective purchasers of real property. Certain transfers of residential property are excluded from the requirements (see § 55-518).

Property Address/
Legal Description: _____

1. **CONDITION:** The undersigned owner(s) of the real property described above makes no representations or warranties as to the condition of the real property or any improvements thereon, and the purchaser(s) is advised to exercise whatever due diligence the purchaser(s) deems necessary including obtaining a certified home inspection, as defined in § 54.1-500, in accordance with the terms and conditions as may be contained in the real estate purchase contract, but in any event, prior to settlement on the parcel of residential real property.

2. **ADJACENT PARCELS:** The undersigned owner(s) makes no representations with respect to any matters that may pertain to parcels adjacent to the subject parcel, and the purchaser(s) is advised to exercise whatever due diligence the purchaser(s) deems necessary with respect to adjacent parcels in accordance with terms and conditions as may be contained in the real estate purchase contract, but in any event, prior to settlement on the parcel of residential real property.

3. **HISTORIC DISTRICT ORDINANCES(S):** The undersigned owner(s) makes no representations to any matters that pertain to whether the provisions of any historic district ordinance affect the property, and the purchaser(s) is advised to exercise whatever due diligence the purchaser(s) deems necessary with respect to any historic district designated by the locality pursuant to §15.2-2306, including review of any local ordinance creating such district or any official map adopted by the locality depicting historic districts, in accordance with terms and conditions as may be contained in the real estate purchase contract, but in any event, prior to settlement on the parcel of residential real property.

4. **RESOURCE PROTECTION AREAS:** The undersigned owner(s) makes no representations with respect to whether the property contains any resource protection areas established in an ordinance implementing the Chesapeake Bay Preservation Act (§ 10.1-2100 et seq.) adopted by the locality where the property is located pursuant to § 10.1-2109, and the purchaser(s) is advised to exercise whatever due diligence the purchaser(s) deems necessary to determine whether the provisions of any such ordinance affect the property, including review of any official map adopted by the locality depicting resource protection areas, in accordance with terms and conditions as may be contained in the real estate purchase contract, but in any event, prior to settlement on the parcel of residential real property.

FIGURE 1.2

Residential Property Disclosures (Cont.)

5. **SEXUAL OFFENDERS:** The undersigned owner(s) makes no representations with respect to information on any sexual offenders registered under Chapter 23 (§ 19.2-387 et seq.) of Title 19.2, and the purchaser(s) is advised to exercise whatever due diligence the purchaser(s) deems necessary with respect to such information, in accordance with terms and conditions as may be contained in the real estate purchase contract, but in any event, prior to settlement pursuant to that contract.

6. **DAM BREAK INUNDATION ZONE(S):** The undersigned owner(s) makes no representations with respect to whether the property is within a dam break inundation zone and the purchaser(s) is advised to exercise whatever due diligence the purchaser(s) deems necessary with respect to whether the property resides within a dam break inundation zone, including a review of any map adopted by the locality depicting dam break inundation zones.

7. **STORMWATER DETENTION:** The undersigned owner(s) makes no representations with respect to the presence of any stormwater detention facilities located on the property and the purchaser(s) is advised to exercise whatever due diligence the purchaser(s) deems necessary to determine the presence of any stormwater detention facilities on the property, in accordance with terms and conditions as may be contained in the real estate purchase contract, but in any event, prior to settlement pursuant to that contract.

8. **WASTEWATER SYSTEM:** The undersigned owner(s) makes no representations with respect to the presence of any wastewater system, including the type or size thereof or associated maintenance responsibilities related thereto, located on the property and the purchaser(s) is advised to exercise whatever due diligence the purchaser(s) deems necessary to determine the presence of any wastewater system on the property, in accordance with terms and conditions as may be contained in the real estate purchase contract, but in any event, prior to settlement pursuant to that contract.

9. **SOLAR ENERGY COLLECTION DEVICE(S):** The owner makes no representations with respect to any right to install or use solar energy collection devices on the property.

FIGURE 1.2

Residential Property Disclosures (Cont.)

Additional Written Disclosure Requirements

FIRST SALE OF A DWELLING: Section 55-518.B. contains other disclosure requirements for transfers involving the first sale of a dwelling because the first sale of a dwelling is exempt from the disclosure requirements listed above. The builder of a new dwelling shall disclose in writing to the purchaser thereof all known material defects which would constitute a violation of any applicable building code.

PLANNING DISTRICT 15: In addition, for property that is located wholly or partially in any locality comprising Planning District 15, the builder or owner, if the builder is not the owner of the property, shall disclose in writing whether the builder or owner has any knowledge of (i) whether mining operations have previously been conducted on the property or (ii) the presence of abandoned mines, shafts, or pits, if any.

The disclosures required by this subsection shall be made by a builder or owner (i) when selling a completed dwelling, before acceptance of the purchase contract or (ii) when selling a dwelling before or during its construction, after issuance of a certificate of occupancy. Such disclosure shall not abrogate any warranty or any other contractual obligations the builder or owner may have to the purchaser. The disclosure required by this subsection may be made on this disclosure form. If no defects are known by the builder to exist, no written disclosure is required by this subsection.

Section 55-519.1 contains a disclosure requirement for properties located in any locality in which there is a military air installation.

Section 32.1-164.1:1 contains a disclosure requirement regarding the validity of septic system operating permits.

See also the Virginia Condominium Act (§ 55-79.39 et seq.), the Virginia Cooperative Act (§ 55-424 et seq.) and the Virginia Property Owners' Association Act (§ 55-508 et seq.).

DPOR 7/13

Legislation enacted in 2011 requires the disclosure on both sales and leasing transactions of known defective drywall on the appropriate REB disclosure form (§55-519.2). As of July 1, 2014, disclosure must be made if the seller has actual knowledge that a home was once used to create methamphetamine, unless the property has been thoroughly cleaned according to Virginia Department of Health guidelines.

At or before settlement, the owner is only required to disclose any material change from the original disclosures. The recertification form was eliminated in 2014.

Time for Disclosure and Purchaser's Options

The disclosure is required before contract ratification by the seller and buyer. If the disclosure is received after contract ratification, the sole remedy for the purchaser is to terminate the contract by giving written notice to the seller. Once the disclosure is received by the buyer, notice to terminate must be given to the seller

- within three days if the notice is hand-carried;
- within five days of postmark, if the notice is mailed;
- prior to settlement;
- prior to occupancy if occupancy occurs before settlement; or
- prior to loan application where the loan application discloses that the right of contract terminations ends when the loan application is taken.

The purchaser may allow the contract to remain valid if she provides a notice of waiver of rights to terminate the contract or remains silent and does nothing.

If the purchaser elects to terminate the contract in accordance with the disclosure law, she may do so without any penalty. Any monies already paid by the purchaser, such as earnest money deposits, must be returned.

Buyer's Recourse

If the buyer learns of defects that either were not disclosed or were misrepresented in the disclosure statement, the buyer is entitled to seek recourse. Any action brought under this act must be commenced within one year from the date the disclosure was delivered. If no disclosure was delivered, action must be commenced within one year of settlement, or within one year of occupancy in the event of lease with option to buy.

The owner is not liable for any error, inaccuracy, or omission of information in the disclosure form if the information was provided to the owner by a reliable third party, such as a surveyor, engineer, appraiser, home inspector, or public authority. The owner is also not liable if she reasonably believed the information to be correct and there was no gross negligence involved.

Liability for Licensee

A real estate licensee cannot be liable for misrepresentation if he relied on information provided by a client, public record, or reliance on representations of another regulated professional (this was clarified as of July 1, 2014). However, a licensee must disclose material adverse facts pertaining to the physical condition of the property that are actually known by the licensee (§54.1-2131B, 18 VAC 135-20-300(2)).

IN PRACTICE A real estate salesperson, is hosting an open house during a rainstorm. While no one is being shown the property, he notices that there is a leak in the attic and water seepage in the basement. He must disclose that information to any prospective buyers as an adverse material defect in the property, regardless of the owner's wishes. If he fails to inform a prospective buyer about the leaking and seepage, he may be found guilty of misrepresentation.

Stigmatized Property

Stigmatized property refers to any property that is made undesirable by some event or circumstance that had no actual effect on its physical structure, environment, or improvements. For example, a house in which a homicide, felony, or suicide occurred may be tainted by that event and be difficult to sell. Buyers may hesitate to make an offer on a property that is reputed to be haunted or one in which the current or former occupant suffered from a communicable disease.

Disclosure of this type of information, which in Virginia has been determined to be immaterial, is not required. In fact, a licensee who represents a seller and discloses stigmatizing information to a buyer could be construed as having breached responsibilities to the client if the buyer cancels the contract due to the disclosure. The failure to disclose this information does not subject either the owner or a licensee to disciplinary action by the courts or the REB. There is also no disciplinary action of a licensee who does disclose such information as long as the seller has approved of such disclosure. The only topic of disclosure that is specifically prohibited is any discussion of HIV or AIDS. If information is disclosed regarding persons infected with HIV, a licensee could be in violation of fair housing laws and the federal privacy act.

■ OTHER LEGISLATION AFFECTING REAL ESTATE PRACTICE

Federal Law

In addition to Fair Housing Law, there are other federal laws that directly affect the practice of real estate.

National Do Not Call Registry

The federal government created the **National Do Not Call Registry** to help consumers avoid unwanted telemarketing calls. Anyone can register online at www.donotcall.gov or by calling 888-382-1222. As of June 2003, cell phone numbers can also be placed on the register. Violators are subject to civil penalties of up to $16,000 per violation.

Exemptions Individuals who use cold calling as a prospecting tool must comply with the provisions of the National Do Not Call Registry. Exemptions to the rule are as follows:

■ Consumers with whom the caller has an existing relationship (this applies to existing clients and customers and extends for up to 18 months after the end of a transaction)

- In response to a consumer inquiry or application (calls can be made for up to three months after the inquiry)
- Persons who have granted express written permission to call

In addition, the rules do not apply to

- charities,
- political organizations,
- telephone surveyors, or
- certain non-profit organizations.

On January 1, 2005, the FTC and FCC rules made it mandatory to check a phone number against a version of the registry that is no more than 31 days old before placing a telemarketing call. An annual fee is charged for accessing individual area codes (the fee per area code in 2014 was $59 or $16.28 for all area codes). Five area codes are available at no cost. A salesperson should always check with the broker before making random calls.

Visit https://telemarketing.donotcall.gov to register and obtain current fees.

CAN-SPAM Act

The **CAN-SPAM Act** of 2003 (Controlling the Assault of Non-Solicited Pornography and Marketing) became effective January 1, 2004. It was designed to create a national standard to control the growing problem of deceptive or fraudulent commercial email and outlines a series of practices that email senders must follow. It does not just apply to bulk email; it covers all electronic mail messages with the primary purpose of advertising or promoting a product or service (for example, an email notice for a new listing in the neighborhood).

Each separate email in violation of the CAN-SPAM Act is subject to a penalty up to $16,000. The main CAN-SPAM requirements are listed below:

- Don't use false or misleading header information.
- Don't use deceptive subject lines.
- Identify the message as an advertisement.
- Tell recipients where you are located (a physical postal address).
- Tell recipients how to opt out of receiving future emails from you.
- Honor opt-out requests promptly (within 10 days).
- Monitor what others are doing on your behalf (for example, even if you hire a marketing company, you are still responsible).

CAN-SPAM information can be found at www.business.ftc.gov/documents/bus61-can-spam-act-compliance-guide-business.

FACTA

The **Fair and Accurate Credit Transaction Act (FACTA)** was enacted in 2003 and is primarily concerned with credit report issues. There is part of the act, however, that deals with protecting the consumer from identity theft that does involve office procedures for a real estate firm.

The FACTA Disposal Rule requires office policies to:

- burn, pulverize, or shred papers containing consumer report information;

- destroy or erase electronic files or media containing consumer report information; and
- conduct due diligence and hire a document destruction contractor to dispose of material identified as consumer report information.

FACTA information can be found at www.ftc.gov and search FACTA.

MAP Rule

A new FTC ruling on Mortgage Acts and Practices – Advertising Rule (MAP Rule), which took effect on August 19, 2011, impacts real estate professionals who provide information about mortgage credit products to consumers. The rule would apply when a licensee provides a buyer with information about a specific mortgage product, for example, rate sheets with current interest rate from a specific lender. Providing a buyer general information about market rates for different types of mortgage products would not be subject to the MAP Rule because these are not related to a specific product. Also, going through a prequalification process with the buyer in order to determine the range of properties that the consumer may be eligible to purchase will not require compliance with the MAP Rule. However, providing the buyer with documentation needed to apply for a preapproval from a lender is covered under the MAP Rule. The rule does not apply to purely informational communications not designed to cause the purchase of a particular good or service.

American Taxpayer Relief Act of 2012

Tax Deductions   The American Taxpayer Relief Act of 2012 was signed into law on January 2, 2013. The bill extends mortgage cancellation relief for homeowners or sellers who had some of their mortgage debt forgiven by a lender, typically in a short sale or foreclosure sale for sellers and in a modification for owners. Without the extension, any debt forgiven would have been taxable. The extension expired at the end of 2013, which may have contributed to the drop in the number of short sales. The deduction for mortgage insurance premiums for tax filers making less than $110,000 also expired at the end of 2013, along with the tax credit for energy-efficient home improvements. Legislation is pending for a continued extension for both issues. Deductions for state and local property taxes remain deductible.

One bright spot as of 2014 is the simplified home-office deduction. Instead of providing detailed expense records, you can now simply deduct $5.00 for every square foot of home office space, up to a maximum of 300 square feet, or $1,500. The simplified expense is reported on Schedule C along with other business expenses.

Tax Rates   The current tax rates were extended for all households earning less than $450,000 and $400,000 for individual filers. For households earning above these limits, tax rates revert to where they were in 2003. That means taxpayers in the highest bracket will pay taxes on ordinary income at a rate of 39.6%, up from 35%. The change in rate can have an impact on net profits for investment properties.

The tax rate on capital gains remains the same at 15% for most households. For those earning above the $400,000 to $450,000 threshold, the rate rises to 20%.

Also included in the legislation is the continued exclusion from taxes for gains on a principal residence sale of up to $500,000 ($250,000 for individuals). However, homesellers with incomes of $450,000 or higher are now required to pay federal taxes on the excess capital gains at the higher rate. For the majority of homesellers, there is no change.

The other key provision is a change in the estate tax so that estates will be taxed at a top rate of 40%, with the first $5 million in value exempted for individual estates and $10 million for family estates.

National Flood Insurance

The ability to obtain flood insurance at a reasonable cost is important to more than 5.6 million business and homeowners throughout the country. In July 2012, Congress passed the Flood Insurance Reform Act, ensuring that the program will remain in effect for another five years. In March 2014, Congress passed the Homeowner Flood Insurance Affordability Act, which calls for a four-year timeout on rate increases triggered by a sale or flood map update. Buyers will now assume the sellers' October 2013 rate. The availability of affordable flood insurance can impact real estate transactions in over 21,000 communities nationwide in areas where the Federal Emergency Management Agency (FEMA) flood maps indicate that flood insurance is required in order to obtain approval for a mortgage loan.

News from RESPA

- The Home Warranty Clarification Act of 2012 was passed by the House in August 2012. This bill restated the original intention by Congress that homeowner warranties are not covered by RESPA regulations. Unfortunately, no action was taken by the Senate. There has long been confusion over whether or not the RESPA regulations allow for a real estate broker to receive a fee from a home warranty company for introducing either a seller or a buyer to a home warranty plan. The fee paid by a warranty company to a broker can be determined to be a form of kickback, which is prohibited by RESPA regulations.
- For some time, many real estate professionals have desired that both the good faith estimate (GFE) required under RESPA and the truth-in-lending (TIL) statement required by the Truth in Lending Act, which are provided to applicants for mortgage loans, be simplified and combined. A proposal was issued on July 9, 2012, by the Consumer Financial Protection Bureau (CFPB) that includes the hoped-for changes to the GFE and TIL along with other provisions. The CFPB proposal also includes some exceptions to the mandatory three-day waiting period required under the Truth in Lending Act. The proposal remains in a comment period during 2014.
- The U.S. Supreme Court ruled on May 24, 2012, that a split of a settlement-service fee paid by a consumer to a real estate settlement-service provider is only a violation of RESPA regulations if the fee is split with a third party.

EPA Delays Proposed Lead Paint Regulations

The Environmental Protection Agency (EPA) has agreed to delay the release of proposed regulations for activities involving lead paint in commercial and public buildings until July 1, 2015. These regulations would have covered proposed renovation, repair, and painting of the exterior of commercial buildings. Any final rule impacting real estate is not expected until late in the year 2016.

New Rules from Consumer Financial Protection Bureau (CFPB)

The Dodd-Frank Wall Street Reform and Consumer Protection Act of 2010 established the Consumer Financial Protection Bureau (CFPB). Its central mission is stated as making consumer financial products and services work better for Americans whether applying for a mortgage, selecting a credit card, or using any type of consumer financial products.

The CFPB has released new rules on how mortgage servicers must treat borrowers that took effect on January 10, 2014, and apply to all mortgage servicers with 5,000 or more loans. The goal of the new regulations is to make sure that servicers cannot take advantage of borrowers who fall behind on their payments. The new CFPB rules are discussed further in Chapter 6.

■ STATE AND LOCAL LAW

Virginia Utility Damage Prevention Act

An additional statute that can have impact on residential property is the Virginia Underground Utility Damage Prevention Act, which requires that anyone planning construction on any site must contact "Miss Utility" so that flags can be placed to protect existing utility lines.

The act states that "no person . . . shall make or begin any excavation or demolition without first notifying the notification center for that area" (§56-265.17 A).

This also pertains to real estate signs placed on utility easements in the front of properties to increase visibility for potential customers. The notification center must be called before excavating to install a sign.

For additional information regarding the act, contact the State Corporation Commission's Division of Utility and Railroad Safety at 800-552-7945 or visit www .scc.virginia.gov/urs/index.aspx.

■ NEW IN 2013

Northern Virginia versus EPA

In January 2013, a federal judge granted relief to landowners by ruling that the U.S. Environmental Protection Agency (EPA) overstepped its authority with its plan to regulate storm water runoff in Fairfax County's Accotink Creek Watershed. The Northern Virginia Association of REALTORS® joined with other members of the development community in supporting the lawsuit filed by the Virginia Department of Transportation (VDOT) and the Fairfax County Board of Supervisors. The suit argued that the EPA could not consider storm water flow a pollutant and that the cost of complying with the proposed regulations would create a financial hardship on VDOT (estimated at $70 million) and Fairfax County (up to $500 million). State and local officials will now work on a new plan for the control of pollution in the Accotink Creek Watershed.

Virginia's Road to the Future

Virginia Governor McDonnell's plan for solving the short and long-term transportation funding needs of the Commonwealth of Virginia became a reality at the conclusion of the 2013 General Assembly. Titled the 2013 Transportation Funding and Reform Package, the plan is expected to generate over $3.1 billion to be invested in the Commonwealth's transportation network over the course of the next five years.

The 2013 transportation legislation:

- eliminates the $0.175 per gallon tax on motor fuel, replaced by 3.5% tax on gasoline and 6% tax on diesel fuel;
- imposes a $64 annual registration fee on hybrid, alternative fuel, and electric motor vehicles;
- raises the sales and use tax across the Commonwealth to 5.3%;
- increases the sales tax on motor vehicles to a total of 4.15% over four years;
- reclassifies texting while driving as a primary offense with fines of $125 for first violation and $250 for any subsequent violation;
- generates additional revenue in Northern Virginia by raising the sales tax to 6%, hotel occupancy tax by 2%, and the real estate grantor's tax to $0.25 per $100; and
- directs $160 million in funding for mass transit capital improvements, operating costs, and special projects beginning in 2014.

The legislation provides for regional self-help provisions allowing localities to address their own specific transportation issues by raising funds independently.

Tysons Transportation Tax District

The Fairfax County Board of Supervisors has voted to create a Transportation Service District to generate funds for transportation improvements to help develop the Tysons area into a walkable urban area. The board will have the ability to levy a tax on all taxable real property within the service district, expected to be between $0.06 and $0.08 per $100 of assessed value. The combination of demographics, traffic congestion, and energy costs are shifting demand throughout the country to urban, walkable neighborhoods, especially for young professionals and retirees.

■ NEW IN VIRGINIA IN 2014

First-Time Homebuyers Savings Accounts

The General Assembly, strongly supported by state REALTORS®, created the First-Time Homebuyers' Savings Accounts to be used for real estate transaction costs listed on the settlement statement (HUD-1). The accounts are to be held at a participating financial institution and may contain cash or other marketable securities. Account holders may contribute up to $50,000 (post-tax) and withdraw the principal and any interest earned up to a total of $150,000 without paying state taxes (federal taxes would still be imposed.). Funds withdrawn for other purposes are subject to recapture taxes and penalties.

Vested Property Rights

The 2014 legislation clarifies the vested rights of owners of properties that were built before current zoning regulations were in effect or where permits can no longer be located. This bill states that so long as the homeowner has been paying taxes on the property for the past 15 years, the structure is deemed legal but non-conforming. When repairing or replacing a vested structure, the homeowner may be asked to bring the structure up to current code, but cannot be forced to remove it.

False Criminal Accusations

In response to a growing trend for plaintiffs suing an agent for false advertising in a civil proceeding to claim that the licensee is guilty of criminal false advertising, legislation now requires attorneys in a civil case to provide supporting evidence, as they would with any other court pleading.

Landlord-Tenant

The trigger number for coverage under the Virginia Residential Landlord Tenant Act (VRLTA) has been lowered from four to two rental properties in addition to a principal residence. This bill also eliminates the payment of interest on security deposits, beginning in 2015.

Flood Insurance Coverage

Mortgage lenders may not require flood insurance coverage exceeding the replacement value of the property's improvements.

CHAPTER 1 QUIZ

1. The term *broker* may refer to all of the following *EXCEPT*
   a. a brokerage firm.
   b. a sole proprietor transacting real estate business.
   c. a managing broker for a branch office.
   d. a principal in a brokerage relationship.

2. By Virginia statutory definition, a salesperson may perform all of the following functions *EXCEPT*
   a. offer a residence for sale.
   b. negotiate an exchange.
   c. serve as a managing broker.
   d. lease rental apartments.

3. Any individual holding a broker's license in Virginia who is *NOT* designated as the principal broker is
   a. a supervising broker.
   b. a managing broker.
   c. an associate broker.
   d. none of the above.

4. When a licensee acts as an independent contractor and *NOT* as a standard agent, the relationship is governed by
   a. the common law of agency.
   b. a standard Virginia REB contractor agreement.
   c. a written agreement between licensee and client.
   d. a buyer agency agreement.

5. An individual wants to sell her own house. Which of the following statements is *TRUE*?
   a. She does not need a real estate license to sell her own property.
   b. In Virginia, anyone who sells real property must have a real estate license.
   c. An individual may obtain a temporary real estate license in order to legally sell her own house.
   d. She may sell her house without a real estate license if she is an attorney.

6. Every principal broker must have all of the following readily available to the public *EXCEPT*
   a. the business firm license.
   b. the managing broker's license.
   c. a roster of all salespersons and brokers affiliated with the firm.
   d. all branch offices' licenses.

7. All of the following are exempt from the state licensing requirements *EXCEPT*
   a. a person acting without compensation as attorney-in-fact.
   b. an attorney involved in a real estate transaction in her normal role as attorney.
   c. an officer of a firm who actively participates in brokerage business.
   d. a licensed auctioneer selling real estate at a public auction.

8. The Virginia Real Estate Transaction Recovery Fund was created to
   a. protect consumers from unscrupulous settlement attorneys.
   b. provide funding for the Virginia Housing Development Authority.
   c. reimburse consumers who suffer monetary loss due to a licensee's misconduct.
   d. establish a fund for research and education of licensees.

9. The Real Estate Board (REB) may assess each active and inactive licensee a proportionate amount whenever the Transaction Recovery Fund falls below a minimum balance of
   a. $20 per licensee.
   b. $400,000.
   c. $1,000,000.
   d. $2,000,000.

10. The maximum amount that any single claimant may recover from the fund based on a single transaction is
    a. $20,000.
    b. $50,000.
    c. $100,000.
    d. unlimited.

11. The Real Estate Board (REB) Rules and Regulations are found in
    a. the Code of Virginia.
    b. the Virginia Constitution.
    c. the Virginia Administrative Code.
    d. the General Assembly Minutes.

12. The Common Interest Community Board (CIC) regulates all of the following EXCEPT
    a. the Condominium Act.
    b. the Real Estate Time-Share Act.
    c. the Real Estate Cooperative Act.
    d. the Residential Property Disclosure Act.

13. Common Interest Community Managers are required to have all of the following EXCEPT
    a. at least one supervisory employee with five years of management experience.
    b. one supervisory employee who has completed an 80-hour training program.
    c. 50% of employees with management responsibility must meet specific experience requirements or attend a 16-hour training program.
    d. 100% of all employees must attend a 16-hour training program annually.

14. Exemptions to the Virginia Residential Property Disclosure Act provisions include all of the following EXCEPT
    a. transfers pursuant to a foreclosure sale.
    b. transfers made without the assistance of a licensed real estate broker.
    c. transfers made between spouses resulting from a divorce.
    d. transfers involving the first sale of a dwelling.

15. As of July 1, 2011, a full list of seller representations is provided to a purchaser by
    a. the listing agent.
    b. the seller.
    c. the REB website.
    d. the buyer agent.

16. If a purchaser does NOT receive the proper property disclosures prior to contract ratification, the contract may be terminated
    a. within three days of occupancy.
    b. within five days of settlement.
    c. prior to settlement.
    d. prior to loan application with no right of contract termination.

17. Which federal organization is responsible for identifying flood areas?
    a. Federal Emergency Management Agency
    b. Department of Housing and Urban Development
    c. Natural Resources Conservation Service
    d. U.S. Fish and Wildlife Service

18. Exemptions to the provisions of the National Do Not Call Registry include all of the following EXCEPT
    a. clients and customers for a period of 18 months from last transaction.
    b. within 18 months of a consumer inquiry.
    c. charitable organizations.
    d. political organizations.

19. Legislation that directly affects the policies and procedures of a brokerage firm include all of the following EXCEPT
    a. cold-calling for prospects (National Do Not Call Registry).
    b. email newsletters (CAN-SPAM).
    c. maintenance of client records (FACTA).
    d. selection of settlement agent (CRESPA).

20. The Fair and Accurate Credit Transaction Act (FACTA) Disposal Rule require office policies to do all of the following EXCEPT
    a. return all client records to the client at settlement.
    b. burn, pulverize, or shred all consumer report information.
    c. destroy or erase electronic files with consumer information.
    d. hire a document destruction contractor to dispose of consumer information.

Brokerage Relationships and Agency

After successfully completing this chapter, you will be able to

- ■ **describe** how to originate and terminate a brokerage relationship,
- ■ **explain** the disclosure requirements for brokerage relationships and agency representation,
- ■ **list** the statutory duties for clients and customers, and
- ■ **discuss** the typical components of listing and buyer agency agreements.

■ KEY TERMS

agency	dual agent or	net listing
brokerage relationship	representative	property management
client	independent contractor	agreement
customer	limited service agent	standard agent
defective drywall	Megan's Law	standard or statutory
designated agent	ministerial acts	agency

The concept of common law of agency as it relates to real estate brokerage no longer exists in Virginia. In 1995, the Virginia General Assembly expressly abrogated the common law of agency in real estate transactions (§54.1-2144). In its place, the legislature enacted an agency statute that codifies the agency relationships between brokers, buyers, sellers, landlords, tenants, and property managers (§§54.1-2130 through 54.1-2146). This is called **standard** or **statutory agency**.

One aspect of the Virginia agency law that differs from the common law of agency is that there is no longer imputed liability on the part of either the client or the broker.

A client is not liable for misrepresentations made by a licensee, nor is a broker liable for misrepresentation on the part of another broker engaged to assist in a real estate transaction. In both cases, liability for another's actions would occur only if the client and/or broker knew, or should have known, of the misrepresentation or failed to take steps to correct it.

Knowledge or information between clients or brokers is not imputed. Each is responsible only for actual knowledge or information, although liability may still occur in a case of unlawful housing discriminatory practices.

■ BROKERAGE RELATIONSHIPS

Definitions

Virginia's statute §54.1-2130 provides the following definitions.

Agency is defined as any relationship in which a real estate licensee acts for or represents a person by such person's express authority in a real estate transaction. Agency includes representation of a client as a standard agent or a limited service agent.

A **brokerage agreement** is the written agreement creating a brokerage relationship between a client and a licensee. A **brokerage relationship** is a contractual relationship between a client and a licensee who has been engaged by the client to procure a seller, buyer, option, tenant, or landlord who is ready, willing, and able to sell, buy, option, exchange, or rent real estate. Although it is often the salesperson who initiates the brokerage relationship with the client, it is, in fact, the broker who has the brokerage relationship with the client. In this context, the *broker licensee* refers to the brokerage firm.

■ **FOR EXAMPLE**   XYZ Realty as a non-broker-owned sole proprietor may have hired Mary Smith to act as principal broker of the firm. The broker/client relationship is with XYZ Realty, not with Mary Smith.

The brokerage relationship is limited to a broker and a client. A **client** is a person who has entered into a brokerage relationship with a broker licensee; any other party to the transaction with whom the licensee does not have a brokerage relationship but for whom the licensee may perform routine services, called *ministerial acts*, is a **customer**.

Ministerial acts are routine acts that a licensee can perform for a person that do not involve discretion or the exercise of the licensee's own judgment.

The parties are free to enter into a brokerage relationship based on a brokerage agreement that specifically states that the licensee is acting as an **independent contractor** and not as an agent. The written agreement, not the statute, governs the relationship. The independent contractor has no obligations required by §§54.1-2131 through 54.1-2135 (duties of a standard agent).

In 2006, in response to changing real estate industry business models, the Virginia General Assembly modified the agency statute by introducing and stating the duties of a limited service representative (now called a **limited service agent**) under §54.1-2138.1.

A licensee may act as a limited service agent only pursuant to a written brokerage agreement. Limited service agents must disclose their status as such and present in writing to the client a list of the services that will be provided, along with a list of the duties required of a standard agent, specifically listing the standard agency duties and services that will not be performed. The following language must be included in the agreement:

> By entering into this brokerage agreement, the undersigned do hereby acknowledge their informed consent to the limited service representation by the licensee and do further acknowledge that neither the other party to the transaction nor any real estate licensee representing the other party is under any legal obligation to assist the undersigned with the performance of any duties and responsibilities of the undersigned not performed by the limited service agent.

A **property management agreement** is the written agreement between a property manager and the owner of real estate for the management of the real estate.

Standard agent is defined as a licensee who acts for or represents a client in an agency relationship. A standard agent has the obligations provided by statute and any additional obligations agreed to by the parties to the brokerage agreement.

A **designated agent** is a licensee assigned by the broker to represent a client when a different client is also represented by the broker in the same transaction. In this way, two licensees from the same brokerage firm can take part in the same transaction while retaining standard agent duties to their clients. This differs from a **dual agent or representative** where a licensee has a brokerage relationship with both seller and buyer, or landlord and tenant, in the same transaction.

Significant changes with regard to both designated and dual agency disclosure went into effect on July 1, 2012. Due to the complexity of the changes, House Bill 1907 also requires that every applicant for relicensure as either a broker or a salesperson must take a minimum three-hour continuing education course on the changes to residential standard agency before renewal or reinstatement of a license. Further discussion and sample disclosure forms will be covered later in this chapter.

Establishing a Brokerage Relationship

In addition to establishing new rules and standards for agency relationships in real estate transactions, the statute provides that neither compensation nor use of a common source information company, such as an MLS, creates a brokerage relationship (§54.1-2140).

Prior to entering into a brokerage relationship, the licensee is required to advise the prospective client of

- the type of brokerage relationship proposed by the broker;
- the broker's compensation; and
- whether the broker will share the compensation with a broker who may have a brokerage relationship with another party to the transaction.

As of July 1, 2012, all brokerage agreements must

- be in writing;
- have a definite termination date (if no date specified, brokerage relationship terminates after 90 days);
- state the amount of the brokerage fees and how and when such fees are to be paid;
- state the services to be rendered by the licensee;
- include such other terms of the brokerage relationship as have been agreed to by the client and the licensee; and
- in the case of brokerage agreements entered into in conjunction with the client's consent to dual representation, the additional disclosures set out in §54.1-2139.

Commencement and Termination of Brokerage Relationship

The brokerage relationship begins at the time the client engages a licensee. Ideally, the relationship terminates when the brokerage agreement's terms have been completely performed. However, the relationship may also be terminated by

- the expiration of the agreement;
- a mutual agreement to terminate;
- a default by any party; or
- the licensee's withdrawal when a client refuses to consent to disclosed dual agency.

All brokerage relationships must have a definite termination date. If no date is specified, the statute establishes a mandatory termination date of 90 days after the commencement of the brokerage relationship (§54.1-2137B).

Once a brokerage relationship has terminated or expired, the licensee owes no further duties to the client. However, the licensee is nonetheless required to account for all monies and property relating to the brokerage relationship and keeping confidential all personal and financial information received from the client.

■ DISCLOSURE REQUIREMENTS

Brokerage Relationships

Virginia agency law requires full disclosure of any existing brokerage relationships. It is essential that the party to the transaction who is not the client of the licensee and who is not represented by another licensee clearly understand that the licensee represents only her client. Although the licensee is required to treat a customer honestly and to disclose any material adverse facts about the physical condition of the property, the agent's primary responsibility is to protect and promote the best interest of the client.

At the time of the first substantive discussion about a specific property with an actual or prospective buyer, seller, landlord, or tenant who is not a client of the licensee and who is not represented by another licensee, a licensee is required to disclose any broker relationship he has with any other party to the transaction. The disclosure will be made in writing at the earliest practical time but no later than the time when specific real estate assistance is provided for sales transactions or at the time of a lease application or in the lease, whichever occurs first. Disclosure is not required for lease terms of less than two months.

As of July 1, 2012, a disclosure of brokerage relationship form must be used, as illustrated in Figure 2.1.

FIGURE 2.1

Disclosure of Brokerage Relationship

DISCLOSURE OF BROKERAGE RELATIONSHIP

The undersigned do hereby acknowledge disclosure that the licensee

_____ (name of broker or salesperson) associated with

_____ (Name of Brokerage Firm) represents the following party in a

real estate transaction:

☐ Seller(s)   or   ☐ Buyer(s)

☐ Landlord(s)   or   ☐ Tenant(s)

_____   _____

Date   Name

_____   _____

Date   Name

Note that this form is required for the person who is not the client of the agent and is not represented by another licensee. Signature of this disclosure by a client is not required because a brokerage relationship has been previously established by an exclusive right to represent, a buyer agency agreement, or an exclusive right to sell.

If the required disclosure is given in combination with other disclosures or information, the disclosure must be conspicuous, printed in bold lettering, all capitals, underlined, or within a separate box (§54.1-2138A). If the licensee's relationship with any party to the transaction changes, all clients and customers involved in the transaction must be informed—in writing—of the change. Copies of all disclosures that are a part of an executed lease or a consummated transaction must be kept for three years.

Disclosed Dual Representation

In Virginia, a licensee may represent both parties in the same real estate transaction—seller and buyer or landlord and tenant—only with the written consent of all clients in the transaction. The client's signature on the written disclosure form is presumptive evidence of the brokerage relationship. Under the July 1, 2012, revisions to agency law, a licensee may act in an agency relationship with a client as either a standard or a limited service agent. A licensee acting as an independent contractor is now called a representative (not an agent). This may create some confusion because before July 1, 2012, the term was limited service representative.

In response to concerns that clients agreeing to dual agency were not being adequately represented, §54.1-2139 was revised, effective July 1, 2012. The new disclosure form points out that the client may be disadvantaged by dual representation. It specifies that the dual agent or representative may not give advice as to terms, offers, or counteroffers or the suitability, condition, or needed repairs of the property and that the licensee will be acting without real knowledge of the client's needs and experience.

The much stronger disclosure form is required as of July 1, 2012. Section 54.1-2139 specifically states that a licensee may not act as either a dual agent or representative without the written consent of all parties to the transaction. The new disclosure form provides for disclosure of the client being represented (seller, buyer, landlord, or tenant) and the type of representation (standard agent, limited service agent, independent contractor). See the sample residential disclosure form in Figure 2.2 and commercial disclosure form in Figure 2.3.

FIGURE 2.2

Disclosure of Dual Agency or Dual Representation in a Residential Real Estate Transaction

RESIDENTIAL REAL ESTATE TRANSACTION

The undersigned do hereby acknowledge disclosure that the licensee

_____ (name of broker or salesperson) associated with

_____ (Brokerage Firm) represents more than one party in this residential

real estate transaction as follows:

A. Brokerage Firm represents the following party (select one):
☐ Seller(s)　　　☐ Buyer(s)　　　☐ Landlord(s)　　　☐ Tenant(s)

As a (select one):
☐ standard agent　　　☐ limited service agent　　　☐ independent contractor

Brokerage Firm represents another party (select one):
☐ Seller(s)　　　☐ Buyer(s)　　　☐ Landlord(s)　　　☐ Tenant(s)

As a (select one):
☐ standard agent　　　☐ limited service agent　　　☐ independent contractor

B. Brokerage Firm disclosure and client acknowledgement of the following (select one):
☐ Brokerage Firm represents two existing clients in the transaction and the undersigned acknowledge the following:
The undersigned understand that the foregoing dual agent or dual representative may not disclose to either client any information that has been given to the dual agent or representative by the other client within the confidence and trust of the brokerage relationship except for that information which is otherwise required or permitted by Article 3 (§ 54.1-2130 et seq.) of Chapter 21 of Title 54.1 of the Code of Virginia to be disclosed.

☐ Brokerage Firm represents one existing client and one new client in the transaction and the undersigned acknowledge the following:
The undersigned understand:
1. That following the commencement of dual agency or representation, the licensee cannot advise either party as to the terms to offer or accept in any offer or counteroffer; however, the licensee may have advised one party as to such terms prior to the commencement of dual agency or representation;
2. That the licensee cannot advise the buyer client as to the suitability of the property, its condition (other than to make any disclosures as required by law of any licensee representing a seller), and cannot advise either party as to what repairs of the property to make or request;
3. That the licensee cannot advise either party in any dispute that arises relating to the transaction;
4. That the licensee may be acting without knowledge of the client's needs, client's knowledge of the market, or client's capabilities in dealing with the intricacies of real estate transactions; and
5. That either party may engage another licensee at additional cost to represent their respective interests.

FIGURE 2.2

Disclosure of Dual Agency or Dual Representation in a Residential Real Estate Transaction (cont.)

The undersigned by signing this notice do hereby acknowledge their informed consent to the disclosed dual representation by the licensee.

_____   _____
Date   Name (One Party)

_____   _____
Date   Name (One Party)

_____   _____
Date   Name (Other Party)

_____   _____
Date   Name (Other Party)

FIGURE   2.3

Disclosure of Dual Agency or Dual Representation in a Commercial Real Estate Transaction

IN A COMMERCIAL REAL ESTATE TRANSACTION

The undersigned do hereby acknowledge disclosure that the licensee

_____ (name of broker or salesperson) associated with

_____ (Brokerage Firm) represents more than one party in this

commercial real estate transaction as follows:

A. Brokerage Firm represents the following party (select one):

   ☐ Seller(s)   ☐ Buyer(s)   ☐ Landlord(s)   ☐ Tenant(s)

As a (select one):

   ☐ standard agent   ☐ limited service agent   ☐ independent contractor

Brokerage Firm represents another party (select one):

   ☐ Seller(s)   ☐ Buyer(s)   ☐ Landlord(s)   ☐ Tenant(s)

As a (select one):

   ☐ standard agent   ☐ limited service agent   ☐ independent contractor

The undersigned understand that the foregoing dual agent or dual representative may not disclose to either client any information that has been given to the dual agent or representative by the other client within the confidence and trust of the brokerage relationship except for that information which is otherwise required or permitted by Article 3 (§ 54.1-2130 et seq.) of Chapter 21 of Title 54.1 of the Code of Virginia to be disclosed.

The undersigned by signing this notice do hereby acknowledge their informed consent to the disclosed dual representation by the licensee.

_____   _____

Date   Name (One Party)

_____   _____

Date   Name (One Party)

_____   _____

Date   Name (Other Party)

_____   _____

Date   Name (Other Party)

A dual agent or representative does not terminate any brokerage relationship by making the required disclosures of dual representation (§54.1-2139E). As mentioned previously, a licensee may withdraw from representing a client who refuses to consent to disclosed dual agency. The licensee may withdraw under such circumstances without liability and may continue to represent the other client. Further, the licensee may continue to represent in other transactions the client who refused dual representation (§54.1-2139F).

Disclosed Designated Agency

The new legislation effective July 1, 2012, also affects designated agents. Section 54.1-2139.1 reestablishes the broker's authority to designate agents or representatives to work with different clients in the same transaction. The required disclosure form is a disclosure of designated agency or representatives as illustrated in Figure 2.4.

FIGURE 2.4

Disclosure of Designated Agency or Representatives

DISCLOSURE OF DESIGNATED AGENTS OR REPRESENTATIVES

The undersigned do hereby acknowledge disclosure that the licensee

_____ (name of Broker and Firm) represents more than one party in this

real estate transaction as indicated below:

☐ Seller(s) and Buyer(s)   ☐ Landlord(s) and Tenant(s)

The undersigned understand that the foregoing dual agent or representative may not disclose to either client or such client's designated agent or representative any information that has been given to the dual agent or representative by the other client within the confidence and trust of the brokerage relationship except for that information which is otherwise required or permitted by Article 3 (§ 54.1-2130 et seq.) of Chapter 21 of Title 54.1 of the Code of Virginia to be disclosed.

The principal or supervising broker has assigned

_____ (broker or salesperson) to act as Designated Agent or Representative for the one party as indicated below:

☐ Seller(s)   ☐ Buyer(s)   ☐ Landlord(s)   ☐ Tenant(s)

As a (select one):

☐ standard agent   ☐ limited service agent   ☐ independent contractor

_____ (broker or salesperson) to act as Designated Agent or Representative for the other party as indicated below:

☐ Seller(s)   ☐ Buyer(s)   ☐ Landlord(s)   ☐ Tenant(s)

As a (select one):

☐ standard agent   ☐ limited service agent   ☐ independent contractor

The undersigned by signing this notice do hereby acknowledge their consent to the disclosed dual representation by the licensee.

_____   _____
Date   Name (One Party)

_____   _____
Date   Name (One Party)

_____   _____
Date   Name (Other Party)

_____   _____
Date   Name (Other Party)

The designated agent or representative must not disclose any personal or financial information to any other party without written consent of the client. The appointment of designated agents or representatives excludes other licensees in the firm from involvement in the transaction. The use of designated agents or representatives does not constitute dual representation if each designee represents only one client in a particular real estate transaction (§54.1-2139.3). The designated agents or representatives are pledged to maintain all confidential information received from their clients. Such information may be shared with the principal or supervising broker who remains in the position of a dual agent or representative with equal responsibilities to both clients.

IN PRACTICE   The principal broker of a brokerage firm, through the actions of agent M, has established a brokerage relationship with a prospective buyer by having her sign an exclusive right-to-represent agreement. The buyer decides to make an offer on a property that is listed with the same firm with agent B as the listing agent. The broker may now designate agent M to be the designated agent for the buyer and agent B to be the designated agent for the seller. Both designated agents will be able to meet all of the statutory obligations of duties to their clients. The principal broker will remain in a dual agency position with equal responsibility to both clients.

If the buyer wished to purchase a property listed with the same firm with agent M as listing agent, agent M could then enter into a disclosed dual agent role where she would have statutory responsibilities to both clients. The brokerage firm would have brokerage relationships with both the buyer, through the signing of an exclusive right-to-represent agreement, and the seller, through the signing of a listing agreement.

Another alternative is for agent M to withdraw from the buyer representation brokerage agreement with the buyer and continue to represent only the seller. The buyer would then be a customer instead of a client. The statutory obligation is to treat the buyer honestly and disclose any adverse material defects in the property. Agent M would also be able to perform ministerial acts for the buyer, but her primary responsibility is to the seller.

In all cases where dual agency or designated agency is practiced, the need for written consent of all parties to the transaction is a requirement of the statute. The disclosure may be combined with other disclosures but shall be conspicuous, printed in bold lettering, all capitals, underlined, or within a separate box.

■ STATUTORY DUTIES

The Virginia agency statute (§§54.1-2131 through 54.1-2135) establishes specific duties for a licensee who is in an agency relationship as a standard agent with a seller, buyer, landlord, or tenant or to manage real estate.

Duties to a Client

The seven specific duties outlined in the statute are basically the same for all clients. The only variation is in the duty to promote the best interests of the client. These variations will be noted separately. Licensees engaged to manage real estate do not have a duty to promote the best interests of the client.

The statutory duties for a client require that licensees

- perform according to the terms of the brokerage relationship;
- promote the best interests of the client by
  - (seller and landlord only) conducting marketing activities seeking a sale or lease at the price and terms established in the brokerage relationship or at a price and terms acceptable to the client (once the property is under contract, the licensee is not obligated to seek additional offers unless required to do so under the brokerage agreement or sales contract),
  - (buyers and tenants) seeking a property at a price and terms acceptable to the client (licensee is not obligated to seek other properties while the client is party to a purchase contract or lease),
  - (sellers and buyers) assisting in the drafting and negotiating of offers and counteroffers, amendments and addenda and in establishing strategies for accomplishing the client's objectives,
  - (landlords and tenants) assisting in the drafting and negotiating of leases or letters of intent,
  - receiving and presenting in a timely manner written offers and counteroffers even when the property is subject to a contract of sale or lease, and
  - providing reasonable assistance to satisfy the client's contract obligations and to facilitate settlement of the purchase contract or finalize a lease;
- maintain confidentiality of all personal and financial information received from the client during the brokerage relationship and any other information characterized as confidential by the client, unless the client consents in writing to its release or its release is required by law;
- exercise ordinary care;
- account in a timely manner for all money and property received in which the client has or may have an interest;
- disclose to the client all material facts related to the property or concerning the transaction of which the licensee has actual knowledge; and
- comply with all requirements of this article, all applicable fair housing statutes and regulations, and all other statutes and regulations that are not in conflict with this article.

In the case of a residential transaction, a licensee must also disclose to the seller the buyer's intent to occupy the property as a principal residence (§54.1-2132B). This disclosure is often stated in the body of a purchase agreement.

Duties to a Customer

The traditional fiduciary responsibilities that were a part of the common law of agency are basically included in the new statutory duties but with far less implied liability.

Customers, the parties with whom the licensee does *not* have a brokerage relationship, must be treated honestly and may not knowingly be given false information. In addition, they must be informed of any material adverse facts regarding the property's physical condition of which the licensee has actual knowledge. As of July 1, 2011, the law specifically requires disclosure of **defective drywall**. As of 2014, disclosure is required if the property was used for the manufacture of methamphetamine. The term *physical condition of the property* refers to the land and any improvements. It does not refer to

- matters outside the boundaries of the land,
- adjacent or other properties in proximity,
- matters relating to governmental land use regulations, or
- matters relating to highways or public streets.

Any such disclosure shall be made in writing. No legal action may be brought against a licensee for making such required disclosures. This was further clarified as of July 1, 2011:

> A licensee shall not be liable for providing false information if the information was (i) provided to the licensee by the licensee's client; (ii) obtained from a governmental entity; (iii) obtained from a non-governmental person or entity that obtained the information from a governmental entity; or (iv) obtained from a person licensed, certified, or registered to provide professional services in the Commonwealth, upon which the licensee relies, and the licensee did not (a) have actual knowledge that the information was false or (b) act in reckless disregard of the truth. (§54.1-2142.1)

A licensee having a brokerage relationship with a client is permitted to assist customers (the party with whom the licensee does not have a brokerage relationship) by performing ministerial acts. The performance of ministerial acts does not violate the licensee's brokerage relationship with the client. Similarly, the brokerage relationship is not violated if the licensee shows alternative properties to prospective buyers (or tenants) or represents other sellers (or landlords).

Property Management

Licensees who are engaged to manage real estate are required by Virginia law to perform according to the management agreement, exercise ordinary care, disclose all material facts concerning the property of which the licensee has actual knowledge (specifically the existence of defective drywall), maintain confidentiality of information, account for all money and property received, and comply with all relevant real estate and fair housing laws and regulations. The licensee is expected to perform services in accordance with the property management agreement. Licensees are permitted to represent other owners in the management of real property and to represent the owner as seller or landlord under a brokerage agreement (§54.1-2135).

As of July 1, 2012, §54.1-2135 has been expanded to require that property management agreements shall be in writing and shall have a definite termination date or duration (if not, the agreement will terminate in 90 days). The agreement must state the amount of the management fees and how they are to be paid, the services to be rendered by the licensee, and include any other terms agreed upon by the owner and the property manager.

■ AGENCY AGREEMENTS

When licensees assist buyers, sellers, tenants, landlords, and property owners, some type of written agreement is required to formalize an agency relationship.

The listing agreement is probably the most widely used instrument for representing a seller in the sale of a property. The buyer agency or buyer representation agreement is technically a listing agreement for buyers.

Listing Forms

Although there are no standard listing or buyer representation forms used throughout the entire Commonwealth, the Virginia Association of REALTORS® (VAR) creates standard forms that are available in print and software versions and are used in many parts of the state. Additionally, several large associations, such as the Northern Virginia Association of REALTORS® (NVAR), have standard forms available for use in large regional, multijurisdictional areas. These are available in print, software, and via online subscription.

It should be noted that while an oral listing or buyer representation agreement may be legal in Virginia; such an agreement would not be enforceable, based on the statute of frauds.

IN PRACTICE   In a listing form, the blanks are rarely optional. All blanks should be filled in. If an item does not apply in a particular transaction, the notation N/A (not applicable) should be used. Finding accurate information for each item may require additional research.

Some items on the listing forms may have to be entered as approximations, such as the mortgage balance—until a payoff statement is available from the lender—or the exact age of the dwelling. Accurate figures should be used wherever possible. Any changes involving financial responsibility, such as a price change, dates, or other major seller commitments, must be authorized in writing by the seller.

■ SELLER REPRESENTATION—SELLER AGENCY AGREEMENT

Types of Listing Agreements

The standard types of listings—open, exclusive agency, and exclusive right-to-sell—are all legal in Virginia. Many brokers will not accept open listings, however, because there is no guarantee of payment for time and money spent on the listings. Also, open listings may not be allowed by many multiple-listing service (MLS) systems. All listing agreements must include a definite termination date. The owner must be furnished a copy of the listing at the time it is signed.

Virginia Real Estate Board (REB) regulations specifically prohibit net listings (18 VAC 135-20-280(5)). A **net listing** is an agreement in which an owner specifies a particular dollar amount that she must net from the sale or rental of a property; the broker may keep any amount over the seller's net that is generated by the transaction. Under a net listing, it is difficult to balance the broker's responsibility to the principal with the broker's own interest in making a profit. Because this practice is not permitted in Virginia, brokers must inform prospective clients that their fee will be a percentage of the selling price, a **commission**, or a flat fee for services.

■ FOR EXAMPLE   A homeowner called a Richmond real estate broker and told her that he wanted to sell his house. "I don't have time to be bothered with percentages and bargaining and offers and counteroffers," he explained. "I just need to walk out of this deal with $150,000 in my pocket. If you sell this place for more than that, you can keep the rest." The broker knew that comparable homes were selling for well over $200,000. Also, the broker knew that net listings are illegal in Virginia. What should the broker do?

The broker should explain that net listings are illegal in Virginia and advise him of the current range of values for properties like his. The broker can then negotiate a commission or fee for the services she will provide, sign a listing agreement with the owner, and proceed to market the property.

Typical Listing Information

A listing agreement (Exclusive Right to Represent Seller) usually contains information such as the following:

- Assurances that the seller has not entered into a listing agreement with another broker
- Complete list of what items (chattels) convey with the property, including items of personal property
- The sales price
- Specific terms of the agreement
- Disclosure of any retainer or administration fees required by the agent or the agent's firm and whether these fees will be refunded to the seller at the conclusion of the transaction
- Statement of the broker's duties; because the document will establish a brokerage relationship, a recital of the statutory duties of a broker is appropriate (see §54.1-2131, Licensees Engaged by Sellers)
- Statement of any duties owed by the client
- Description of the purpose of the agreement
- Complete disclosure of how the broker will be paid
- Recital of disclosed dual or designated agent representation. Statement of applicability of federal, state, and local disclosures include, but are not limited to, the following:
  — Lead-based paint
  — Mold
  — **Megan's Law** (information about registered sex offenders must be made available to the public)
  — Defective drywall
  — Disclosure statements
  — POA or condominium inclusion
- Local disclaimer information; some local multiple-listing service (MLS) systems have regional disclosure information or information that sellers should know prior to entering into a sales agreement
- Fair housing statement
- Recital of any other provisions pertaining to the brokerage relationship
- Statement describing how the listing agreement may be terminated by either party

A property owner is now allowed to opt out of having the property displayed on the internet. The owner can also either authorize or not authorize specific elements on the broker's website, such as showing third-party comments or reviews, and/or an automated estimate of the market value of the property. Electronic signatures are now allowed as long as all parties agree to use them as shown on the form.

See Appendix A for a sample listing agreement.

Buyer Representation—Buyer Agency Agreement

A buyer's agent establishes a brokerage relationship with a client through a buyer representation agreement. A typical buyer's representation agreement is shown in Appendix B.

An exclusive right-to-represent buyer agreement typically contains information such as the following:

- Assurances that the buyer has not entered into a buyer representation agreement with another broker
- Information about other properties that the buyer may have been shown by other agents
- Specific terms of the agreement
- Disclosure of any retainer or administration fees required by the agent or the agent's firm and whether these fees will be refunded to the buyer at the conclusion of the transaction
- Statement of the broker's duties; because the document will establish a brokerage relationship, a recital of the statutory duties of a broker is appropriate (see §54.1-2132, Licensees Engaged by Buyers)
- Statement of any duties owed by the client
- Description of the purpose of the agreement
- Complete disclosure of how the broker will be paid
- Recital of disclosed dual or designated agent representation local disclaimer information; some local MLS systems have regional disclosure information on information that buyers should know before entering into a purchase agreement
- Fair housing statement
- Recital of any other provisions pertaining to the brokerage relationship
- Statement describing how the listing agreement may be terminated by either party

All of the statutory requirements for brokerage relationships and agency can be found in the Code of Virginia under Title 54.1, Chapter 21, 54.1-2130 through 54.1-2146.

Search the Code of Virginia on the Virginia General Assembly Legislative Information System (LIS) website at http://leg1.state.va.us/lis.htm.

CHAPTER 2 QUIZ

1. An agency relationship is *BEST* described as one in which a licensee
   a. has a signed agreement establishing a brokerage relationship.
   b. has a separate independent contractor agreement with a buyer.
   c. performs ministerial acts for a seller.
   d. acts for or represents another person in a real estate transaction.

2. Routine services that do *NOT* involve a licensee's experience or discretion are called
   a. transactional acts.
   b. routine brokerage.
   c. ministerial acts.
   d. customer service.

3. A brokerage relationship can be terminated by any of the following *EXCEPT*
   a. one party's unilaterally firing the other.
   b. expiration of the agreement.
   c. a default by either party.
   d. a licensee's withdrawal when the client refuses to consent to dual agency.

4. A listing agent places a property in the local MLS stating that the house is connected to the public sewer when in fact it is on a septic system. Six months after settlement, the septic system fails and the purchaser wants to sue the seller for misrepresentation. Which of the following statements is *TRUE*?
   a. The new owner can collect the cost of connecting to public sewer from the seller.
   b. The new owner can sue the seller for damages.
   c. The seller is not responsible for misrepresentations made by the listing agent.
   d. The contract will be voided.

5. Broker A is representing a buyer in the purchase of a town house listed with broker B. Broker A has a signed exclusive right-to-represent contract with the buyer. He will need to have a Disclosure of Brokerage Relationship form signed by
   a. the buyer.
   b. the sellers of the town house.
   c. both the buyer and the sellers of the town house.
   d. no one because the sellers have their own agent.

6. Salespersons M and T are licensees who are both affiliated with the same realty firm. M has listed a house, and T has a likely buyer. What should the supervising broker do?
   a. The broker should do nothing because neither salesperson wishes to act as disclosed dual agents.
   b. The broker should insist that one of the salespersons sign a disclosed dual agency agreement with the buyers and sellers.
   c. The broker may assign the salespersons as designated agents, providing a disclosure form to the sellers only.
   d. The broker may assign the two salespersons as designated agents and provide a disclosure form to both the sellers and the prospective buyers.

7. A prospective buyer calls the listing agent on a home she is interested in. She tells him that she has a signed buyer agency agreement with another licensee, but he is out of town and she would like the listing agent to show her the home. When should the listing agent make an agency disclosure to the prospective buyer?
   a. Immediately, over the phone
   b. When he shows her the listing
   c. After she signs a new buyer agency agreement with him
   d. Never; none will be needed

8. A prospective buyer calls a licensee and spends 20 minutes talking about her real estate needs. They agree to meet and go for a drive to look at neighborhoods but never discuss or visit any specific property. The licensee should provide her with agency disclosure

   a. when she gets in the car.
   b. while they are talking on the phone.
   c. when she gets back to the caller's home.
   d. no disclosure is required since no specific assistance was given.

9. All of the following are specific duties owed to a seller or buyer client EXCEPT

   a. to perform to the terms of the contract.
   b. to protect and promote the best interests of the client.
   c. to always be obedient to the client's demands.
   d. to maintain confidentiality forever.

10. The specific duty that falls under the duty to promote the best interests of the client that only applies to sellers and landlords is the duty to

    a. conduct marketing activities.
    b. seek a price and terms acceptable to the client.
    c. assist in the drafting and negotiating of offers and counteroffers.
    d. providing assistance to satisfy the client's contract obligations.

11. The term *physical condition of the property* refers to

    a. a gas station on the corner.
    b. the empty field behind the house.
    c. defective drywall in the house.
    d. plans for widening the street.

12. A licensee would not violate her brokerage relationship with her seller client by doing any of the following EXCEPT

    a. performing ministerial acts for a buyer customer.
    b. showing alternative properties to prospective clients.
    c. representing other clients in other transactions.
    d. disclosing confidential information to the buyers.

13. A seller offers a broker a listing agreement that contains the following clause: "Seller must receive the amount of $60,000 from the sale of this property. Seller agrees that the selling agent will receive, as his or her total compensation, any proceeds that remain beyond that amount after satisfaction of seller's mortgage loan and any closing costs incurred by seller." Based on these facts, the broker

    a. must decline this listing agreement because the clause violates REB regulations.
    b. must decline this listing agreement because it is not the standard form used in Virginia.
    c. may accept this listing agreement because the clause is standard in an open listing.
    d. may accept this listing agreement because it specifically limits the amount of the compensation.

14. Which of the following is the CORRECT way to enter the termination date on a listing form?

    a. 90 days from today
    b. July 1, 2008
    c. Until property is sold
    d. Until seller decides to cancel

15. Seller B has been best friends with broker A for 30 years. He wants to have broker A sell his farm based on a handshake agreement. In Virginia, this is

    a. illegal, based on the Statute of Frauds.
    b. illegal, based on Virginia Agency Law.
    c. legal and fully enforceable, based on Virginia Agency Law.
    d. legal but not enforceable, based on the Statute of Frauds.

Interests and Forms of Ownership

■ **LEARNING OBJECTIVES**   *After successfully completing this chapter, you will be able to*

■ **explain** a transfer of interest through eminent domain, descent and distribution, or easement;

■ **define** the different types of tenancy used in Virginia;

■ **describe** forms of ownership, including cooperative, condominium, and time-share; and

■ **review** the elements of the Virginia Property Owners' Association Act.

■ KEY TERMS

augmented estate	homestead exemption	resale certificate
automatic survivorship	intestate	tacking
condemnation	joint tenancy	tenancy by the entirety
condominium	just compensation	tenancy in common
cooperative	land trust	tenancy in partnership
easement by necessity	law of descent and	testate
easement by prescription	distribution	time-share ownership
elective share	property	unsecured debts
eminent domain	public offering statement	
estate	(POS)	

An estate in land is the character and extent of ownership interest that a person has in real property. Virginia recognizes all the major estates in land, such as inheritable fee simple absolute, defeasible, and determinable estates and noninheritable life estates, including conventional, ordinary with rights of remainder, reversion, or *pur autre vie*. Specific areas of ownership interest will be covered in this chapter.

Land trusts are permitted in Virginia. A **land trust** is a trust in which the assets consist of real estate. While the deed to a trustee may appear to confer full powers to deal with the real property and complete legal and equitable title to the trust property, the trustee's powers are in fact restricted by a trust agreement mentioned in the deed. The agreement typically gives the beneficiary full powers of management and control. However, even the beneficiary cannot deal with the property as if no trust existed. Land trusts generally continue for a definite term.

■ **FOR EXAMPLE** The deed of trust used as collateral in the financing of a property.

■ TRANSFER OF OWNERSHIP

The most common method of transfer of ownership is through the purchase and sale of a property. There are, however, other legal ways to accomplish a transfer of property that are provided for in the Virginia Constitution and statutes.

Eminent Domain

In Virginia, the power of eminent domain is provided by both state constitution and statutes. Virginia law provides that easements, ingress and egress rights, flowage rights, and all similar rights and uses constitute property. As a result, just compensation must be paid if they are taken or damaged by the Commonwealth through the power of **eminent domain**, sometimes called a taking. This process is called **condemnation**.

In November 2012, an amendment to the constitution was passed that limits the state's power of eminent domain to only taking private property for public use and not giving it to a private landowner even if it would result in job creation.

Just compensation means the fair market value of the property at the time of the taking. Payment of just compensation is a prerequisite to passing of title to the property. In addition, the Commonwealth must have made a genuine but ineffectual effort to purchase the property directly before beginning condemnation proceedings.

If the parties do not agree on what constitutes just compensation for the land, commissioners are appointed to hold a hearing and determine the amount. Virginia's Condemnation Act provides for a two-stage proceeding. First, the court determines the fair market value of the land taken and the damage, if any, to the remaining land. Second, if payment occurs, the court determines the rights and claims of all persons entitled to compensation.

Required Disclosure Real estate licensees are required to disclose to all interested parties that a condemnation is planned for a parcel or an entire area. If a seller is aware that a governmental authority has made an offer to acquire the property and that condemnation proceedings are contemplated, prospective buyers should be made aware of this information. Because condemnation can affect the value of both the condemned property and neighboring properties, it is an important consideration for buyers and sellers alike.

■ **FOR EXAMPLE** A portion of a homeowner's property was condemned for street construction. This had an adverse impact on the value of the homeowner's remaining property. However, the value of adjacent parcels increased as a result of the improved access provided by the street.

Descent and Distribution in Marital Estates

In 1991, the Virginia legislature abolished the concepts of dower and curtesy. The Augmented Estate and Elective Share Act defines to whom a deceased person's property is distributed if the individual dies **intestate**, that is, without having executed a valid will. The **law of descent and distribution** is similar to the old dower and curtesy statutes because it establishes the rights of ownership to property by a surviving spouse and others.

The statute defines **property** or **estate** as including

■ insurance policies,
■ retirement benefits (exclusive of Social Security),
■ annuities,
■ pension plans,
■ deferred compensation arrangements, and
■ employee benefit plans.

Intestate Distributions This discussion of descent and distribution is a simplified overview of a very complex law (see the Code of Virginia, Table of Contents, Title 64.1 Wills and Decedents' Estates, at http://leg1.state.va.us/lis.htm for more detailed information).

The act defines the rights of natural children, adopted children, children by previous marriages, illegitimate children, children of surrogates, and children born by in vitro fertilization.

IN PRACTICE Real estate licensees are cautioned that their involvement in real estate transactions involving part of an estate can open the door to complications that may arise from claims by the heirs.

If a person dies **testate**, that is, having executed a valid will, but fails to specifically devise or bequeath all property, the undistributed property is treated as if the person died intestate.

When a person dies intestate, distribution is made first to the surviving spouse. If there are children or their descendants, two-thirds of the estate passes to the children with the remaining third to the surviving spouse. If there is no surviving spouse or children, the estate is distributed in accordance with the Virginia Code rules of descent and distribution (§64.1-1).

■ **FOR EXAMPLE** A man died without having made a valid will. His estate, valued at $785,950, was distributed among his surviving spouse and three children as follows:

The surviving spouse: $261,983.33 = ⅓ of $785,950

Each of the children: $174,655.55 each = ⅔ divided by 3

If he had left a valid will disposing of $500,000 of the estate, the remaining $285,950 would be distributed to his spouse and children as follows:

Surviving spouse: $95,316.67 = ⅓ of $285,950

Each of the children: $63,544.44 each = ⅔ of $285,950 divided by 3

Although a surviving spouse could be named in a will to receive certain property and to be further entitled to receive a share of the surplus, it is possible for the spouse to renounce the will and claim an **elective share** of the augmented estate with the same distribution as if the deceased died intestate.

Augmented Estate   An **augmented estate** consists of the property, both real and personal, owned by the deceased at the time of death. The value of the augmented estate is the value that remains after the payment of funeral expenses, the cost of the estate administrator, and personal debts of the decedent.

Items that can be excluded from the augmented estate include

- property owned by the surviving spouse;
- property owned by the decedent and another, with right of survivorship;
- property conveyed during the marriage with the consent of the surviving spouse;
- property acquired by the decedent as a gift, by will or intestate succession from someone other than the surviving spouse; and
- property transferred prior to January 1, 1991, if such transfer was irrevocable as of that date.

If a claim for an elective share is made, the surviving spouse receives one-third of the estate if there are children. If there are no children or descendants of children, the surviving spouse is entitled to one-half of the estate (§64.1-16).

Other Considerations   A surviving spouse has the right to possess and occupy the principal family residence during the period of time that the estate matters are being settled although the residence may be a part of the augmented estate of the deceased.

If a husband or wife willfully deserts or abandons his or her spouse until the death of the deserted spouse, the deserting spouse is barred from all interest of the other by intestate succession, elective share, exempt property, family allowance, and homestead allowance.

A surviving spouse may be entitled to the Virginia Homestead allowance of $15,000. If there is no surviving spouse, the $15,000 is divided equally among any minor children. The homestead allowance is in lieu of any share passing to the spouse or children by will or intestate distribution.

■ VIRGINIA HOMESTEAD EXEMPTION

Under Virginia's **homestead exemption**, a householder is entitled to hold a certain amount of real or personal property exempt from unsecured debts. The total value of the property may not exceed $5,000, plus $500 for each dependent. If the householder is 65 or older or a veteran with 40% or more disability, the allowance is $10,000.

Only a householder or head of a family may have the benefit of the homestead exemption. A husband and wife living together may both be deemed householders if each contributes to maintaining the household.

The exemption does not apply against

- ■ claims for the purchase price of the homestead property,
- ■ mechanics' liens, and
- ■ claims for taxes.

The claim to homestead must be made by deed in the case of real property or by an inventory under oath for personal property. The owner of the homestead may sell or encumber the homestead property.

The key words in the homestead exemption are **unsecured debts**. For example, a credit card balance is an unsecured debt. On the other hand, because a mortgage or a deed of trust is secured by real property, it has priority over the homestead exemption. The property may be sold at foreclosure to satisfy a secured debt.

In addition to the homestead estate, the householder is entitled to hold certain other items of real and personal property exempt from sale for the satisfaction of a debt, such as a family bible, wedding and engagement rings, family portraits and heirlooms, a burial plot, $1,000 worth of clothing, $5,000 worth of household furnishings, one firearm worth no more than $3,000, all pets, health aids, items needed for an occupation or trade up to $10,000 in value, and an unsecured automobile up to $6,000 in value.

IN PRACTICE   A real estate agent may be unaware that a homestead deed has been filed. The exemption is usually revealed in a title search conducted by an attorney or title examiner. The agent should be aware that the filing could indicate financial difficulties or even pending bankruptcy, or that judgments may be recorded.

A full discussion of the Virginia Homestead Exemption can be found in the Code of Virginia, Title 34.

■ EASEMENTS

Simply put, an **easement** is a right to use someone else's land. The most common easement is a utility company's right to access and use a landowner's land (property) for the purposes of delivering the utility either to the landowner or other landowners.

Creating an Easement

An easement may be acquired by express grant or may be created by covenant or agreement. In Virginia, the owner of a dominant tenement may convey the land without the easement. When the easement is not an **easement by necessity**, that is, not necessary for access to the property, and the appurtenance is expressly excluded by the grant, it will not convey. When a grantor conveys land by a deed that describes the property as bounded by a road or street that the grantor owns, the grantor is implying that a right-of-way exists. The grantee acquires the benefit of the easement automatically.

If the width of a right-of-way is not specified in the grant, it is limited to the width as it existed at the time of the grant. An **easement by prescription** is somewhat similar to the acquisition of property by adverse possession and the two terms are often confused. An easement by prescription differs from adverse possession in significant ways, as shown in Figure 3.1.

FIGURE 3.1

Easement by Prescription versus Adverse Possession

Criteria	Easement by Prescription	Adverse Possession (See Chapter 8)
Use of the property	Use of the property occurs with the knowledge and acquiescence of the landowner	Use of the property is hostile and without the true owner's permission
Prescriptive period	20 years	15 years
Tacking allowed?	Tacking is permitted	Tacking is not permitted

In an action to establish an easement by prescription in Virginia, the court must find that use of the property was

- adverse,
- under a claim of right,
- exclusive,
- continuous,
- uninterrupted, and
- with the knowledge and acquiescence of the landowner.

In Virginia, the prescriptive period is 20 years. **Tacking**—combining successive periods of continuous uninterrupted use by different parties—is permitted in Virginia.

When an easement is terminated, no document needs to be recorded in the clerk's office of the county where the land is located.

■ FORMS OF HOMEOWNERSHIP

There are many forms of homeownership available in Virginia, including several types of ownership by two or more parties. The first part of this section deals with co-ownership of a single property; the second half is dedicated to co-ownership within a greater complex of other homeowners.

Co-Ownership

An individual is said to own property in severalty. When two or more people purchase a property, the term is *tenancy*. The significant part of which type of tenancy is selected is concerned with rights of inheritance.

Joint Tenancy   Virginia's **joint tenancy** is similar to that of most other states, insofar as the four unities of time, title, interest, and possession must be present. However, Virginia's interpretation of *unity of interest* is that one joint tenant cannot be a tenant for life and another for years. Similarly, one tenant cannot be a tenant in fee and another a tenant for life. Joint tenancy is always created by an act of the parties, never by descent or operation of law.

The doctrine of **automatic survivorship** has been abolished in Virginia. The legislature intended to place joint tenants in the same situation as tenants in common as far as augmented estates were concerned. If the deed expressly creates a joint tenancy with right of survivorship (as in common law), then on the death of a joint tenant, the entire estate continues in the surviving tenant or tenants. The surviving spouse of the deceased joint tenant has no liability, and the deceased's creditors have no claim against the enlarged interests of the surviving tenants. Property owners who wish to have a property pass at their death to particular persons frequently create a joint tenancy as a substitute for a will.

A tenant in common or a joint tenant who commits waste may be liable to the other cotenant(s) for damages. By statute, a joint tenant or a tenant in common may demand an accounting from a cotenant who receives more than her fair share of rents and profits from the property. Similarly, joint tenants or tenants in common who improve a common property at their own expense are entitled to file a partition suit to divide and sell the property to obtain compensation for the improvements. However, if one tenant makes improvements without the consent of the other, the amount of compensation is limited to the amount by which the value of the common property has been enhanced.

Tenancy in Common   In Virginia, **tenancy in common** may be created by

- an express limitation to two or more persons to hold land as tenants in common;
- a grant of part interest in one's land to another;
- a devise or grant of land to two or more persons to be divided between them;
- a breakup of estates in joint tenancy; and
- the dissolving of a tenancy by the entirety as a result of the divorce or mutual agreement of the parties.

A tenant in common may convey undivided interest; however, a contract by one tenant in common relating to the whole estate is voidable by any cotenant who did not join in the contract.

A deceased cotenant's interest, in passing through his will or to his heirs, is subject to the statute of Wills and Decedents Estates, which protects the rights of the surviving spouse (see Augmented Estate earlier in this chapter). Tenancy in common carries no right of survivorship, and the interest of the deceased does not automatically pass to a surviving cotenant.

Tenancy by the Entirety   **Tenancy by the entirety** is a special type of joint tenancy created between husband and wife that is honored in Virginia. There is no right to partition or to convey a half interest. The tenancy is indestructible except by mutual agreement or divorce, in which case the tenancy by the entirety is converted into a tenancy in common.

Property held by husband and wife as tenants by the entirety is legally an asset of both parties. If one spouse contracts to convey the property, that spouse cannot do so alone. The conveying spouse would be answerable to the would-be purchaser for the inability to perform.

IN PRACTICE   If a married woman has retained her maiden name, the deed should grant to "John Doe and Mary Jones, husband and wife, as tenants by the entirety," not to "Mary Doe, also called Mary Jones."

Neither spouse alone may encumber the property. Any debts that could become liens on the property must be entered into jointly by both parties.

Community Property   There are no community property laws in Virginia.

Tenancy in Partnership   A partnership may own real property, but each individual partner's interest is considered personal property. A partner is co-owner with the other partners of real property as a tenant in partnership.

Tenancy in partnership has the following features:

- A partner (subject to the partnership agreement) has an equal right with the other partners to possess the property for partnership purposes but may not possess it for any other purpose without the other partners' consent.
- A partner's right in a property is not assignable unless all the partners assign their rights in the same property.
- A partner's right in the property is not subject to creditors, except for a claim against the partnership itself. When partnership property is attached for a partnership debt, no rights can be claimed under homestead exemption laws by any partner or by the representative of a deceased partner.
- On the death of a partner, that partner's interest in partnership property passes to the surviving partners. If the decedent was the last surviving partner, her right in the property vests in her legal representative. The surviving partner, or legal representative, has no right to possess the property for anything other than a partnership purpose.
- A partner can transfer property on behalf of all the partners if acting within the scope of the firm's business and purposes. Partners may transfer partnership property among themselves, provided all partners consent.

IN PRACTICE   Whenever a real estate licensee represents a buyer who is purchasing partnership-owned property, the licensee should have an attorney review the partnership agreement to ensure that a general partner with power to bind all other general partners executes conveyance. It is desirable to have a written resolution of the partnership authorizing the sale.

Corporations   A corporation may acquire and convey real property in its corporate name. A contract entered into by a corporation under an assumed name may be enforced by either party. If an instrument bears both a corporate seal and the signatures of the responsible corporate officers, it is presumed to be a corporate instrument, even if it lacks the required number of signatures or the corporate name.

IN PRACTICE Anyone who purchases real estate from a corporation should require a written corporate resolution that duly authorizes the sale of property by the corporation.

Co-Ownership Within a Community

Some forms of ownership involve the use of a **public offering statement (POS)**. The sale of a cooperative, a condominium, or a time-share requires the POS to fully and accurately disclose the characteristics of the project. Additionally, the Virginia Property Owners Association Act may require the use of the POS.

Condominiums, cooperatives, time-shares, and the property owner associations now fall under the authority of the Common Interest Community (CIC) Board. A Common Interest Community Manager is defined as a person or entity that provides management services to an association for a fee or other compensation. Management services may include the following:

- Acting for the association in its business, legal, financial, or other transactions
- Executing the resolutions and decisions of an association or enforcing the rights secured by law
- Collecting, disbursing, or otherwise controlling money or other property
- Preparing budgets, financial statements, or other financial reports
- Arranging, conducting, or coordinating meetings of the association or its governing body
- Negotiating contracts or arranging for services on behalf of the association
- Offering or soliciting to perform any services on behalf of an association

The Common Interest Community Manager must be licensed by the CIC.

New legislation in 2011 states that no association or CIC manager can require payment at the time requests are made for packets, certificates, or updates. The fees are to be collected at settlement. If settlement does not occur within 90 days, the fees may be assessed against the lot or unit owner. (For non-CIC managed associations the law is unclear as to time of payment.)

The law does not require a signed receipt for the hand-delivery but does when delivered by electronic means.

IN PRACTICE A licensee should make sure that a purchaser signs a receipt for delivery of a resale packet or certificate that states that the packet received should contain all the required disclosures, not that the packet is complete. This allows time for the purchaser to review the packet within the three-day right-of-recession period.

Cooperative Ownership

Cooperative ownership is governed by the Virginia Real Estate Cooperative Act. (§§55-424 through 55-506) The Common Interest Community Board (CIC) is charged with administrative responsibility for the Virginia Cooperative Act. A **cooperative** is "real estate owned by an association, each of the members of which is entitled, by virtue of his or her ownership interest in the association, to exclusive possession of a unit."

A cooperative is created by a *Declaration of Cooperative*, filed in the clerk's office of the circuit court in the district in which the real estate is located. A cooperative has both common elements and limited common elements. When an individual purchases a cooperative unit, he is purchasing shares in the corporation (considered personal property) and signing a proprietary lease that allows for use of that particular unit.

The cooperative association may adopt and amend bylaws, rules, and regulations; adopt and amend budgets; hire and discharge management agents; regulate the use, maintenance, and repair of common elements; impose charges; and exercise other powers conferred by the declaration and bylaws.

Unless otherwise provided by the cooperative declaration, the association is responsible for the common elements and the proprietary lessee is responsible for the individual unit. The association has a lien on the cooperative interest for unpaid assessments. Nonpayment of assessment may be cause for eviction and resale of the cooperative interest.

Sale of a Cooperative Interest   In the case of an initial sale of the cooperative, the purchaser must be given a Public Offering Statement (POS). The POS must be provided before conveyance and not later than the date of the contract. If this does not occur, the seller has a financial liability (§55-483).

Before the contract for the resale of a cooperative interest is executed or before conveyance, the purchaser must be given, among other things, a proprietary lease, a copy of the declaration, bylaws, and rules and regulations of the association, and a certificate containing the following statements:

- Disclosure of the effect of any right of first refusal or other restraint on transferability
- The amount of the monthly common expense assessment, as well as any unpaid expense currently due or payable from the sale and from the lessee
- Any other fees payable by proprietary lessees
- Any capital expenditures anticipated by the association for the current and next two succeeding fiscal years
- The amount of reserves for capital expenditures designated for specific projects
- The most recent regularly prepared balance sheet and income/expense statement
- The current operating budget of the association
- Unsatisfied judgments and pending suits
- Insurance coverage
- Health or building code violations against the unit or common elements
- Remaining term of any leasehold estate and provisions for extensions or renewal, if any

- Disclosure that the Public Offering Statement (POS) is available for inspection
- Deductibility of any real estate taxes and interest
- Restrictions in the declaration that may affect the amount received by the proprietary lease holder on sale, condemnation, or loss to the unit or cooperative upon termination of the cooperative
- Certification that the association has filed the required reports to the CIC

Alternately, the documents can be provided after the ratification of a contract when the contract is made contingent on the receipt of such documents and when it provides for the statutory rescission period to the purchaser.

IN PRACTICE In the sale of a cooperative interest, it is the seller's obligation to provide a buyer with the required information. The real estate licensee, however, may facilitate the transfer of information from the seller to the buyer as a service to the client.

Buyer's Right to Rescind In Virginia, purchasers of a cooperative interest have certain rights to rescind the contract. In an initial sale, (the first time the cooperative interest is sold after the cooperative is established), the buyer has the right to rescind within 10 days following ratification of the contract or after receiving the Public Offering Statement, whichever is later. When a cooperative unit is resold, that is, by an owner to a buyer, the purchase contract is voidable by the purchaser until the certificate has been provided and for five days thereafter or until conveyance, whichever occurs first (§55-484).

Condominium Ownership

The Common Interest Community (CIC) Board is charged with the administrative responsibility for the Virginia Condominium Act (§§55-79.39 through 55-79.103).

A **condominium** can be a multiunit structure, an attached single-family dwelling, such as a town home, or a detached single-family dwelling. Commercial properties may also be condominiums. It is important to recognize that a condominium is a form of ownership and not a type of property or structure. The owner of property may convert the property to condominium status. The owner is called the declarant because she must declare her intent to have the property considered a condominium.

The declarant must provide declaration instruments to the CIC Board that includes the following:

- Name of the condominium (the name must include the word *condominium)*
- Name of city and county where the condominium is located
- Legal description by metes and bounds
- Description or delineation of the horizontal and vertical boundaries of each unit
- Description or delineation of all common elements and any limited common elements

- The allocation to each unit of the undivided ownership interest in the common elements
- A statement of the declarant's obligation to complete improvements not yet completed (specific to type and quality, size or capacity, and time for completion)

There may be additional requirements if the condominium contains any convertible land is an expandable, contractible, or leasehold condominium.

In addition, the declarant must submit a copy of the *bylaws* under which the condominium will operate. The bylaws shall be specific regarding such issues as

- the form of self-governance for the unit owners;
- whether there are to be trustees, a board of directors, or other officers;
- their exact duties and the means by which they are to be appointed or elected;
- the extent to which the governing or executive body may delegate responsibilities to a management agent;
- the accounting and management records that will be maintained;
- a schedule of meetings of all owners and of the executive body;
- statutory requirements for meeting notices (21 days); and
- the rules and regulations that will apply to all owners.

Condominium Public Offering Statement   The declarant must also provide a Public Offering Statement (POS). The POS discloses all characteristics of the condominium and makes known all unusual and material circumstances or features. The POS shall include

- the name and principal address of the declarant;
- a narrative description of the condominium, including the number of units and future plans for the addition of more units;
- copies of the declaration and bylaws, a projected budget, and provisions for reserves;
- copies of any management contract or lease of recreational areas, including a statement of the relationship between the declarant and the managing agent;
- a description of the status of construction, zoning, permits, or other compliance with state or local statute or regulation;
- the terms of any encumbrances, liens, or easements that affect the title;
- the terms and conditions of any financing offered to purchasers;
- provisions of warranties;
- a statement that purchaser may cancel the contract within 10 days of delivery of the POS, or within 10 days of the contract date, whichever is later;
- a statement of the declarant's obligation to complete planned improvements;
- a statement identifying the common and limited common elements along with any user fees;
- a statement of any limitation on the number of persons who may occupy a unit; and
- a statement setting forth any restrictions or limitation on the right to display the flag of the United States, including size, place, and manner of display (§55.79-90).

Initial Sale of a Condominium Unit   At the initial sale of a condominium unit, the purchaser receives a copy of the POS along with the sales contract. The first purchaser of a condominium unit has the right to rescind a ratified contract, without penalty, within five days (reduced from 10 days in 2014), for any reason. The five-day period begins with the date of contract ratification or on receipt of the POS, whichever is later. The right to rescind cannot be waived. The right to cancel must be listed on the first page of the purchase contract in bold, 12-point type.

At closing, the purchaser acquires a fee simple interest in the individual unit and an undivided percentage interest in the common elements as a tenant in common with the other unit owners. At this time, the purchaser assumes responsibility for the individual unit purchased.

The declarant remains responsible for all unsold units and for the overall management and maintenance of the condominium development until 75% of the units are sold. At that point, responsibility for maintenance and management of the property shifts to the owners' association. The declarant becomes a member of the association as owner of the remaining units.

Voting Rights   Each unit owner has an assigned ownership interest and voting rights in the governance of the condominium. This interest is usually in proportion to the size of each individual unit and the amenities of the unit. The exact percentage of ownership interest is established in the declaration.

Bylaw Changes   The Condominium Act states that two-thirds of the total voting interest is required to change the bylaws.

Termination   Once a property has been declared a condominium, its status can be changed by abandoning or dissolving it; 80% of the voting interest must approve the termination of a condominium's status.

Statutory Lien Rights   The unit owners' association has a statutory lien on every unit for unpaid assessments levied against the unit. This lien is secondary to real estate tax liens and other liens recorded prior to the filing of the original condominium declaration.

Resale of a Condominium Unit   All unit owners have the right to resell their individual units. In the event of an intended resale, the seller must obtain certain documents from the unit owners' association. These documents are collectively called the **resale certificate**.

The unit owners' association shall furnish the resale certificate upon the written notice request of any unit owner within 14 days of the receipt of such request. Payment of actual costs of preparing the resale certificate may be required of the unit owner requesting it as a prerequisite to its issuance, but the total fee shall not exceed a total of $150 for two hard copies or $125 for an electronic version. An additional expedite fee (certificate must be delivered within five days) may be charged up to $50. An additional hard copy may be ordered for $25. The declarant may also charge a $100 fee for inspection of the unit as a requirement for preparing the resale certificate (§55.79.97:1).

In response to complaints from agents that condos and POAs were overcharging, HB 1674 was passed by the General Assembly, effective July 1, 2011, that explicitly prohibits unauthorized resale packet fees. The bill also amends the Condo Act to include a right of cancellation if a resale packet is unavailable.

The resale certificate shall be current as of the date specified on the resale certificate but not more than 12 months old. This means that the seller may obtain the certificate in advance of any purchase contract and have it immediately available for the purchaser. The buyer's rights to receive the certificate and to cancel the contract are waived if the right is not exercised prior to settlement.

Right to Rescind   The certificate must be provided to the purchaser. The purchaser may cancel the contract under the following conditions:

- Within three days after the date of the contract if the certificate was provided to the purchaser on or before the date that the purchaser signs the contract
- Within three days after receiving the certificate if hand-delivered or by electronic means
- Within six days of the postmark date if the certificate is mailed (§55.79.97)

Legislation passed in 2011 allows buyers to electronically deliver notice of cancellation under the POA and Condominium Acts.

Condominium Disclosure Packet   The documents required in the resale certificate include the following:

- A statement of any expenditure of funds requiring an assessment in addition to the regular assessment
- A statement of all assessments and other fees or charges currently imposed
- A statement whether there is any other entity or facility to which the unit owner may be liable for fees or charges
- A statement of the status and amount of any reserve or replacement fund
- A copy of the current budget and statement of current financial position
- A statement of any pending suits or judgments
- A statement setting forth what insurance coverage is provided for all unit owners
- A statement that any improvements or alterations made to the unit are not in violation of the condominium instruments
- A copy of the current bylaws, rules and regulations, and architectural guidelines
- A statement of whether the condominium is subject to the Property Owners' Association Act
- A copy of notice given to the unit owner of any current or pending rule or architectural violation
- A copy of approved minutes of unit owners' association meetings for previous six months
- Certification that the association has filed the annual report to the Common Interest Community Board
- A statement of any limitation on number of persons who may occupy a unit
- A statement setting forth any restrictions on right of unit owner to display the flag of the United States (55-79.97)

Time-Share Ownership

Following are two types of **time-share ownership** recognized by the Virginia Time-Share Act (§55-360 et seq.):

- *Time-share estate* means a right to occupy a unit, or any of several units, during five or more separate time periods over a period of at least five years. The time-share estate includes renewal options, coupled with either a freehold interest or an estate for years, that is, a lease, in all or part of a time-share project.
- *Time-share use* means a right to occupy a time-share unit or any of several time-share units, during five or more separate time periods over a period of at least five years, including renewal options, not coupled with a freehold estate or an estate for years in a time-share project. Time-share use does not mean a right subject to a first-come, first-served, space-available basis that exists in a country club, motel, or health spa.

The Common Interest Community Board is charged with the administrative responsibility for the Time-Share Act.

Creation of a Time-Share   The developer of a time-share project must file and record with the CIC a time-share instrument that defines the project being created. This process establishes a time-share association in accordance with the Virginia Nonstock Corporations Act (§13.1-801).

A time-share association must be set up before any time-share estates may be sold. The project must be named, and the name must include the words *time-share*, *time-share interest*, *interval ownership*, *vacation ownership*, or other terms recognized in the industry.

Some of the items that are to be included in the time-share instrument include

- the name of the time-share project;
- the complete address and legal description of the project; and
- a description of the property (§55.367).

Time-Share Public Offering Statement   The POS filed for a time-share project is similar to the POS filed for a condominium. The developer may not convey any interest or advertise the property until the POS has been approved. If the time-share is being converted from another type of ownership, additional information is required regarding repairs made during the preceding three years and the physical condition of the structure. The purpose and value of reserve funds must be disclosed.

If the property to be converted is currently leased, tenants must be given 90 days' notice of the intent to convert the property to a time-share project. The tenants then have 60 days in which to contract with the developer to purchase the unit currently occupied if that unit is to be part of the overall project. Tenants on month-to-month leases must be given 120 days' notice to vacate.

Right to Rescind   The purchaser of a time-share interest at the project's initial sale has seven calendar days from execution of contract in which to cancel the contract without penalty. The developer is required to deliver the POS to the purchaser prior to the execution of the contract. The cancellation period commences on the date of contract ratification. If the seventh day falls on a Sunday or legal holiday, the right to cancel will expire on the day following the Sunday or legal holiday. The purchaser's right of cancellation cannot be waived, which must be identified in the contract.

Further, if there are material changes to the POS prior to settlement and after the initial time of contracting to purchase, the developer must provide the purchaser with the amended statement. The purchaser's right of cancellation is reinstated.

Deposits   Money received by the developer as earnest money deposits or down payments must be placed in an escrow account established by the developer and held there through the rescission period. The developer also must post a surety bond with the REB in the amount of $25,000 or the amount of the deposits received, whichever is greater. If any purchaser exercises the statutory right of rescission, the developer has 45 days in which to refund all monies paid by the purchaser.

Advertisements   Advertisements used for the marketing of time-share interests that offer gifts or prizes must clearly disclose the retail value of the gift or prize offered. The ad must also disclose the terms and conditions under which the gift is offered, the odds of actually winning a prize, and the number of gifts or prizes to be awarded. The ad must include the offer's expiration date and a statement that the offer is made for the purpose of soliciting the purchase of a time-share estate.

Transfer of Control   The developer remains in control of the project until 90% of the time-share estate has been sold or when all amenities and facilities have been completed, whichever is later. This is called the *developer control period*. The developer control period may not exceed 10 years after the sale of the first time-share interest. At the conclusion of the developer control period, the time-share owners' association assumes control and responsibility for the management and maintenance of the project. The developer must transfer control of the project to the owners' association without charging any fee. The owners' association may appoint or elect a managing agent for the project.

The owners' association has a statutory lien on every time-share estate in the project for unpaid regular and special assessments. The bylaws of the association may be changed by a vote of the owners. Should the owners decide to terminate the time-share project, approval by 51% of the voting interest of the association is required.

Resale of Time-Share   A *resale* of a time-share interest by any person other than the developer is subject to rules similar to those governing the resale of a condominium. The seller must obtain a resale certificate from the owners' association. The certificate contains a copy of the time-share instruments; current financial statements; current bylaws; current rules and regulations of the association; fees and assessments; a disclosure of any liens that may be pending on the time-share for nonpayment of fees; and a statement of pending litigation against the developer, owners' association, or managing entity relative to the time-share project. The association may charge up to $50 for the certificate of resale.

The buyer in a time-share resale has the right to rescind the contract within five days following receipt of the certificate of resale or actual transfer, whichever occurs first. This right is without penalty and may be for any reason. Once the contract has closed, however, all rights of rescission are waived.

Statute of Limitations   Any action for misrepresentation of information in the project instruments, the POS, or any contract must be initiated within two years of the date of the contract.

■ VIRGINIA PROPERTY OWNERS' ASSOCIATION ACT

The Virginia Property Owners' Association (POA) Act sets forth requirements for the formation and operation of the property owners' association. Each association subject to the act is governed by covenants, deed restrictions, POSs, bylaws, and other restrictions designed to manage, regulate, and control the specific development, community, subdivision, or neighborhood and their common areas, if any. The specifics of the various governing documents vary among associations (Code of Virginia, Title 55, Chapter 26, §§55-508 through 55-516.2).

The Common Interest Community (CIC) Board is charged with the administrative responsibility for the Virginia POA Act.

An association may be either self-managed or an independent management company may be employed to manage the affairs of the association. The act allows for a board of directors that may consist of property owners, developer representatives, and even representation from the independent management company, if used. Actions of the board, meetings, records, budgets, reports, and other association functions are governed by the act and the specific association documents. The board has the power to establish, adopt, and enforce rules with respect to the use of common areas and/or other areas of responsibility as established in the original declaration. A majority of votes from a quorum of the property members is usually required to repeal or amend rules and regulations. Violations of rules and regulations by the member property owner may result in the member being suspended from use of the common area facilities.

Property owners may be assessed routine fees, as allowed by the association documents, for the maintenance and upkeep of the association and common areas. Special assessments may be levied by the association. These special assessments usually require a majority vote of the property owners in accordance with the association's bylaws. Failure of a property owner to pay the authorized assessments entitles the association to place a lien on the property (§55-516).

Exemptions

Condominiums, cooperatives, time-shares, and campgrounds are exempt from the POA act. However, if one of these types of ownership is located within an area that has been declared to be under the POA Act, the property is subject to both sets of regulations.

IN PRACTICE   Reston, Virginia, is a very large planned unit development (PUD) and properties there are subject to POA fees. There are also several condominium projects within the PUD that are subject to both condo and POA fees.

Additional exemptions to disclosure requirements include disposition of a lot by gift, pursuant to court order, by foreclosure, sale at auction, or to a person not acquiring the lot for a personal resident.

Disclosure Requirements

Because each association may impose certain restrictions and fees on the member property owners, potential purchasers must receive sufficient information prior to settlement about the association in order to make an informed decision to continue with the purchase. Therefore, any party who sells property subject to the act must include a statement in the sales contract to the effect that

- the property is located in a development that is subject to the POA Act;
- the act requires that the seller obtain a disclosure packet from the POA and provide that packet to the buyer;
- the buyer may cancel the contract within three days after receiving the packet or being advised that the packet will not be provided;
- the buyer has the right to request an update of the packet; and
- the rights to cancel the contract are waived if those rights are not exercised prior to closing.

If the contract does not contain these disclosures, the sole remedy for the buyer is to rescind the contract prior to closing (§55-511).

POA Disclosure Packet

The information in the POA disclosure packet must be current as of the date of the packet. This allows the property owner to have a packet available for the buyer at the time of contract.

The association is required to make the packet available within 14 days after an owner/member, or an owner/member's authorized agent, files a written request. The association may charge a fee reflecting the actual cost for preparation of the packet but shall not exceed $150 for two hard copies or $125 for an electronic version. An additional hard copy can be purchased for $25. The association's failure to deliver the packet in a timely manner waives any claim for delinquent assessments or fines (§55-509.5).

An association that is not professionally managed may charge $0.10 per page or a total of $100 for actual costs in preparing the packet. The cost for a disclosure packet update cannot exceed $50.

Contents of the POA Disclosure

Each disclosure packet must include the name of the association plus the name and address of the registered agent, if incorporated. The packet must also include

- a statement of any expenditure that would require an additional assessment during the current or succeeding fiscal year;
- a statement of all assessments and other fees currently imposed;
- a statement whether there is any other entity or facility to which the lot owner may be liable for fees or charges;
- the current reserve report and a statement of the status and amount of any reserve or replacement fund;

- a copy of the current budget plus statement of income and expenses, including a statement of the balance on any loans;
- a statement of any pending suit or unpaid judgment;
- a statement of what insurance coverage is provided for lot owners and what is expected of each individual lot owner;
- plans for any improvement or alteration of lot or uses of common areas;
- any restrictions on the placement of For Sale signs or flags;
- a statement setting forth any restriction, limitation, or prohibition on the right of a lot owner to display any flag, including restrictions as to size, place, and manner of placement; and
- certification that the association has filed with the CIC Board the required annual report.

The Association Disclosure Packet must include the following attachments, if any:

- A copy of the current declaration, articles of incorporation and bylaws, and all rules and regulations or architectural guidelines adopted by the association
- A copy of notice given to the lot owner of any current or pending violation of rules
- Copies of last six months' minutes of the association meetings

An informational form prepared by the CIC Board must accompany all POA disclosure packets. The purpose of this form is to describe the special circumstances and the relationship between lot owners and the association in order to educate the prospective purchasers and foster a better understanding between the property owners and the association. A copy of this form is available on the Virginia Association of REALTORS® website.

Purchaser's Right to Request Update

The purchaser may submit a copy of the contract to the association with a request for updating of the disclosure packet. The association must respond within 10 days and has the right to charge the purchaser a fee for preparation of the new packet that reflects the actual cost but not to exceed $50. The purpose of this request for update of the packet is to both assure the buyer that there have been no changes and to identify the specifics of any material changes. If there have been any material changes, the buyer has no recourse for cancellation of the contract unless that right had previously been agreed on in the purchase contract.

IN PRACTICE When purchasing a property bound by a POA, it is wise to include terms in the contract allowing the purchaser to request an update and to be able to void the contract if an update to a previously provided POA packet is not forthcoming within a specified period of time.

Purchaser's Right to Rescind

The purchaser has the right to cancel the contract

- within three days after the date of the contract, if the packet or notice that the packet is unavailable was provided before signing of the contract;

- within three days after receiving the packet or notice that the packet is not available (if hand-delivered or by electronic means); or
- within six days after the postmark date of either the packet or the notice that the packet is not available was sent by U.S. mail.

The purchaser may also cancel the contract any time prior to settlement if not notified that the disclosure packet will not be available nor the packet delivered.

If the purchaser elects to rescind, the notice of rescission must be hand-delivered or sent by U.S. mail, return receipt requested, to the owner. Rescission is without penalty, and the purchaser is entitled to a full refund of any earnest money given. Any rights to rescind the contract must be exercised prior to closing.

Legislation allows buyers to electronically deliver notice of cancellation under the POA and Condominium Acts.

A complete discussion of interests and forms of ownership of real estate in Virginia may be found in the Code of Virginia, Title 55—Property and Conveyances; see the table of contents, Title 55, at http://leg1.state.va.us/lis.htm.

Changes Made by 2014 General Assembly

Several miscellaneous items regarding condominium or property-owner associations were passed by the 2014 General Assembly, including the following:

- The process for members of a Condo or Property Owners' Association to inspect association records was clarified. Residents are permitted to inspect records during normal business hours with 5 business days' written notice to a professionally managed association or 10 business days' written notice to a self-managed association.
- Associations may not assess a late fee of more than 5% for non-payment of assessments unless otherwise stated in the association documents.
- Associations may not charge separate inspection fees for unimproved lots or charge sellers for website access to request the resale disclosure packet. The choice of electronic delivery is at the option of the seller. Five electronic copies are to be provided for the same fee to the seller, seller's agent, purchaser, purchaser's agent, and one additional person. If the resale packet is delivered using a commercial mail delivery service, the right of cancellation is set at three days following delivery.
- An association may take action against a unit owner in general district or circuit court for violations of the condo or POA instruments. The owner must be given written notice and time to correct the violation. The prevailing party may recover court costs and reasonable attorneys' fees.
- No association may ban the installation of solar collection devices unless the ban is specifically outlined in the recorded declarations.

CHAPTER 3 QUIZ

1. Which of the following does *NOT* constitute the exercise of eminent domain by the process of condemnation?
   a. A county taking a farmer's cropland for a highway
   b. The state taking from private woodland for the construction of a roadside visitor center
   c. A county zoning ordinance change
   d. Port Authority of Hampton Roads taking riparian rights for a pier

2. All of the following items could be excluded from an augmented estate *EXCEPT*
   a. a condominium owned by the deceased wife.
   b. a small farm willed to the deceased by his grandmother.
   c. a beach property sold with the wife's consent.
   d. a 52-foot sailboat purchased during the marriage.

3. Which of the following statements concerning the homestead exemption is *TRUE*?
   a. Exemption is automatic; every homeowner has one.
   b. The homeowner's filing for homestead exemption indicates financial difficulties.
   c. The homestead exemption is protection against claims for taxes, mechanics' liens, and deeds of trust against the property.
   d. The family bible, wedding rings, and burial plots are in addition to the $5,000 exemption.

4. All of the following are true of an easement by necessity *EXCEPT*
   a. it must be an appurtenant easement.
   b. both the dominant and the servient estates must have at some time in the past been owned by the same person.
   c. the only reasonable means of access is over the servient estate.
   d. inconvenience is a basis for the easement.

5. A married couple owns real property as tenants by the entirety. The husband dies owing money to creditors. In this situation, the wife owns the property
   a. in severalty and is liable to the creditors.
   b. and is not liable to the creditors.
   c. except for a share owned by the creditors.
   d. held by her husband, and the creditors cannot make any claim to the property.

6. Which of the following is *TRUE* regarding Virginia's community property laws?
   a. Since 2001, the Virginia statute is patterned after California's statute.
   b. Virginia only recognizes some community property provisions.
   c. Augmented estates are the same as community property provisions.
   d. Virginia is not a community property state.

7. Two partners in a successful accounting practice are in the process of purchasing a small office condominium for their practice. They would *NOT* be able to take title as
   a. tenants by the entirety.
   b. tenants in common.
   c. joint tenants.
   d. tenants in partnership.

8. Contracts for the initial purchase of a cooperative interest may be rescinded without penalty how many days after either contract ratification or receipt of the POS?
   a. 5 days
   b. 10 days
   c. 14 days
   d. 21 Days

9. If a condominium unit owner fails to pay the homeowners association's assessment against his unit, the association may
   a. place a lien against the unit.
   b. garnish the owner's wages.
   c. do nothing; as a stockholder, the unit owner has priority.
   d. revoke the unit owner's privileges and rights.

10. A recently retired woman has a ratified contract to purchase a two-bedroom condominium unit. She is now suffering from buyer's remorse and wishes to back out of the contract. She has not yet received the condominium documents. After hand-delivery of the documents, she will have how many days to cancel the contract?

    a. 3 days
    b. 5 days
    c. 7 days
    d. 10 days

11. When the owner's interest in a time-share includes either a freehold interest or an estate for years, it is what type?

    a. Time-share use
    b. Time-share estate
    c. Time-share fee
    d. Time-share demise

12. A young man recently visited a brand-new time-share project on the Eastern Shore. If he decides to make an offer on the property, how long will he have to cancel the contract without penalty?

    a. None; he is bound to the contract
    b. 3 days after ratification of contract
    c. 7 days after ratification of contract
    d. 10 days after ratification of contract

13. A military couple has decided they no longer wish to purchase the town house that they currently have under contract. The town house is covered by the POA Act. The couple can cancel their contract

    a. whenever they wish.
    b. within 10 days after ratification of contract.
    c. within 3 days after receiving the POA disclosure packet.
    d. within 14 days after receiving the property disclosure packet.

14. Both the Condominium Act and the Property Owners' Association Act have a set limit on the amount that may be charged for preparation of the required document packet of

    a. $150 for two hard copies.
    b. up to $325.
    c. actual cost of copying.
    d. any amount they choose.

15. Administration of the Virginia Property Owners' Association Act comes under the

    a. REB.
    b. CIC Board.
    c. VAC.
    d. DPOR.

Real Estate Taxes and Other Liens

■ **LEARNING OBJECTIVES**   *After successfully completing this chapter, you will be able to*

■ **describe** taxation liens, including exemptions and special assessments;

■ **explain** a mechanic's lien and how it may be implemented; and

■ **define** judgments and other types of liens.

■ **KEY TERMS**

broker's lien	money judgment	vendor's lien
landlord's lien	principle of uniformity	writ of execution
lis pendens	"run with the land"	writ of possession
mechanic's lien	special assessment	

Real estate taxes in Virginia are levied according to the provisions of Article X of the Virginia Constitution. The article specifies that all property shall be levied at fair market value and shall be uniform upon the same class of subjects within the territorial limits of the authority levying the tax (i.e., residential, commercial). This **principle of uniformity** does not prevent differences in taxation or the classification for taxation purposes of properties according to use in a business, trade, or occupation. The General Assembly is given the authority to legislate laws for the levying and collecting of real estate taxes and to provide for a difference in the rate of taxation in certain circumstances. Virginia real and personal property tax records are managed by the County Assessor Office in each Virginia County. Many counties provide an online searchable database where searches can be made by address, owner name, or map number.

■ TITLE 58.1 – TAXATION

Title 58.1 of the Code of Virginia contains the general laws regarding taxation (§§58.1-3200 et seq.). Based on Article X, Section 4 of the Virginia Constitution, all taxable real estate is to be assessed for local taxation. Taxable real estate includes a leasehold interest in a case where the land or improvements are exempt from taxation by the owner.

Exemptions

Section 6 of Article X of the Constitution provides for the following exemptions from taxation:

- Property owned by the Commonwealth
- Real estate and personal property owned and used by churches or religious bodies for worship or residence of ministers
- Private or public non-profit burying grounds or cemeteries
- Property owned by non-profit public libraries or institutions of learning
- Intangible personal property
- Property used for religious, charitable, patriotic, historical, benevolent, cultural, or public park and playground purposes
- Property subject to a perpetual easement permitting inundation by water
- Property of any veteran determined to have a 100% service-connected disability who occupies the property as a personal residence (there will be a referendum on the November 2014 ballot to exempt from taxation the real property of the surviving spouse of a soldier killed in action as long as the assessed value of the property does not exceed the average value for the locality; the exemption would apply to both dwelling and land, not to exceed one acre).

The governing body of any county, city, or town may provide for the exemption or deferral of taxation for real estate owned and occupied by anyone at least 65 years old or permanently and totally disabled (see §58.1-3217). As of March 24, 2011, the law authorizes local governments to establish annual income or financial worth limitations as a condition of eligibility. Partial exemptions may also be granted for property in a redevelopment or conservation area, for certain rehabilitated, renovated, or replacement residential structures, and energy-efficient buildings.

Buildings that are listed on the Virginia Landmarks Register, not including the real estate or land on which they are located, are declared as a separate class of property and may be levied at a different rate as long as the building is maintained so as to retain the characteristics for which it was originally listed.

The controlling factor in determining whether private property is exempt from taxation is the use of the property. Public property, however, may be exempted from taxation without regard to its use. All non-exempt tangible personal property is subject to taxation by the local authority. Examples include aircraft, mobile homes, campers, and watercraft assessed at market value.

Transportation Issues

As part of Virginia's transportation plan, regional localities are now allowed to address their own specific transportation issues by raising funds independently. For example, earlier legislation had allowed counties and cities within the Northern Virginia Transportation Authority and the Hampton Roads metropolitan planning areas to permit real property zoned for commercial or industrial uses to be declared a separate class of real property for local taxation. All regional localities will now have this option.

The 2014 legislation also repealed the $64 annual license tax on hybrid electric motor vehicles that had been imposed in 2013. The DMV was directed to issue refunds for portions of the hybrid license taxes paid for registration years beginning on or after July 1, 2014.

Assessments

Taxes **"run with the land,"** meaning that the owner is responsible for paying real estate taxes for the current tax year from the date of purchase until the end of the year. In Virginia, the buyer is said to own the property on the date of closing or settlement. Taxes should be prorated between the seller (vendor) and the buyer (vendee) as of the day of settlement. Any delinquent taxes should be paid by the seller at closing. Penalties and interest on delinquent taxes are established by law.

IN PRACTICE Unpaid taxes are a lien on real property. The settlement agent must verify that prior years' taxes have been paid and ascertain the status of the current year's taxes. Any other information should be obtained from city or county tax offices.

Taxes are generally not payable in advance of the due date. However, each city and county has its own particular manner of assessing taxes and setting the due date. Real estate licensees should be aware of four phases of taxes:

1. Past-due taxes
2. Taxes currently due and payable
3. Taxes not yet due
4. Prepaid taxes

The taxes for the first two phases will be collected from the seller's proceeds and paid to the proper authority by the settlement attorney. In the third and fourth phases, there are no taxes to be paid at the time a sale is closed. The closer will prorate the taxes between buyer and seller.

In phase three, the seller will be charged with the portion of the taxes that represents the number of days she occupied the property. The buyer will be credited with the same amount.

In phase four, where the taxes have been prepaid, the seller will receive a credit for the amount of taxes already paid for the period of time that he will not be occupying the property. The buyer will be charged with the same amount.

Estimating Taxes

Sometimes, past-year taxes cannot be used to estimate current taxes. On occasion, a licensee may desire to prepare either a seller or buyer an illustration (through the use of a Net Sheet) of the costs associated with the transaction. If this occurs, the licensee should obtain tax information directly from the tax assessor's office or from the owner's records.

New Construction

In the case of new construction, the taxes on the land are prorated based on taxes for the past year. The licensee should alert the purchaser that the taxes for the previous year are artificially low because they are based on the value of the land only and not the improvement (new home) recently constructed on it. Taxes on the new improvements are estimated using the purchase price multiplied by the county or city assessment rate. Taxes are estimated from the date the certificate of occupancy is issued, or a partial assessment may be levied against new construction not yet completed. Any additional tax bills should be presented to the settlement agent for proper disposition and prorating of additional taxes to be paid. The settlement agent can address the finalization of tax costs at closing.

Leases

As a general rule, the landlord under any ordinary lease is responsible for the taxes on the property; however, this does not apply to a perpetual leaseholder who is, in effect, the owner of the property and is entitled to its use forever. In such a case, the burden of taxation is placed on the lessee. In the case of net leases, the tenant is usually responsible for payment of the taxes.

Tax Liens

Delinquent real property taxes are both a personal debt and a lien against the property. A tax lien on real property has priority over all other liens except court costs. A tax lien overrides a vendor's lien, even though the vendor's lien may have been first. A tax lien is also prior to the landlord's lien for rent. The Virginia statutes give real estate taxes priority over a deed of trust in the distribution of proceeds under a foreclosure sale. The foreclosing trustee must satisfy all outstanding deficiencies before distributing the remaining proceeds to other creditors. If the statute's requirements are not complied with, delinquent taxes remain a debt against the purchaser at the sale.

A lien in favor of the United States for unpaid taxes, interest, and penalties may arise against all real and personal property belonging to a taxpayer. The lien is perfected under Virginia law by filing a notice of tax lien in the circuit court for the jurisdiction in which the taxpayer resides. The tax lien remains in effect until the taxes are paid.

When taxes on real estate in a county, city, or town are delinquent on December 31 following the third anniversary of the date on which the taxes became due, the real estate may be sold to collect the tax.

■ **FOR EXAMPLE**   An individual's property tax was due on June 10, 2012, but was never paid. If the tax is still delinquent on December 31, 2015, the property may be sold for taxes on January 1, 2016.

At least 30 days before taking any action to sell the property, the tax-collecting officer must send a notice to the last known address of the property owner. Notice of the sale must be published in a newspaper of general circulation in the area 30 to 60 days prior to the commencement of the sale proceedings.

The sale proceedings are initiated by filing a suit in the circuit court of the county or city where the real estate is located. Owners of real estate, or their heirs, successors, and assigns, have the right to redeem the real estate prior to the sale date by paying all taxes, penalties, and interest due, plus costs, including the cost of publication and a reasonable attorney's fee set by the court. The former owner of any real estate sold for delinquent real estate taxes is entitled to any receipts from the sale in excess of the taxes, penalties, interest, and costs.

Special Assessments

There is a distinction between special assessments and general tax levies for purposes of funding government services and operations. **Special assessments** are taxes levied against specific benefited properties to pay for limited local improvements. They are founded on the theory of benefits brought about by improvements to adjacent properties. This public improvement enhances the value of a specific property—a sidewalk, for example, or a repaved alley. A special assessment is distinguished from an improvement that benefits the entire community, such as a park.

The statute specifically provides that notice must be given to abutting landowners of the contemplated improvements before the ordinance authorizing the improvements is put into effect. This gives the landowner an opportunity to be heard concerning the adoption or rejection of such an ordinance. The statute provides for special assessments relating to sewers, street paving, and other local public improvements.

The only properties subject to special assessments are those of abutting landowners. Local improvements may be ordered by a town or city council (with costs to be defrayed by special assessment) following receipt of a petition from not less than three-fourths of the landowners who will be affected by the assessment. However, the council may issue such an improvement order without a petition.

The amount of special assessment for a local improvement constitutes a lien on the property benefited by the improvement, enforceable by a suit in court. Property owners have the right to appear before the municipal authorities and protest both the authorization of the improvements and the assessments.

For a complete discussion of real estate taxes, see Code of Virginia, Table of Contents, Title 58.1—Taxation, at http://leg1.state.va.us/lis.htm.

■ LIENS OTHER THAN TAXES

There are numerous other types of liens that may be filed against real property. The mere issuance of an attachment creates no lien on the real estate. To create a lien, it is necessary for the officer to show that levy (actual attachment or seizure) was made.

A **lis pendens**, or pending suit, does not bind or affect a subsequent purchaser of real estate unless a memorandum is properly recorded giving notice of the suit. The memorandum of notice states the title of the suit, its general object, and the court in which it is pending. The notice declares the amount of the claim, describes the property, and names the person whose estate is intended to be affected.

If the lis pendens is not docketed as provided by the statutes, a purchaser without notice of the pending suit takes good title, with no lien on the land by virtue of the pending suit.

Mechanic's Lien

One of the most common types of lien affecting the sale of real property is a **mechanic's lien**. Anyone who performs labor or furnishes material with a value of $150 or more for the construction, removal, repair, or improvement of any building or structure has a right of lien on both the land and the building. The object of the law is to give laborers and materialmen the security of a lien on the property to the extent that they have added to its value. No lien will attach to the property for repairs and/or improvements that were not ordered by the owner, or the owner's agent.

The Virginia Mechanics' Lien Disclosure Act, Code of Virginia, Title 43, Chapter 1, requires that the seller of property disclose in the sales contract a warning that an effective mechanic's lien may be filed against the real property even after settlement.

The act's purpose is to protect contractors, brokers, purchasers, title agents, and insurers from builders or owners who contracted for improvements, sold the property, and never paid the contractor. The act requires that each residential sales contract include the following:

> NOTICE Virginia law §43.1 et seq. permits persons who have performed labor or furnished materials for the construction, removal, repair, or improvement of any building or structure to file a lien against the property. This lien may be filed at any time after the work is commenced or the material is furnished, but not later than the earlier of (1) 90 days from the last day of the month in which the lienor last performed work or furnished materials, or (2) 90 days from the time the construction, removal, repair, or improvement is terminated.
>
> An effective lien for work performed, prior to the date of settlement, may be filed after settlement. Legal counsel should be consulted.

While inclusion of the statement is mandatory, failure to include it will not void the contract.

Perfecting the Lien A general contractor or a subcontractor may perfect a mechanic's lien by filing a memorandum of mechanic's lien with the clerk of court in the jurisdiction in which the property or structure is located. The filing must be within 90 days of the last day of the month in which the contractor last performed labor or furnished materials. However, under no circumstances may filing occur later than 90 days from the time the building is completed or the work otherwise terminated.

Written notice must be given to the owner of the property. The notice memorandum must include

- the name of the owner of the property;
- the name of the claimant;
- the amount of the claim;
- the time when the amount is due and payable; and
- a brief description of the property.

A mechanic's lien is enforced by a suit filed within six months of recording the memorandum of lien or 60 days from the completion or termination of work on the structure, whichever is later. If the person who ordered the work owns less than the fee simple estate in the land, only his actual interest is subject to the lien.

When a buyer constructs a building or structure, or undertakes repairs to an existing building or structure before the transaction has closed, the owner's interest will be subject to any mechanic's lien if the owner knows about the activity.

When a lien, such as a deed of trust, is created on land before work is begun or materials furnished, the deed of trust is a first lien on the land and a second lien on the building or structure. A deed of trust that is recorded before the work began is entitled to priority to the extent of the estimated value of the property without improvements for which the lien is claimed.

Typically, the seller must execute an affidavit at closing that declares no work has been performed or any materials furnished within 120 days before the date of closing. This declaration ensures that no mechanic can file a lien on the property after closing for labor performed or materials furnished prior to closing. Nonetheless, a buyer should be advised to obtain additional assurances that no mechanic's lien can be filed.

Closing agents are charged with the responsibility to advise buyers of possible mechanic's lien filings and must inform buyers about title insurance protection.

A lien waiver should be demanded for new construction stating that all amounts have been paid for labor performed and materials furnished in connection with the construction. The waiver should be executed by the general contractor and all subcontractors. However, no waiver is required if affirmative mechanic's lien coverage is provided by a title insurance company.

Judgments

Every **money judgment** rendered in Virginia by any court, or by confession of judgment, constitutes a lien on any real estate the judgment debtor owns or may own in the future. The lien is effective from the date the judgment is docketed, that is, indexed by the clerk of court. It is prudent to docket the judgment in the city or county in which the debtor's property is located. If the debtor currently has no property, it is wise to docket the judgment wherever property is located that may become the debtor's in the future (for example, property owned by family members).

A **writ of execution** may be issued and the judgment enforced within 20 years from the date the judgment was rendered. A judgment may be extended beyond its 20-year life by a motion made in the circuit court, following notice to the judgment debtor and redocketing of the judgment.

If the real estate is conveyed to a grantee for value subject to a judgment lien, the judgment creditor must bring the suit to enforce the judgment lien within 10 years from the date the grantee's deed was recorded.

If the judgment is for recovery of specific real property, a **writ of possession** is needed. If the judgment debtor owns real estate outside Virginia, the debtor may be required to convey it to a sheriff.

Within 30 days of the satisfaction, that is, payment of a judgment, a judgment creditor must release the judgment wherever it is docketed. Failure to do so within 10 days of demand by the judgment debtor makes the creditor subject to a fine.

Estate and Inheritance Tax

There is no Virginia estate tax for decedents whose death occurred on or after July 1, 2007.

Vendor's Lien

In Virginia, if any person conveys any real estate and the purchase money remains unpaid at the time of the conveyance, the vendor will not have a lien for the unpaid purchase money unless the lien is expressly reserved on the face of the deed. The object of this statute is to make the lien a matter of record, putting all persons who deal with the property on notice of all liens and encumbrances. The extent of the **vendor's lien** does not depend on the extent of the vendor's interest in the land conveyed but on the contract of the parties as gathered from the deed itself.

Landlord's Lien

The Virginia statutes give a landlord a right of lien. It exists independently of the right to hold property for payment of rent. When the **landlord's lien** for rent is obtained, it relates back to the very beginning of the tenancy and takes precedence over any lien that any other person has obtained or created against goods (personal property) on the leased premises since the tenancy began. A lien legally attaches to all property on the premises when it is asserted or on the premises within 30 days prior to attachment of lien. The landlord can seize the tenant's goods only to the extent necessary to satisfy the rent justly believed to be due.

See Chapter 9 for more information on landlord and tenant rights and obligations.

Commercial Broker's Lien

A commercial real estate broker has a **broker's lien** on the rent paid by the tenant in the amount of the compensation (commission) agreed on by the owner and the broker.

CHAPTER 4 QUIZ

1. Which of the following is *TRUE* of uniform real estate taxation in Virginia?
   a. Tax rates and assessments must be uniformly applied to similar properties.
   b. All properties pay the same amount of tax.
   c. Only the tax rate needs to be uniform.
   d. Uniformity is a common-law principle.

2. A single family house is located near the end of a block right next to a bakery shop. How must these properties be treated for real estate tax purposes?
   a. There can be no difference between them.
   b. They will be classified differently, according to use.
   c. The bakery will not subject to taxation because it is for public use.
   d. Because the bakery abuts a residential zone, it must be treated as a residence.

3. All of the following types of real property are exempt from real property taxation *EXCEPT*
   a. for-profit cemetery.
   b. government-owned land.
   c. land owned by nonprofit educational institutions.
   d. land owned by a totally disabled veteran.

4. Which of the following statements is *FALSE* regarding taxes on new construction?
   a. Taxes are prorated based on the previous year's taxes.
   b. Taxes are estimated from the date of the certificate of occupancy.
   c. The first year taxes may be artificially low.
   d. Taxes are estimated based on comparable values for the area.

5. In Virginia, the owner of property on the date of sale is
   a. the buyer.
   b. the seller.
   c. the buyer and seller, divided evenly.
   d. either, depending on negotiation.

6. Which of the following liens would have first priority?
   a. Deed of trust
   b. Mechanic's lien
   c. Property tax lien
   d. Landlord's lien

7. How long after the work was done may a mechanic wait before filing a mechanic's lien?
   a. No more than 30 days
   b. No more than 60 days
   c. No more than 90 days
   d. No more than 6 months

8. How soon after filing the lien must the mechanic enforce it by filing suit?
   a. Within three months
   b. Within six months
   c. Within nine months
   d. Within one year

9. Based on the Virginia Mechanic's Lien Disclosure Act, disclosure of the possibility for a mechanic's lien must be made
   a. as part of the sales contract exactly as written in the act.
   b. as an addendum to the contract.
   c. any time prior to settlement.
   d. within three days after ratification of the contract.

10. A creditor on a judgment must enforce the judgment once it is rendered within
    a. 6 months.
    b. 1 year.
    c. 5 years.
    d. 20 years.

11. If a lien against the property of a decedent is made, it remains enforceable for
    a. 6 months.
    b. 18 months.
    c. 2 years.
    d. 10 years.

12. A lis pendens notice must declare all of the following *EXCEPT*

a. the amount of the claim.
b. the description of the property.
c. the name of prospective purchaser.
d. the name of the person whose estate is affected.

CHAPTER 5

Real Estate Contracts

■ **LEARNING OBJECTIVES**   *After successfully completing this chapter, you will be able to*

- ■ **identify** methods of describing real estate in Virginia;
- ■ **list** items typically found in a sales contract;
- ■ **describe** types of contingencies and statutory inclusions in a contract; and
- ■ **discuss** other contract procedures, including warranties.

■ KEY TERMS

as-built survey	house location survey	power of attorney
attorney-in-fact	land surveyor	Statute of Frauds
boundary survey	lot-and-block method	structural defect
caveat emptor	metes-and-bounds	subdivision plat
equitable title	method	walk-through inspection
four-corners doctrine	parol evidence	

The Code of Virginia allows real estate licensees—brokers and salespersons—to prepare written contracts for the sale, purchase, option, exchange, or rental of real estate as long as the contract is incidental to a specific real estate transaction and there is no additional charge for preparing the contract (§54.1-2101.1). In some states, brokers and salespersons are not authorized to prepare contracts. In Virginia, the operative word is *incidental*.

■ **FOR EXAMPLE**   While a licensee assists a buyer in a variety of functions, such as locating property, arranging financing, selecting a settlement agent, and so on, the preparation of the sales contract is incidental to the variety of services provided. In the situation of a seller who hires the licensee, the licensee performs a variety of services, such as marketing the property, advertising, showing the property to buyers, and so on. As in the case of the buyer example, the preparation of the sales contract is incidental to the transaction.

■ STATUTE OF FRAUDS

The English law passed in 1667 called the **Statute of Frauds** requires that the transfer of real estate be in writing. Virginia contract law prevents the enforcement of an oral contract or promise (§11.1). The statute does not invalidate oral contracts; rather, it addresses the contract's enforceability. The statute bars any action concerning a contract for the sale of real estate or for a lease on real property for more than one year unless the document is in writing. Although an oral lease for a term of more than one year is unenforceable and the parties cannot be compelled to perform, they are nonetheless free to make and comply with such an agreement. Further discussion of the Statute of Frauds may be found in the Code of Virginia, Title 8.2A-201 (Commercial Code).

The actual contract used for the purchase and sale of real property may take any form. The only requirement is that it be in enough detail to clearly state the agreement between the parties. One important point of clarification is an accurate legal description.

■ LEGAL DESCRIPTIONS

The most common method of describing real estate in Virginia is a combination of the **metes-and-bounds method** and the **lot-and-block method**.

Licensees should use great care in describing property. Both the real estate plat map and county or city tax records, as well as at least one deed by which the land was conveyed in the past, may be checked to verify that the proper legal description is being used. The description should enable the parties or a court to determine exactly what land the parties intended to convey.

Although the street address is usually given on a purchase contract, this is not an adequate legal description due to the fact that street addresses are frequently changed.

Methods of Description

The description of land by any of the following methods is legally sufficient, if the county or city and state are included:

■ By courses and distances with an identifiable starting point (metes-and-bounds method)
■ As bounded by natural or artificial objects or by the land of named persons (monuments method)
■ By reference to a recorded map, plat, survey, deed, or other writing (lot-and-block method)
■ By number or code on a recorded subdivision (subdivision method)

- By geodetic survey of townships, ranges, meridians, and so forth (rectangular government survey method)
- By house number and named street, where there is an established system of numbering (in many cases, this is not considered to be an adequate legal description because house numbers and street names are frequently subject to change)
- By any name by which the land is generally known and identifiable
- As occupied or acquired by a named person at a definite time
- As being all the land of the grantor in a designated way or acquired in a specific way

■ **FOR EXAMPLE**   This is a common property description:

"All those certain lots, pieces, or parcels of land, situated in the city of Norfolk, Virginia, known, numbered, and designated on the Plat of Estabrook Corporation, made by S.W. Armistead, C.E., February, 1920, and recorded in the clerk's office of the Circuit Court of the City of Chesapeake, Virginia, in Map Book 17, page 4, as Lots No. 35 and 36, located on the North side of Amherst Street in Block 'E' in said Subdivision called Estabrook, and appurtenances thereunto belonging said lots being 25 × 100 feet each."

A shortened form is frequently used in listing agreements and sales contracts:

"Lots 35 and 36, Block E, Plat of Estabrook, Norfolk, Virginia 23513, also known and described as 36 Amherst Street."

The following would also be an acceptable description:

"All that land called Warrone Crossing, as purchased by Nicholas Lilly on June 17, 1984, and bounded on the north by Richmond Hwy., on the south by Muddy Run, on the east by the farm belonging to John Evans, and on the south by the Redly Estate owned by Elizabeth Davies."

A false description does not invalidate the deed if, after rejecting the false description, enough information remains to permit reliable identification of the land to be conveyed. A complete description can be found in the deed that conveyed the property to the seller. The identical description should be used to convey the land to the buyer.

Disputed boundaries between two adjoining lands may be settled by express agreement. Virginia law provides for a court proceeding to establish boundaries. In conflicts concerning true boundaries, Virginia law gives preference to methods of description in the following order:

- Natural monuments or landmarks
- Artificial monuments and established lines
- Adjacent boundaries or lines of adjoining tracts
- Calls for courses and distances
- Designation of quantity, such as "approximately 3.5 acres"

This preference will not be applied where it would frustrate the intent of the parties.

In disputes among purchasers of a lot shown on a plat, the metes and bounds established accurate survey, and corresponding calls of courses and distances that are noted on the plat will supersede errors in the plat and will control dimensions and configuration of the lots.

Surveying and Surveys

To engage in the practice of land surveying in Virginia, a person must hold a valid surveyor's license, unless exempted by the statute (i.e., a licensed architect or engineer when surveying is incidental to a particular project). A **land surveyor** must pass a Board examination and complete a minimum of 16 hours of continuing education per biennium.

Lenders are not allowed to require that a particular surveyor perform the survey in connection with making a loan to purchase real property. Surveys are recorded in the clerk's office of the circuit court where the land is located.

Four Types of Surveys   The following are four types of surveys commonly used in Virginia:

- A **subdivision plat** is a map of each parcel of land. The plat shows subdivided lots, streets, and similar features. The plat is generally created from a tract of land to subdivide it. The subdivided lots may or may not be staked on the ground once the plat has been created.
- A **boundary survey**, as opposed to a subdivision plat, shows the boundary or perimeter of the parcel as taken from and applied to the ground. Corner stakes or other physical landmarks appear.
- A **house location survey** is a boundary survey with the location of the house shown.
- An **as-built survey** (also called a *physical survey*) is a house location survey with all other physical features of the subject property shown, including water courses, utility lines, fence lines, outbuildings, and similar features.

A recently recorded survey of a subject property may reveal matters not shown in the record.

The attorney is primarily the person obligated to examine the survey. The following conditions suggest that potential problems may exist and should be brought to the attention of an attorney:

- Property boundaries that do not conform with the recorded plat
- Structural encroachments by the property onto neighboring properties, or by neighboring structures onto the subject property
- Fences that are not on the boundary line
- Party walls
- Riparian rights of others in streams, lakes, and other bodies of water
- Utilities that service other properties
- Old roadways
- Cemeteries
- Violation of setback, side, or rear building lines
- Property that may be landlocked

Any defect shown on the survey should be reported and corrective action taken where necessary.

Plat Maps   In areas of Virginia where recorded plat maps are used in lieu of individual surveys, the appropriate lot must be identified and lot dimensions must be legibly shown. Necessary endorsements to the title insurance policy must be issued pertaining to easements, deed restrictions, and property identification. The closing lawyer is responsible for obtaining the endorsements.

Subdivision Plat   In Virginia, a subdivision plat must contain all the necessary approvals of county or city officials. In addition, the dedications or consents of all owners, trustees, and other similar parties must be properly recorded. The law provides that the mere recordation of a plat transfers the streets, alleys, and other areas set aside for public use to the county or municipality in fee simple.

■ THE CONTRACT

The actual contract used for the purchase and sale of real property may take any form. The only requirement is that it be in enough detail to clearly state the agreement between the parties.

When two parties agree to form a contract, they attempt to write down all of the specific terms of the agreement (drafting the contract). Occasionally, however, one party later feels that all the terms of the agreement were not included in the written document and wishes to introduce evidence of prior oral agreements to alter the terms of the existing contract.

Parol evidence, that is, evidence of facts and circumstances not included in the deed or contract, is admissible in a court proceeding if the facts were well known in the community at the time the deed was made.

Parol evidence should not be confused with the Statue of Frauds, which requires that any contract for the sale of real estate be in writing in order to be enforceable.

Contract Provisions

Typically, a sales contract contains information covering the following:

■ Real property
— Personal property, fixtures, and utilities
— Equipment, maintenance, and condition
■ Legal description
■ Price and financing
— Deposit
— Down payment
— Loan application, approval, and appraisal
■ Inspections
— Access to property
— Well and septic system inspection
— Termite and wood-destroying pest inspection
— Repairs
■ Damage or loss
■ Title and settlement
— Conveyances, deed(s) of trust

— Possession date
— Settlement
— Fees: broker's, attorney's, adjustments
■ Disclosures and notices

Earnest Money Deposit (EMD)

Although not legally required as part of a contract for the purchase of real estate, an earnest money deposit is usually submitted along with the original offer to purchase. The earnest money serves to show that the potential buyer is indeed "in earnest" about going through with the purchase. No specific amount is recommended, but the larger the EMD, the most risk there is for the buyer; a large EMD should provide some assurance for a seller that the buyer will not back out.

IN PRACTICE An all-cash offer often includes a large earnest money deposit since there is no third party involved in confirming the financial status of the purchaser.

The Virginia Real Estate Board Regulations are very specific about the disposition of any earnest money deposit:

■ The money must be deposited in the broker's escrow account within five business days of ratification of the contract.
■ The earnest money deposit may not be released from the escrow account until
— it is credited toward the sales price at settlement,
— the seller and the purchaser agree in writing as to its disposition,
— a court orders a disbursement of the funds, or
— it is disposed of in any other manner authorized by the Real Estate Board.

If the earnest money deposit is to be placed in an interest-bearing account, the contract must state who is to receive the interest.

Contract Forms

Local real estate associations often have standard sales contract forms to be used by their members. As business practices change and regulations increase, contract documentation and forms change to meet these new requirements. Because a sales contract often contains information specific to a given geographic area, you should contact your local real estate association or multiple-listing service (MLS) for information on how to obtain up-to-date contract forms.

It is customary for real estate licensees to assist buyers and sellers with the preparation of the contract by filling in the blanks on the form. As with any printed form, all blanks should be filled in. If the item does not apply, the notation N/A (not applicable) should be inserted. Licensees should be careful when striking out whole paragraphs or sections of a contract because important beneficial language often can be inadvertently deleted. Licensees should use a proper addendum of clauses or amendments to alter terms specifically spelled out in the contract.

IN PRACTICE As with all legal matters, real estate brokers and salespersons should refrain from trying to explain the legal technicalities. Improper or misunderstood explanations could subject the licensee to legal action later.

Though the word *contract* may imply the use of a single document, in actual practice, the average real estate contract for a given transaction is a series of documents, the most important of which is the actual sales agreement between the seller and the purchaser. Other documents and forms are typically added to the basic sales contract forms to meet compliance with federal, state, and local requirements for the sale and transfer of property. It is not uncommon for these pages of the transaction contract to exceed the number of pages in the standard sales contract. For example, Virginia has a Residential Property Disclosure Law, which requires that a disclosure be made as a part of the contract. The Environmental Protection Agency (EPA) requires a disclosure on all properties constructed prior to 1978 when lead-based paint was used in construction.

Builder Contracts

When new construction is involved, the entire contract package is typically provided by the builder, although some associations have published New Homes Sales Contracts. In a transaction that involves the sale of land, a contract specifically designated for that purpose should be used.

Builder negotiation on contract terms is rare when there are multiple buyers interested in one property. Things to be aware of when dealing with a builder contract include the following:

- *Substitutions.* The contract may allow the builder to make substitutions. If the purchaser wants certain specifications, they should be noted in the contract with a right to terminate the contract if substitutions are not acceptable.
- *Warranties.* Section 55-70.1 provides a solid warranty for new homes, but homebuyers may be asked to waive that warranty. Any such waiver should be inconspicuous, large type in order to be easily identified. The standard warranty may be replaced by a third-party warranty only covering specific items.
- *Deposits and/or Advance Payments.* Any such payments must be placed in a separate escrow account, with no accessibility by the builder. A builder having financial difficulties could result in an uncompleted house with unpaid liens against it.
- *Four-Corner Doctrine.* Virginia abides by the **four-corner doctrine** that says all agreements must be present within the "four corners" of the contract in order to be valid. An oral agreement between builder and buyer is not valid. The best advice to give a new homebuyer client is to suggest seeking legal counsel to review the contract.

While it is impractical to include every scenario in which a particular form is required, Figure 5.1 provides an approximation of how certain forms might be included in a total contract package.

FIGURE   5.1

Contract Form

Standard Form	# of Pages
Agency Disclosure: An appropriate disclosure for the type of agency used in the transaction is included.	1
Sales Contract: Contains the basics of the sales transaction between the purchaser and the seller.	10
Jurisdictional Addendum: Some contracts, such as the Regional Contract used by NVAR, require the use of a regional addendum for the appropriate jurisdiction.	5
Contingencies and Clauses Addendum: Special contingencies (e.g., home inspections, radon inspection, third-party approval, or post-occupancy agreements) and optional standard paragraph clauses are far too numerous to include in the standard sales contract.	3
Property Disclosure: Virginia Residential Property Disclosure	1–2
Lead-Based Paint Disclosure: Required by EPA if the property was constructed prior to 1978.	1
FHA Home Inspection Notice: If FHA financing is used, a notice of information on a home inspection is required.	1
Approximate Total Pages (minimum)	24

■ CONTINGENCIES

Once a contract is prepared for presentation to the seller, certain conditions of the purchase can appear in the form of contingencies to contract on ratification. Typical contingencies include a home inspection or a well and septic system inspection. These contingencies, while important, are generated by the wishes of the purchaser or as a requirement of the lender. There are other contingencies, however, that are generated by statute. If a property is a condominium or is in a subdivision bound by a property owners' association (POA), the seller must provide the purchaser with an opportunity to review the condominium resale packet or POA disclosure packet regarding the referenced property. This requirement of the law automatically creates a contingency to the contract and must be afforded to the purchaser exclusive of any other terms or conditions of the contract.

Request for Property Owners' Association Disclosure Packet

The Virginia POA Act requires that the seller request and furnish the disclosure packet regarding the referenced property. By the provisions of Virginia Code Section 55-512, this packet must be delivered to the seller within 14 days of the request. Payment by seller is currently required to be made at settlement.

Request for Condominium Disclosure

The Virginia Condominium Act requires that the seller request the condominium resale packet regarding the referenced property and furnish it to the buyer. By the provisions of Virginia Code Section 55-79.97, this packet must be delivered within 14 days of the request. Payment by seller is made at settlement.

■ STATUTORY INCLUSIONS

Federal and state laws require that certain disclosures be made during the course of a real estate transaction. Although disclosures were covered in Chapter 2, the information is reiterated here because it is in the actual assembly of a sales contract that these documents again come into play. The average sales contract will contain the required statutory disclosures as proof that they were actually made to the parties to the contract as required by law. Additionally, many firms and brokers require stricter standards than those required by laws of the state. These practices by some firms and brokers help to ensure maximum compliance with state regulations.

Disclosure of Brokerage Relationship

According to Virginia Real Estate Board regulations, a disclosure of brokerage relationship must be made to nonrepresented buyers on the first substantive discussion about a specific property. Good real estate practice dictates this be done prior to showing any property to a nonrepresented buyer.

Disclosed Dual Representation (§54.1-2139)   In Virginia, a licensee may represent both parties in the same real estate transaction—seller and buyer or landlord and tenant—only with the written consent of all clients in the transaction. The client's signature on the written disclosure form is presumptive evidence of the brokerage relationship. The disclosure must be substantially in the same form as shown in Chapter 2.

A dual standard agent does not terminate any brokerage relationship by making the required disclosures of dual representation (§54.1-2139C). As mentioned previously, a licensee may withdraw from representing a client who refuses to consent to disclosed dual agency. The licensee may continue to represent in other transactions the client who refused dual representation (§54.1-2139D).

Designated Representation   A principal or supervising broker may assign different affiliated licensees as designated standard agents to represent different clients in the same transaction. The appointment of designated representatives excludes other licensees in the firm from involvement in the transaction. The use of designated representatives does not constitute dual representation if each designee represents only one client in a particular real estate transaction. The designated representatives are pledged to maintain all confidential information received from their clients. Such information may be shared with the principal or supervising broker, who remains in the position of a dual representative with equal responsibilities to both clients. The disclosure must be made in writing and must be similar to the form shown in Chapter 2. See Code of Virginia §54.1-2139E for more detail.

Limited Services Agency

A licensee may act as a limited service agent only pursuant to a written brokerage agreement. Limited service agents must disclose their status as a limited services agent and present the client with a written disclosure that compares the services to be provided with the duties and services required of a standard agent that the licensee will not perform.

Residential Property Disclosure Documentation

The Virginia Residential Property Disclosure Act requires that the owner of residential real property consisting of one to four dwelling units furnish a purchaser with a Residential Property Disclosure Statement. This requirement is effective whether or not the transaction is with the assistance of a licensed real estate broker or salesperson. A complete discussion of the act was covered in Chapter 1.

IN PRACTICE   A licensee must make sure that a Property Disclosure Statement and a Rights and Obligations Form are given to a buyer prior to ratification of a contract. The purchaser is directed to a DPOR website maintained by the Real Estate Board with a full list of seller representations.

Lead-Based Paint Disclosure Requirements

Since 1996, the Environmental Protection Agency (EPA) has required that all prospective buyers and tenants receive an EPA pamphlet describing the hazards of lead-based paint for any property built before 1978. A lead-based paint disclosure form must be a part of all contracts and leases (see Figure 5.2). In July 2008, EPA passed a rule requiring that all repairs, renovations and painting projects affecting more than 6 square feet of interior space or 20 square feet of exterior on properties built before 1978 be done by an EPA-certified contractor. This rule went into effect April 2010.

FIGURE 5.2

Sale: Disclosure and Acknowledgement of Information on Lead-Based Paint and/or Lead-Based Paint Hazards

SALE: DISCLOSURE AND ACKNOWLEDGMENT OF INFORMATION ON LEAD-BASED PAINT AND/OR LEAD-BASED PAINT HAZARDS

For the sale of the Property at: _____

Lead Warning Statement

Every purchaser of any interest in residential real property on which a residential dwelling was built prior to 1978 is notified that such property may present exposure to lead from lead-based paint that may place young children at risk of developing lead poisoning. Lead poisoning in young children may produce permanent neurological damage, including learning disabilities, reduced intelligence quotient, behavioral problems, and impaired memory. Lead poisoning also poses a particular risk to pregnant women. The seller of any interest in residential real property is required to provide the buyer with any information on lead-based paint hazards from risk assessments or inspections in the seller=s possession and notify the buyer of any known lead-based paint hazards. A risk assessment or inspection for possible lead-based paint hazards is recommended prior to purchase.

Seller's Disclosure (initial)

_____ / _____ (a) Presence of lead-based paint and/or lead-based paint hazard (check one below):

☐ Known lead-based paint and/or lead-based paint hazards are present in the housing (explain):

_____

_____

☐ Seller has no knowledge of lead-based paint and/or lead-based paint hazards in the housing.

_____ / _____ (b) Records and Reports available to the seller (check one below):

☐ Seller has provided the purchaser with all available records and reports pertaining to lead-based paint and/or lead-based paint hazards in the housing (list documents below):

☐ Seller has no reports or records pertaining to lead-based paint and/or lead-based paint hazards in the housing.

Purchaser's Acknowledgment (initial)

_____ / _____ (c) Purchaser has received and had an opportunity to review copies of all information listed above.

_____ / _____ (d) Purchaser has received the pamphlet *Protect Your Family From Lead in Your Home.*

_____ / _____ (e) Purchaser has (check one below):

☐ Received a 10-day opportunity (or mutually agreed upon period) to conduct a risk assessment or inspection for the presence of lead-based paint or lead-based paint hazards; or

☐ Waived the opportunity to conduct a risk assessment or inspection for the presence of lead-based paint and/or lead-based paint hazards.

Sales Associates' Acknowledgments (initial)

_____ / _____ (f) Listing and Selling Sales Associates are aware of their duty to ensure compliance with 42 U.S.C. 4852d. These Associates have informed the Seller of the Sellers' obligations under this law as evidenced by Seller and Purchaser having completed this form.

Certification of Accuracy

The undersigned have reviewed the information above and certify that to the best of their knowledge the information they have provided is true and accurate.

SELLER: **PURCHASER:**

_____ / _____   _____ / _____
Date   Signature   Date   Signature

_____ / _____   _____ / _____
Date   Signature   Date   Signature

_____ / _____   _____ / _____
Date   Signature of Listing Associate   Date   Signature of Selling Associate

Contingencies, Addenda, and Amendments

Sometimes additional conditions must be met before a sales contract becomes in full force. The contingency may be a part of the original contract or can be attached as an addendum or an amendment. In all cases, the signatures (or initials) of all parties are required in order for the contingency to be enforceable. A contingency should always include

- reference to the original contract with names of all parties and the correct date,
- a clear statement of what action is to be performed,
- any changes clearly marked with a cross-hatch for initials of all parties, and
- copies provided for all parties.

An addendum is new information that is to be included as part of the original contract. An amendment is a change to information that is already a part of the original contract. An addendum or amendment is usually prepared sometime after the original contract has been ratified. It requires the approval of all parties before it can become enforceable as part of the sales contract.

A contingency to a contract must be satisfied, removed, or approved before the parties can move forward with the other terms of the contract.

FOR EXAMPLE A home inspection contingency typically permits the purchaser to inspect the property with the aid of a certified or licensed professional. The contract is then said to be contingent on a mutual resolution between the purchaser and the seller of the outcome of the inspection. If a mutual resolution cannot be reached, typically the contract dies (becomes void). For a contingency to be enforceable, it must contain an expiration date and/or time plus a list or description of options available to the parties.

CONTRACT PROCEDURES

Use of a standard form does not excuse the licensee from pointing out to both parties that the contract is a legally binding document and that legal advice should be sought if either party has legal questions. The parties may make the agreement contingent on review and approval by an attorney.

Power of Attorney

Sometimes, a party cannot be present at the closing and must be represented by an **attorney-in-fact** acting under a **power of attorney**. In Virginia, a specific power of attorney specifying the transaction and the parties involved, is generally preferred, rather than a general power of attorney. The power of attorney must be notarized and recorded with the deed.

It is not a good business practice and perhaps may even be a conflict of interest for licensees to perform as attorneys-in-fact for their seller or buyer clients. It is best to suggest that the client engage a licensed attorney to serve as an attorney-in-fact. Additionally, if a buyer is using a power of attorney, the buyer should be counseled to consult with the lender and the settlement company to ensure that the power of attorney document will be acceptable for loan purposes.

IN PRACTICE   Many military notaries are from outside Virginia and may not comply with the requirements of the Virginia Code. Most settlement companies use their own form of power of attorney; always check with them first.

Spousal Consent

If property is owned in severalty and the owner is married, the seller's spouse should join in the contract so that no claims can be made later. If one or the other spouse does not sign, the courts will not order specific performance on the contract unless the buyer is willing to accept a deed that remains subject to the spousal interest. The buyer may still sue the seller for breach of contract because the seller could not convey the property with a clear title.

The capacity in which each signer executes the contract should be clearly stated. The contract should indicate whether the signer is an individual, a married couple, a partnership, a corporation, a limited liability company, or any other legal entity.

Title

The buyer under a real estate sales contract expects to receive marketable title to the property from the seller. Marketable title and insurable title are not necessarily the same because a title insurance policy may list exceptions against which it does not insure.

Equitable Title

When the buyer and seller have ratified, that is, signed, the sales contract, the buyer's interest is called **equitable title**. A buyer's equitable title gives the buyer an insurable interest in the property. While Virginia law places the risk of damage to the property during this period on the buyer, most sales contracts in Virginia provide that the seller bears the risk of loss. Licensees should ensure that this point is addressed in the contract.

■ WARRANTIES

The principle of **caveat emptor** (Latin for "let the buyer beware") is still the law in Virginia regarding previously owned homes.

Buyers and sellers should ensure that the sales contract is sufficiently complete in order to provide for the identification and resolution of deficient items for which they may have concern. These actions may include, but are not limited to, property inspection contingencies, such as lead-based paint, radon, or mold inspections; exterior insulation finishing system (EIFS) or defective drywall; wood-destroying pests and moisture inspections, and other appropriate property reviews, such as well and septic inspection; and a final **walk-through inspection**. Many real estate jurisdictions have local consumer disclosure forms that alert the buyer to issues that may be pertinent to the locale, such as a Megan's Law disclosure. If in doubt, buyers should insist on a study period (contingency) in the sales contract to provide sufficient time to investigate various issues.

Existing Homes

In most areas, the seller will warrant that the heating, plumbing, electrical, and air-conditioning systems are in normal working order at the time of settlement. The buyer usually has the opportunity for a walk-through inspection prior to settlement to verify that no material changes have occurred since the signing of the sales contract (such as storm damage, vandalism, or the removal of fixtures). If there have been any changes, the seller is required to inform the buyer of them, regardless of whether a walk-through is to be performed. It is a buyer's responsibility to determine what conditions beyond the property's boundaries may affect its value.

New Construction

For new homes, the builder normally supplies a detailed warranty, primarily to limit liability, which includes either a 5-year or 10-year warranty against foundation defects. At the time of closing, there is an implied warranty that the dwelling and its fixtures (to the seller's best actual knowledge) are free from structural defects and constructed in a professional manner. A **structural defect** is a flaw that reduces the stability or safety of the structure below accepted standards or that restricts the normal use of the structure. The implied warranties continue for one year after the date of transfer of title or the buyer's taking possession, whichever occurs first.

Homeowner Warranty

Several companies offer a homeowner warranty that allows for repair or replacement of various systems and appliances within the home for a one-year period. The warranty may be purchased by either the seller or the buyer and does not require an inspection.

CHAPTER 5 QUIZ

1. All of the following are satisfactory legal descriptions in Virginia *EXCEPT*
   a. "Lot 7, Block D, Plat of Red Valley, Martin County, Virginia."
   b. "the entire 77.5 acres purchased by Edna Kelly on June 20, 1991, and called Seaside Neck, Roanoke."
   c. "727 Olean Drive, Fletcherton, Virginia."
   d. "proceeding 120 feet due west of the intersection of the east line of J Street and the north line of 11th Street to a point; thence north 10 degrees 31 minutes west 100 feet."

2. A deed contains the following description: "Lots 7 and 8, Block F, Section 3, Plat of Greydon, otherwise called 14 Havers Drive, Venus, Virginia." In fact, Block F has only six lots, and the street address is Lot 5. Is this deed valid?
   a. No, a false element in a description invalidates the deed.
   b. No, because the lot description is faulty, a new deed is needed.
   c. Yes, it's valid if the buyer knows which property is meant.
   d. Yes, enough correct information remains to permit identification.

3. A lender wishes to use the services of only licensed surveyors and says he will *NOT* accept the surveys of unlicensed or nonexempt surveyors. Is this practice legal?
   a. Yes, a lender may use the services of either licensed or exempt surveyors, but the lender cannot require that a particular surveyor conduct the survey.
   b. Yes, as long as the lender always uses the same surveyor, this practice is legal.
   c. No, surveyors are selected by the clerk's office.
   d. Yes, the lender can require that a particular surveyor conduct the survey.

4. The survey for a property shows the location of the house, the garage, the fence, utility lines, and the children's playhouse in the backyard. This is MOST likely which type of survey?
   a. Subdivision plat
   b. Boundary survey
   c. House location survey
   d. As-built survey

5. The buyer and seller agree to the sale of a home for $150,000. No written contract is signed, but the seller accepts payment in full from the buyer and delivers the deed. Which of the following statements is *TRUE*?
   a. The sale is without legal effect; the seller continues to own the home.
   b. The sale violates the Statute of Frauds' maximum amount for oral contracts.
   c. The sale is enforceable in a court of law under the Statute of Frauds, due to the parties' compliance.
   d. The sale is unenforceable under the Statute of Frauds, but the parties are free to comply with its terms.

6. An actual contract used for the purchase and sale of real property
   a. must be on a form approved by the Real Estate Board.
   b. must be drafted by an attorney licensed to practice in the Commonwealth of Virginia.
   c. may take any form.
   d. does not need enough detail to clearly state the agreement between the parties.

7. A sales contract contains all of the following *EXCEPT*
   a. the type of sewage system.
   b. the amount of the down payment.
   c. the ages of the parties to the contract.
   d. the possession date.

8. All of the following are statutory contingencies required by law *EXCEPT*

   a. condominium resale packet.
   b. property owners' association disclosure packet.
   c. well and septic system disclosure.
   d. property disclosure.

9. The disclosure of lead-based paint and/or lead-based paint hazards is required on all

   a. sales contracts.
   b. residential sale contracts.
   c. residential contracts for properties constructed prior to 1978.
   d. residential contracts for sale to purchasers with small children.

10. All of the following are required disclosure forms that must be included with a sales contract *EXCEPT*

   a. brokerage relationship.
   b. property disclosure.
   c. home inspection disclosure.
   d. lead-based paint disclosure.

11. Two weeks after a buyer and seller signed a sales contract on a house, the house burned to the ground. If the contract is silent on the issue, which party is liable?

   a. The buyer only, under his equitable title interest
   b. The buyer and seller share the risk of loss equally
   c. The seller because she continues to possess title to the property
   d. The seller, under the implied condition of good faith

12. During construction of a new house, the foundation cracked and the builder decided to build the bearing walls of a lighter material to keep the entire structure from collapsing. A structural engineer told him that a strong wind would probably blow the house down. Nonetheless, the cracked foundation and structural shortcuts were easily covered over, and the house was sold to a first-time homebuyer without mentioning the defects. Two weeks after closing, the house collapsed in a thunderstorm. Is the builder liable?

   a. No, under caveat emptor
   b. No, because the buyer never asked about specific defects
   c. Yes, due to the implied warranty against foundation defects
   d. Yes, due to the failure to have the property inspected

13. Do *marketable title* and *insurable title* mean virtually the same thing?

   a. Yes, they are synonymous.
   b. Yes, if it is marketable, it is insurable.
   c. No, insurable title list exceptions for which it will not insure.
   d. No, insurable title is the same as equitable title.

14. The implied warranty supplied by a builder on new construction continues for a period of

   a. 1 year.
   b. 5 years.
   c. 10 years.
   d. indefinitely.

15. A married man is selling a property that he owns in severalty. Which of the following statements is *TRUE*?

   a. The wife will not need to sign the contract.
   b. The court will order specific performance on the contract.
   c. The buyer cannot sue the seller for breach of contract.
   d. The buyer can accept a deed that remains subject to the spousal interest.

Real Estate Financing

■ **LEARNING OBJECTIVES** *After successfully completing this chapter, you will be able to*

> ■ **describe** financing options for home mortgage loans;
>
> ■ **explain** the purpose and actions of the Virginia Housing Development Authority; and
>
> ■ **review** the process for foreclosing on a deed of trust.

■ KEY TERMS

acknowledgement	Home Affordable	promissory note
alienation clause	Modification Program	purchase-money
beneficiary	(HAMP)	financing
deed of trust	home equity line of credit	qualified residential
deferred purchase money	(HELOC)	mortgage (QRM)
due-on-sale clause	judicial foreclosure	short sale
government-sponsored	loan origination fee	title theory
enterprise (GSE)	mixed-use development	trustee
grace period	nonjudicial foreclosure	usury
grantor	power of sale clause	

This chapter briefly discusses the financing of single-family residential real estate in Virginia. It does not address commercial or more sophisticated transactions, but many of the concepts addressed will apply to such transactions.

■ PURCHASE CONTRACTS AND FINANCING

A licensed real estate broker or agent who has negotiated a sale may prepare a routine contract for the transaction. If a first deed of trust loan is to be obtained, the contract usually is made contingent on the purchaser's obtaining the loan. The real estate licensee must be careful in describing the loan because of the complexity of the terms. The seller may add the provision that the purchaser must apply for the loan promptly; should the purchaser not notify the seller by a certain date that loan approval has been obtained, the contingency shall be deemed waived. Typically, preprinted real estate contracts provide that the purchaser has a specified number of days from the date of the contract in which to apply for financing. The contract should specifically state what type of financing is contemplated: cash, assumption, seller financed, FHA, VA, or conventional loan obtained through an institutional lender.

The contract should provide a ceiling on the interest rate the borrower will accept. If this condition is not included, the purchaser could be bound by the contract even if the interest rate rises several percentage points between the date the contract is ratified and the date the purchaser locks in the interest rate with a lender. The lack of an interest rate cap could end up significantly increasing the cost of the home for the buyer.

If an existing loan is to remain on the property, the contract should specify whether it will be assumed or whether title will be taken subject to the existing loan.

■ INSTITUTIONAL FINANCING

In Virginia, a **deed of trust**, rather than a mortgage, is the instrument used to establish collateral in a residential sales transaction. Three parties are involved in a deed of trust: the borrower, the lender (**beneficiary**), and a **trustee** (a neutral third party) who holds the deed of trust for both the borrower and the lender. By signing the note and deed of trust, the borrower waives various rights, including the right to a court hearing in case of foreclosure. It is extremely important that the borrower fully understands the nature of the note and deed of trust. The **promissory note** defines the amount of debt and method of repayment. Even though collateral for the loan is established by a deed of trust, the term *mortgage* is still used generically when referring to a mortgage loan, getting a mortgage, mortgage payment, and so on. The note and deed of trust give the lender, in the event the borrower should default, the right to declare the entire debt due and payable. In that situation, the **power of sale clause** in the deed of trust gives the trustee the right to sell the property (foreclose) without going to court. This is called a **nonjudicial foreclosure**. Some states require the use of a mortgage that requires court action to foreclose and is called a **judicial foreclosure**.

The Note and Deed of Trust   The note and deed of trust are generally prepared by the lender. Standard forms are available for specialized loans, such as those insured (e.g., FHA) or guaranteed (e.g., VA) by the government. The note is not usually recorded although the deed of trust should always be promptly recorded.

The note and deed of trust should be signed in the exact manner and in the same name as the title is held. No witnesses are necessary. The deed of trust must be **acknowledged** (notarized) to permit its recordation in the land records of the circuit court where the property is located. Further, VA and FHA notes and notes to be sold out of state require notarization with a seal. Good sources of information on residential financing are available at the following locations:

- FHA: www.hud.gov
- VA: www.va.gov
- Fannie Mae: www.fanniemae.com
- Freddie Mac: www.freddiemac.com

Due-On-Sale Clauses

Loans that contain a **due-on-sale clause**, also called an **alienation clause**, are not assumable unless the lender chooses to waive the due-on-sale clause. Due-on-sale clauses are enforceable in Virginia. When a loan containing a due-on-sale clause is made on real property comprising not more than four residential dwelling units, the deed of trust must contain the following language, either in capital letters or underlined:

> "NOTICE—THE DEBT SECURED HEREBY IS SUBJECT TO CALL IN FULL OR THE TERMS THEREOF BEING MODIFIED IN THE EVENT OF SALE OR CONVEYANCE OF THE PROPERTY CONVEYED."

■ RELEASES

Whenever the borrower pays off any note, a marginal release is made on the face of the instrument wherever the document is recorded. Alternatively, a certificate of satisfaction or a partial satisfaction form is filed in the deed books in the clerk's office in the county where the land is located.

Lender Charges   Many conventional first deeds of trust loans contain a provision for a late charge if a monthly payment is not made within a certain period of time after the due date (called a **grace period**). The fact that a late charge may be collected must be disclosed in the loan's truth-in-lending statement. In Virginia, late charges may not exceed 5% of the installment due and cannot be collected unless the payment is not made within seven calendar days after the due date. Most lenders permit 15 days. The late charge must be specified in the contract between the lender and the borrower. Late charges in excess of the statutory amount are void only with regard to the excess amount; an inflated late charge does not affect the underlying obligation.

In addition to such charges as points, late charges, and escrows, Virginia law permits lenders to charge a **loan origination fee** for granting a loan.

Other allowable closing costs are the fees charged for title examination, title insurance, recording charges, taxes, hazard insurance, mortgage guarantee insurance, appraisals, credit reports, surveys, document preparation, real estate tax service fees, lender inspection, and attorney or settlement agent charges for closing the loan and settlement on the property.

The lender generally requires a house location survey. The survey must be current (within the past six months), and the survey must be done by a certified land surveyor.

Home Mortgage Loans

Home loans generally fall into two categories: conventional and government. Conventional loans are those that conform to standards set by Fannie Mae and Freddie Mac. Non-conforming loans do not meet the Fannie/Freddie standards and will not be purchased by them (for example, a jumbo loan that exceeds the current Fannie/Freddie loan limit).

In the past, Fannie Mae and Freddie Mac were independent agencies called **government-sponsored enterprises (GSEs)**. In 2008, regulation of Fannie Mae and Freddie Mac was given to the Federal Housing Finance Administration (FHFA), which also has the authority to establish conforming mortgage loan limits. For current loan limits, visit www.hud.gov and select "FHA Mortgage Limits" under the Resources tab.

Government loans include FHA, VA, Rural Housing Service (RHS), and certain loans provided by local or state financing authorities. FHA loans are insured by the Federal Housing Administration; VA loans are guaranteed by the Department of Veterans Affairs.

Consumer Financial Protection Bureau

The Consumer Financial Protection Bureau (CFPB) was created as part of the Dodd-Frank legislation in 2010. The CFPB established new rules for mortgage servicers that went into effect January 10, 2014. Despite concern in the mortgage lending industry regarding the thousands of pages of rules and new processes that would now be required, lenders were able to develop coping strategies and to implement the new regulations in a timely fashion.

The new CFPB rules require the servicer to

- provide billing information in writing;
- provide at least two months' warning if there is going to be a change in an adjustable-rate mortgage interest rate that means payments are about to change;
- promptly credit mortgage payments;
- respond quickly when asked about paying off a loan;
- not charge for insurance that is not needed, or overcharge for force-placed insurance;
- quickly resolve complaints and share information;
- have and follow good customer service policies and procedures;
- contact the borrower to help when the borrower is having trouble making payments;
- work with the borrower who is having trouble paying the mortgage, before starting or continuing foreclosure; and
- allow the borrower to seek review of the mortgage servicer's decision about a loan workout request.

This information is available in the CFPB brochure *What the New Mortgage Servicing Rules Mean for Consumers*. The brochure also provides contact information for any consumer who does not believe that the lender is following the mortgage servicing rules. This brochure and other CFPB resources are available at www .consumerfinance.gov.

Qualified Residential Mortgage (QRM)

The CFPB has been working on developing qualifying standards for the **qualified residential mortgage (QRM)**. The original concept for the QRM is that it would greatly simplify the qualifying process for a mortgage loan, making it possible to go to settlement more quickly. A major concern for future borrowers was the requirement for a 20% down payment. The CFPB sought additional information with regard to debt-to-income (DTI) ratios, amount of down-payment, and other factors involved in the development of a qualified mortgage (QM) test. The QM rule is widely expected to be the standard for lending in years to come, although without requiring a 20% down-payment.

Another part of the Dodd-Frank legislation would have required the lender to retain a percentage of a mortgage loan that did not meet the QRM standards. Lawmakers continue to work on developing a standard that can work for both lenders and consumers.

Real Estate Settlement Procedures (RESPA) and Truth in Lending Act (TILA) Forms

Two new forms are anticipated by August of 2015. The first will be the Loan Estimate Form, which is to be delivered to the borrower within three days of loan application. The second is the Closing Disclosure Form, which will replace the current Settlement Statement (HUD-1).

■ VIRGINIA HOUSING DEVELOPMENT AUTHORITY

The Virginia Housing Development Authority (VHDA) was created in 1972 by the Virginia General Assembly. Its purpose is to make housing more affordable for those with low or moderate incomes. VHDA is self-supporting, and funding for its programs is provided by the private sector through the sales of VHDA bonds. Federal and state tax dollars are not used to fund VHDA lending programs. Basic VHDA services include the following:

■ Single-family loan programs—creative and lower interest rate loans for low-income to moderate-income homebuyers who have not had an ownership interest in their primary residences during the three years prior to making application for the loan
■ Multifamily loan products—mortgage loans to developers of multifamily projects (primarily for rentals for low-income and moderate-income tenants)
■ Administration of the federal low-income housing Tax Credit Program
■ Administration of the federal Section 8 and Section 236 rent subsidy programs
■ Virginia Housing Fund—loans for multifamily housing that will serve low-income and moderate-income residents in difficult situations or locations
■ Administration of some functions of the Virginia Housing Partnership Fund

VHDA offers a variety of different loan programs, including those made in conjunction with FHA, VA, and Rural Housing Service (RHS). A homeownership education course is required of first-time buyers.

Specific guidelines for the various VHDA loan products may be obtained from a local lender or by contacting VHDA headquarters in Richmond or online at www.vhda.com.

VHDA also builds and operates residential housing, nursing care facilities, and nursing homes providing medical and related facilities for the residence and care of the elderly.

Virginia Housing Partnership Fund

The Virginia Housing Partnership (Revolving) Fund was created to address the serious shortage in the Commonwealth of safe and decent residential housing at prices that persons and families of low and moderate incomes can afford. Housing developments and housing projects funded through the fund are intended to provide additional affordable housing opportunities for low-income and moderate-income Virginians by preserving existing housing units, by producing new housing units, and by assisting persons with special needs with obtaining adequate housing.

This fund was renamed the Virginia Housing Trust Fund by the 2013 General Assembly, and $7,000,000 was allocated to the fund to be administered by the VHDA along with the Department of Housing and Community Development (DHCD). Eighty percent of the money is to be used for low-interest loans made through eligible organizations, with the remaining 20% directed to reducing homelessness in the Commonwealth.

■ FHA FINANCING

Many Virginians obtain Federal Housing Administration (FHA) insured mortgage loans for either first-time or subsequent purchases of a home. Both current loan limits (based on geographic area) and FHA mortgage insurance premiums are subject to frequent change. As of April 1, 2013, the standard mortgage limit for a one-unit dwelling is $271,050. In an FHA-considered high-cost area, the limit is $625,500. The loan limits for two, three, or four-unit dwellings can be found at www.fha.com.

FHA mortgage insurance premiums (MIPs) undergo frequent changes. As of April 1, 2013, the upfront mortgage insurance premium is 1.75% of the loan amount, except for some special loan programs. The annual premium as of April 1, 2013, for a 30-year mortgage is 1.30% of loan amount for loans with more than 5% down and 1.35% for loans with less than 5% down. The upfront MIP is amortized over the term of the loan (usually 30 years) and has less impact on the monthly payment. The annual fee, however, is divided by 12 and added to the monthly payment, which can make a significant difference in the amount due each month.

HUD-1 Settlement Statement and Good Faith Estimate

Changes were made to the Settlement Statement (HUD-1) and Good Faith Estimate (GFE) required under the Real Estate Settlement Procedures Act (RESPA) to help consumers shop for the lowest cost mortgage and avoid costly and potentially harmful loan offers (see Figures 6.1 and 6.2). Copies of the current forms are available through www.hud.gov.

FIGURE 6.1

Settlement Statement (HUD-1)

OMB Approval No. 2502-0265

A. **Settlement Statement (HUD-1)**

B. Type of Loan

1. ☐ FHA	2. ☐ RHS	3. ☐ Conv. Unins.	6. File Number:	7. Loan Number:	8. Mortgage Insurance Case Number:
4. ☐ VA	5. ☐ Conv. Ins.				

C. Note: This form is furnished to give you a statement of actual settlement costs. Amounts paid to and by the settlement agent are shown. Items marked "(p.o.c.)" were paid outside the closing; they are shown here for informational purposes and are not included in the totals.

D. Name & Address of Borrower:	E. Name & Address of Seller:	F. Name & Address of Lender:
G. Property Location:	H. Settlement Agent:	I. Settlement Date:
	Place of Settlement:	

J. Summary of Borrower's Transaction		**K. Summary of Seller's Transaction**	
100. Gross Amount Due from Borrower		**400. Gross Amount Due to Seller**	
101. Contract sales price		401. Contract sales price	
102. Personal property		402. Personal property	
103. Settlement charges to borrower (line 1400)		403.	
104.		404.	
105.		405.	
Adjustment for items paid by seller in advance		Adjustment for items paid by seller in advance	
106. City/town taxes to		406. City/town taxes to	
107. County taxes to		407. County taxes to	
108. Assessments to		408. Assessments to	
109.		409.	
110.		410.	
111.		411.	
112.		412.	
120. Gross Amount Due from Borrower		**420. Gross Amount Due to Seller**	
200. Amount Paid by or in Behalf of Borrower		**500. Reductions In Amount Due to seller**	
201. Deposit or earnest money		501. Excess deposit (see instructions)	
202. Principal amount of new loan(s)		502. Settlement charges to seller (line 1400)	
203. Existing loan(s) taken subject to		503. Existing loan(s) taken subject to	
204.		504. Payoff of first mortgage loan	
205.		505. Payoff of second mortgage loan	
206.		506.	
207.		507.	
208.		508.	
209.		509.	
Adjustments for items unpaid by seller		Adjustments for items unpaid by seller	
210. City/town taxes to		510. City/town taxes to	
211. County taxes to		511. County taxes to	
212. Assessments to		512. Assessments to	
213.		513.	
214.		514.	
215.		515.	
216.		516.	
217.		517.	
218.		518.	
219.		519.	
220. Total Paid by/for Borrower		**520. Total Reduction Amount Due Seller**	
300. Cash at Settlement from/to Borrower		**600. Cash at Settlement to/from Seller**	
301. Gross amount due from borrower (line 120)		601. Gross amount due to seller (line 420)	
302. Less amounts paid by/for borrower (line 220)	( )	602. Less reductions in amounts due seller (line 520)	( )
303. Cash ☐ From ☐ To Borrower		**603. Cash** ☐ To ☐ From Seller	

The Public Reporting Burden for this collection of information is estimated at 35 minutes per response for collecting, reviewing, and reporting the data. This agency may not collect this information, and you are not required to complete this form, unless it displays a currently valid OMB control number. No confidentiality is assured; this disclosure is mandatory. This is designed to provide the parties to a RESPA covered transaction with information during the settlement process.

FIGURE 6.1

Settlement Statement (HUD-1) (cont.)

L. Settlement Charges

700. Total Real Estate Broker Fees		Paid From Borrower's Funds at Settlement	Paid From Seller's Funds at Settlement
Division of commission (line 700) as follows :			
701. $ to			
702. $ to			
703. Commission paid at settlement			
704.			

800. Items Payable in Connection with Loan			
801. Our origination charge	$ (from GFE #1)		
802. Your credit or charge (points) for the specific interest rate chosen	$ (from GFE #2)		
803. Your adjusted origination charges	(from GFE #A)		
804. Appraisal fee to	(from GFE #3)		
805. Credit report to	(from GFE #3)		
806. Tax service to	(from GFE #3)		
807. Flood certification to	(from GFE #3)		
808.			
809.			
810.			
811.			

900. Items Required by Lender to be Paid in Advance			
901. Daily interest charges from to @ $ /day	(from GFE #10)		
902. Mortgage insurance premium for months to	(from GFE #3)		
903. Homeowner's insurance for years to	(from GFE #11)		
904.			

1000. Reserves Deposited with Lender			
1001. Initial deposit for your escrow account	(from GFE #9)		
1002. Homeowner's insurance months @ $ per month $			
1003. Mortgage insurance months @ $ per month $			
1004. Property Taxes months @ $ per month $			
1005. months @ $ per month $			
1006. months @ $ per month $			
1007. Aggregate Adjustment -$			

1100. Title Charges			
1101. Title services and lender's title insurance	(from GFE #4)		
1102. Settlement or closing fee	$		
1103. Owner's title insurance	(from GFE #5)		
1104. Lender's title insurance	$		
1105. Lender's title policy limit $			
1106. Owner's title policy limit $			
1107. Agent's portion of the total title insurance premium to	$		
1108. Underwriter's portion of the total title insurance premium to	$		
1109.			
1110.			
1111.			

1200. Government Recording and Transfer Charges			
1201. Government recording charges	(from GFE #7)		
1202. Deed $ Mortgage $ Release $			
1203. Transfer taxes	(from GFE #8)		
1204. City/County tax/stamps Deed $ Mortgage $			
1205. State tax/stamps Deed $ Mortgage $			
1206.			

1300. Additional Settlement Charges			
1301. Required services that you can shop for	(from GFE #6)		
1302. $			
1303. $			
1304.			
1305.			

1400. Total Settlement Charges (enter on lines 103, Section J and 502, Section K)			

FIGURE 6.1

Settlement Statement (HUD-1) (cont.)

Comparison of Good Faith Estimate (GFE) and HUD-1 Charrges		Good Faith Estimate	HUD-1
Charges That Cannot Increase	**HUD-1 Line Number**		
Our origination charge	# 801		
Your credit or charge (points) for the specific interest rate chosen	# 802		
Your adjusted origination charges	# 803		
Transfer taxes	# 1203		

Charges That In Total Cannot Increase More Than 10%		Good Faith Estimate	HUD-1
Government recording charges	# 1201		
	#		
	#		
	#		
	#		
	#		
	#		
	#		
	Total		
	Increase between GFE and HUD-1 Charges	$ or	%

Charges That Can Change		Good Faith Estimate	HUD-1
Initial deposit for your escrow account	# 1001		
Daily interest charges $ /day	# 901		
Homeowner's insurance	# 903		
	#		
	#		
	#		

Loan Terms

Your initial loan amount is	$
Your loan term is	years
Your initial interest rate is	%
Your initial monthly amount owed for principal, interest, and any mortgage insurance is	$ includes ☐ Principal ☐ Interest ☐ Mortgage Insurance
Can your interest rate rise?	☐ No ☐ Yes, it can rise to a maximum of %. The first change will be on and can change again every after . Every change date, your interest rate can increase or decrease by %. Over the life of the loan, your interest rate is guaranteed to never be **lower** than % or **higher** than %.
Even if you make payments on time, can your loan balance rise?	☐ No ☐ Yes, it can rise to a maximum of $
Even if you make payments on time, can your monthly amount owed for principal, interest, and mortgage insurance rise?	☐ No ☐ Yes, the first increase can be on and the monthly amount owed can rise to $. The maximum it can ever rise to is $
Does your loan have a prepayment penalty?	☐ No ☐ Yes, your maximum prepayment penalty is $
Does your loan have a balloon payment?	☐ No ☐ Yes, you have a balloon payment of $ due in years on .
Total monthly amount owed including escrow account payments	☐ You do not have a monthly escrow payment for items, such as property taxes and homeowner's insurance. You must pay these items directly yourself. ☐ You have an additional monthly escrow payment of $ that results in a total initial monthly amount owed of $. This includes principal, interest, any mortgage insurance and any items checked below: ☐ Property taxes ☐ Homeowner's insurance ☐ Flood insurance ☐ ☐ ☐

Note: If you have any questions about the Settlement Charges and Loan Terms listed on this form, please contact your lender.

FIGURE 6.2

Good Faith Estimate (GFE)

OMB Approval No. 2502-0265

Good Faith Estimate (GFE)

Name of Originator	Borrower
Originator Address	Property Address
Originator Phone Number	
Originator Email	Date of GFE

Purpose

This GFE gives you an estimate of your settlement charges and loan terms if you are approved for this loan. For more information, see HUD's *Special Information Booklet* on settlement charges, your *Truth-in-Lending Disclosures,* and other consumer information at www.hud.gov/respa. If you decide you would like to proceed with this loan, contact us.

Shopping for your loan

Only you can shop for the best loan for you. Compare this GFE with other loan offers, so you can find the best loan. Use the shopping chart on page 3 to compare all the offers you receive.

Important dates

1. The interest rate for this GFE is available through _____ . After this time, the interest rate, some of your loan Origination Charges, and the monthly payment shown below can change until you lock your interest rate.

2. This estimate for all other settlement charges is available through _____ .

3. After you lock your interest rate, you must go to settlement within ____ days (your rate lock period) to receive the locked interest rate.

4. You must lock the interest rate at least ____ days before settlement.

Summary of your loan

Your initial loan amount is	$
Your loan term is	years
Your initial interest rate is	%
Your initial monthly amount owed for principal, interest, and any mortgage insurance is	$ per month
Can your interest rate rise?	☐ No ☐ Yes, it can rise to a maximum of %. The first change will be in .
Even if you make payments on time, can your loan balance rise?	☐ No ☐ Yes, it can rise to a maximum of $
Even if you make payments on time, can your monthly amount owed for principal, interest, and any mortgage insurance rise?	☐ No ☐ Yes, the first increase can be in and the monthly amount owed can rise to $. The maximum it can ever rise to is $
Does your loan have a prepayment penalty?	☐ No ☐ Yes, your maximum prepayment penalty is $
Does your loan have a balloon payment?	☐ No ☐ Yes, you have a balloon payment of $ due in years.

Escrow account information

Some lenders require an escrow account to hold funds for paying property taxes or other property-related charges in addition to your monthly amount owed of $ _____ .

Do we require you to have an escrow account for your loan?

☐ No, you do not have an escrow account. You must pay these charges directly when due.

☐ Yes, you have an escrow account. It may or may not cover all of these charges. Ask us.

Summary of your settlement charges

A	Your Adjusted Origination Charges *(See page 2.)*	$
B	Your Charges for All Other Settlement Services *(See page 2.)*	$
A + B	Total Estimated Settlement Charges	$

FIGURE 6.2

Good Faith Estimate (GFE) (cont.)

Understanding
your estimated
settlement charges

*Some of these charges
can change at settlement.
See the top of page 3 for
more information.*

Your Adjusted Origination Charges

1. Our origination charge
This charge is for getting this loan for you.

2. Your credit or charge (points) for the specific interest rate chosen

☐ The credit or charge for the interest rate of [＿＿＿] % is included in "Our origination charge." (See item 1 above.)

☐ You receive a credit of $[＿＿＿] for this interest rate of [＿＿＿]%. This credit **reduces** your settlement charges.

☐ You pay a charge of $[＿＿＿] for this interest rate of [＿＿＿]%. This charge (points) **increases** your total settlement charges.

The tradeoff table on page 3 shows that you can change your total settlement charges by choosing a different interest rate for this loan.

A Your Adjusted Origination Charges | $

Your Charges for All Other Settlement Services

3. Required services that we select
These charges are for services we require to complete your settlement. We will choose the providers of these services.

| Service | Charge |

4. Title services and lender's title insurance
This charge includes the services of a title or settlement agent, for example, and title insurance to protect the lender, if required.

5. Owner's title insurance
You may purchase an owner's title insurance policy to protect your interest in the property.

6. Required services that you can shop for
These charges are for other services that are required to complete your settlement. We can identify providers of these services or you can shop for them yourself. Our estimates for providing these services are below.

| Service | Charge |

7. Government recording charges
These charges are for state and local fees to record your loan and title documents.

8. Transfer taxes
These charges are for state and local fees on mortgages and home sales.

9. Initial deposit for your escrow account
This charge is held in an escrow account to pay future recurring charges on your property and includes ☐ all property taxes, ☐ all insurance, and ☐ other [＿＿＿＿＿].

10. Daily interest charges
This charge is for the daily interest on your loan from the day of your settlement until the first day of the next month or the first day of your normal mortgage payment cycle. This amount is $[＿＿＿]per day for [＿＿] days (if your settlement is [＿＿＿＿＿]).

11. Homeowner's insurance
This charge is for the insurance you must buy for the property to protect from a loss, such as fire.

| Policy | Charge |

B Your Charges for All Other Settlement Services | $

A + B Total Estimated Settlement Charges | $

FIGURE 6.2

Good Faith Estimate (GFE) (cont.)

Instructions

Understanding which charges can change at settlement

This GFE estimates your settlement charges. At your settlement, you will receive a HUD-1, a form that lists your actual costs. Compare the charges on the HUD-1 with the charges on this GFE. Charges can change if you select your own provider and do not use the companies we identify. (See below for details.)

These charges **cannot increase** at settlement:	The total of these charges **can increase up to 10%** at settlement:	These charges **can change** at settlement:
■ Our origination charge ■ Your credit or charge (points) for the specific interest rate chosen (*after you lock in your interest rate*) ■ Your adjusted origination charges (*after you lock in your interest rate*) ■ Transfer taxes	■ Required services that we select ■ Title services and lender's title insurance (*if we select them or you use companies we identify*) ■ Owner's title insurance (*if you use companies we identify*) ■ Required services that you can shop for (*if you use companies we identify*) ■ Government recording charges	■ Required services that you can shop for (*if you do not use companies we identify*) ■ Title services and lender's title insurance (*if you do not use companies we identify*) ■ Owner's title insurance (*if you do not use companies we identify*) ■ Initial deposit for your escrow account ■ Daily interest charges ■ Homeowner's insurance

Using the tradeoff table

In this GFE, we offered you this loan with a particular interest rate and estimated settlement charges. However:

■ If you want to choose this same loan with **lower settlement charges,** then you will have a **higher interest rate.**

■ If you want to choose this same loan with a **lower interest rate,** then you will have **higher settlement charges.**

If you would like to choose an available option, you must ask us for a new GFE.

Loan originators have the option to complete this table. Please ask for additional information if the table is not completed.

	The loan in this GFE	The same loan with lower settlement charges	The same loan with a lower interest rate
Your initial loan amount	$	$	$
Your initial interest rate [1]	%	%	%
Your initial monthly amount owed	$	$	$
Change in the monthly amount owed from this GFE	No change	You will pay $ **more** every month	You will pay $ **less** every month
Change in the amount you will pay at settlement with this interest rate	No change	Your settlement charges will be **reduced** by $	Your settlement charges will **increase** by $
How much your total estimated settlement charges will be	$	$	$

[1] For an adjustable rate loan, the comparisons above are for the initial interest rate before adjustments are made.

Using the shopping chart

Use this chart to compare GFEs from different loan originators. Fill in the information by using a different column for each GFE you receive. By comparing loan offers, you can shop for the best loan.

	This loan	Loan 2	Loan 3	Loan 4
Loan originator name				
Initial loan amount				
Loan term				
Initial interest rate				
Initial monthly amount owed				
Rate lock period				
Can interest rate rise?				
Can loan balance rise?				
Can monthly amount owed rise?				
Prepayment penalty?				
Balloon payment?				
Total Estimated Settlement Charges				

If your loan is sold in the future

Some lenders may sell your loan after settlement. Any fees lenders receive in the future cannot change the loan you receive or the charges you paid at settlement.

Changes Regarding Condominiums

In the past, it has often been difficult to obtain FHA financing for condominiums because of the limitations on the percentage of investor owners. An FHA mortgagee letter issued September 13, 2012, focused on four major concerns:

1. Treatment of delinquent dues
2. Property certification requirements
3. Owner-occupancy requirements
4. Treatment of commercial space

Changes covered in this letter to lenders included the following:

- A developer or a single investor may own up to 50% of the total units at the time of project approval.
- **Mixed-use developments** are defined as developments with a combination of any of the following: commercial, residential, retail, office, or parking space (half of the space may be devoted to commercial use as long as the commercial space does not have a negative impact on the residential character of the project).
- No more than 15% of the total units can be in arrears (more than 60 days past due) on condominium association fee payments.
- The Project Owner's Certification document has been revised. For more details, see www.hud.gov.

Assistance for Disaster Areas

A November mortgagee letter published guidance for families with FHA-insured mortgages struggling to repair or rebuild homes in the wake of major disasters like Hurricane Sandy. Provisions of the letter include the following:

- A 90-day moratorium of foreclosures on properties located in presidentially declared disaster areas is outlined.
- Servicers must consider a full range of benefits for affected borrowers, including mortgage modifications, partial claims, use of FHA, HAMP, or other refinance options, and a waiver of late charges.
- Lenders are to release homeowners' insurance proceeds to the borrower rather than retaining such proceeds to make up for missed payments.
- HUD's Section 203(h) mortgage insurance product to assist disaster victims is summarized, and reference is made to HUD's Section 203(k) rehabilitation mortgage insurance product.

■ VA LOANS

The Department of Veterans Affairs (VA) adjustable-rate mortgage (ARM) was made a permanent loan product in August 2012 as part of the Honoring America's Veterans and Caring for Camp Lejeune Families Act of 2012. Another part of this law reinstated the higher loan limits for VA-guaranteed loans through 2014. The VA loan limit for most counties in Virginia is $417,000, but the loan limit may be as high as $843,750 in high-cost areas, such as Northern Virginia and Virginia Beach.

■ PURCHASE-MONEY FINANCING AND SELLER FINANCING

Purchase-money financing occurs when a mortgage or deed of trust is given as part of the purchaser's consideration for the purchase of real property. Purchase-money financing may be provided by a third party, such as an institutional lender or the seller. When provided by the seller, it commonly refers to a seller taking back a second trust in lieu of cash to make up the difference between the first trust from the institutional lender and the selling price for the property.

■ **FOR EXAMPLE** A seller wants $100,000 for his property. The purchasers are able to secure a $70,000 loan secured by a first deed of trust from an institutional lender. Because they have only $10,000 in cash available for a down payment, they ask the seller to accept a purchase-money deed of trust (seller financing) for $20,000. The rate and terms must be agreed on between the seller and the purchasers.

A purchase-money deed of trust has priority over other claims or liens against the purchaser except for property tax or IRS tax liens.

■ DEFERRED PURCHASE-MONEY DEED OF TRUST

Sellers with no immediate need for cash from the proceeds of a sale may choose to defer the income of the sale and obtain an installment tax treatment by creating an annuity in the form of a **deferred purchase money** deed of trust, held by the seller. One advantage to sellers is that they usually receive a substantial down payment. Such an arrangement may be prohibited, however, if there is to be a first deed of trust to an outside (institutional) lender. A purchase-money deed of trust held by the seller should state that it is granted to secure *deferred purchase money*, while a purchase-money deed of trust to a third (institutional lender) party states that it is granted to secure *purchase money*. If it is a second deed of trust, it can be for a short term with a balloon payment at the end. The first lender's guidelines must be followed. If it is subordinated, the purchase-money second deed of trust should include a provision that any default in a senior encumbrance or lien will also be considered a default on a second deed of trust.

■ **FOR EXAMPLE** A seller wants $400,000 for his property but does not want to take the proceeds of the sale in one tax year. He offers to take back financing in the form of a deferred purchase-money deed of trust. He will accept a $20,000 down payment from the purchasers and hold a note for $380,000 that balloons in 10 years. The rate and terms must be agreed on between the seller and the purchasers.

HELOCS or Credit Line Deeds of Trust

Sometimes called *credit line deeds of trust*, a **home equity line of credit (HELOC)** permits the note holder to make advances from time to time secured by the real estate described in the deed. Most HELOCs are second trusts and are sometimes made at the same time as the first trust with the same lender. The total amount of advances may not exceed the maximum credit line extended to the borrower. Virginia law permits credit line deeds of trust, subject to certain rules. The trust document must identify itself as a credit line deed of trust on the front page in capital letters and underscored type. The phrase *this is a credit line deed of trust* gives notice that the note holder named in the deed of trust and the grantors and other borrowers identified in the deed have an agreement.

From the date of the recording of a credit line deed of trust, the lien has priority over all other deeds, conveyances, and other instruments or contracts in writing that are unrecorded at that time and of which the note holder has no knowledge. The credit line deed of trust also has priority over judgment liens subsequently docketed. However, if a judgment creditor gives notice to the note holder at the address indicated on the credit line deed of trust, the deed of trust has no priority over the judgment for any advances or extensions of credit subsequently made under the deed of trust.

■ FORECLOSURES

There are three ways to foreclose a deed of trust in Virginia:

1. Decree of court (strict foreclosure)
2. Conveyance of the property by the grantors and the trustees to the beneficiary in consideration of the debt (deed in lieu of foreclosure)
3. Sale by the trustee pursuant to a power of sale (trustee sale)

Although an exhaustive discussion of foreclosure procedures is not included here, it is important for licensees to be aware that bankruptcy of the mortgagor is an automatic stay of foreclosure. If a lien is foreclosed, that is, no bankruptcy was granted, the lien and all inferior liens are wiped out. Superior liens, however—those that have priority over the foreclosed lien—are not affected. A purchaser takes the property subject to any prior liens.

Foreclosure of VA and FHA loans is subject to certain additional requirements. For example, the loan must have been in default for three months prior to the commencement of foreclosure; notices must be given to both the debtor and the insuring agency; and the lender must take affirmative steps to avoid foreclosure, including personal interviews and acceptance of partial payments.

Trustee's Powers and Duties

Virginia is a **title theory** state.

Legal title to the property conveyed by the deed of trust is vested in the trustee for the benefit of the note holder. The trustee can act only in a manner authorized by statute or the express or implied terms of the trust.

The trustee is the agent for both the **grantor** (the homeowner) and the beneficiary (the lender) and is bound to act impartially between them. The trustee is obliged to seek every possible advantage to the trust in the course of any sale. This includes using all reasonable diligence to obtain the best price possible. The trustee may adjourn the sale from time to time to meet any unexpected occurrences, but the re-advertisement of the sale must be in the same manner as the original advertisement.

The terms of the deed of trust will determine how the property is advertised. Even if the number of advertisements meets the terms, Virginia law provides that the sale may take place no earlier than the eighth day after the first advertisement and no later than 30 days after the last advertisement.

If it is clear at the sale that the property will be sold for a grossly inadequate or sacrificial price, it is the trustee's duty to adjourn the sale. In addition, if the trustee knows of facts that might keep bidding low, such as a cloud on title, he must adjourn the sale and remove the hindrance.

By statute, the trustee must ascertain whether there are any real estate tax liens against the property being sold. The trustee is obligated to pay the taxes out of the proceeds of sale and give the tax lien priority over the deed of trust. In addition, the purchaser is required to see that the taxes are paid. If the taxes are not paid, the trustee may be liable personally and the purchaser takes the land subject to the tax lien (though not personally liable for its payment). The trustee should also pay the prorated portion of the current year's real estate taxes.

Potential Conflict of Interest

A trustee may not purchase the property held in trust without written permission from the trustor. The trustee is bound by law to secure the highest possible price for the property, while a purchaser seeks to procure the property at the lowest possible price. The trustee's duty to the trust transcends any potential personal interest she may have or acquire in the property.

The sale must be held in accordance with the terms of the deed of trust, which specifies the time, manner, and place of sale. Unless the deed of trust states otherwise, the sale is held at the property itself, near the circuit court building, or at some other place selected by the trustee in the city or county in which the property is located

At the sale, the trustee sells the property to the highest bidder, and the successful purchaser executes a memorandum of sale. The trustee obtains the deposit from the purchaser.

The trustee cannot convey a greater interest than the deed of trust gives authority to sell. The sale is subject to encumbrances that have priority over the deed of trust. Accordingly, the trustee's deed should contain only a special warranty of title. However, the form of the deed and the title conveyed must conform to the manner in which the property was advertised.

Disbursement of Proceeds

The trustee must apply the proceeds of sale in the following order:

- Discharge the expenses of executing the trust, including a commission to the trustee of 5% of the gross proceeds
- Discharge all taxes, levies, and assessments with costs and interest, if they have priority over the deed of trust

- Discharge, in the order of their priority, any remaining debts and obligations secured by the deed of trust and any liens of record inferior to the deed of trust, with interest
- Render the residue of the proceeds to the grantor (foreclosed mortgagor) or his assigns

When the sale is made under any recorded deed of trust, the trustee must file a report and accounting with the commissioner of accounts within four months of the sale.

Short Sales

In an effort to avoid foreclosure, some homeowners are able to reach an agreement with their mortgage loan lender to accept a **short sale**, an amount that is less than what is actually due on the mortgage loan. The federal government has prepared standardized rules and forms for short sales. Many homeowners have been very distressed when their short sale has fallen through.

Fannie Mae and Freddie Mac have issued new guidelines to enhance and streamline the short sale process. Hardship eligibility has been increased and improvements have been made to the valuation process.

IN PRACTICE The REB advises licensees who perform or intend to perform transactions involving foreclosures or short sales to complete adequate training prior to offering their service to the public.

The rule of *caveat emptor* (let the buyer beware) applies in foreclosure sales, with regard to both the quality of title and the condition of the property.

Loan Modification Programs

Since 2008, the government has taken steps to help at-risk homeowners avoid foreclosure. The **Home Affordable Modification Program (HAMP)** was created in March 2009 as part of the Making Home Affordable initiative. All lenders participating in the government's program must agree to follow very specific procedures and formulas. The HAMP program has given some homeowners an opportunity to modify or refinance their mortgage in order to make the monthly payments affordable and avoid foreclosure.

The Home Affordable Refinance Program (HARP) made refinancing available for many homeowners regardless of hardship conditions.

■ USURY

Usury is the loan of money at a greater rate of interest than allowed by law. Virginia law provides that loans secured by a first deed of trust on real estate may be lawfully enforced with no limitation on the amount of interest, if that arrangement is properly stated in the instrument or separate agreement. The contract generally is considered to be the promissory note. Most prudent lenders insert the rate in the note.

The law provides that disclosure of charges may be contained in an interest disclosure statement if such disclosure is not otherwise specified in the note. It further provides that an interest rate that varies in accordance with any exterior standard or that cannot be ascertained from the contract without reference to exterior circumstances or documents is enforceable as agreed in the signed contract. For example, a note providing for an interest rate of 3% above the stated prime rate of a specific bank is enforceable.

Allowable Interest Rates

Where the seller in a bona fide real estate transaction takes back a purchase-money deed of trust, the promissory note may provide for any rate of interest agreed to by the parties. Usury is not applicable to such a transaction because the interest rate is considered a part of the purchase price.

CHAPTER 6 QUIZ

1. When borrowers sign a note and deed of trust, they are giving the lender the right to
   a. request a court hearing within 30 days of default.
   b. set the time and place of the court hearing.
   c. initiate a non-judicial foreclosure.
   d. initiate a judicial foreclosure.

2. The responsibility for preparing the note and deed of trust involved in a closing belongs to the
   a. seller's broker.
   b. settlement attorney.
   c. lender.
   d. buyer.

3. The Consumer Financial Protection Bureau was created to
   a. protect the interests of the consumer.
   b. regulate the FHA.
   c. oversee Fannie Mae and Freddie Mac.
   d. administer the Virginia Housing Trust Fund.

4. What is the maximum late charge that may be assessed on a mortgage loan payment?
   a. No limit if the charge is stated in the loan contract
   b. 5%
   c. 10%
   d. 15%

5. An individual purchased a house with a conventional first deed of trust loan. The annual payment is $18,540, with monthly payments due on the tenth of each month. The loan has no provision for a grace period. If the borrower makes a payment on June 18, can the lender legally impose a late charge?
   a. Yes, but no more than $154.50
   b. Yes, but no more than $77.25
   c. Yes, but no more than an amount equal to one month's interest
   d. No, because late fees on conventional first deeds of trust are illegal in Virginia

6. A deed of trust that permits the borrower to receive advances from time to time up to a maximum amount secured by real property is called
   a. a conventional loan.
   b. an escrow credit loan.
   c. a mortgage loan deed of trust.
   d. a credit line deed of trust or a home equity line of credit (HELOC).

7. The new rules for mortgage servicers established by the Consumer Financial Protection Bureau include all of the following EXCEPT
   a. provide two month's warning for any rate increase.
   b. promptly credit mortgage payments.
   c. work with the borrower before starting foreclosure proceedings.
   d. allow a six month's moratorium for delinquent loans.

8. The primary purpose of the Virginia Housing Development Authority is to
   a. encourage more housing development in Virginia.
   b. make housing more affordable for low-income and moderate-income buyers.
   c. obtain funds from state tax dollars.
   d. replace VA and FHA funding in Virginia.

9. The Virginia Housing Development Authority (VHDA) is funded by
   a. HUD.
   b. Virginia income tax.
   c. sale of bonds in the private sector.
   d. federal subsidy programs.

10. In addition to providing loans for affordable housing, VHDA also builds and operates all of the following EXCEPT
    a. schools.
    b. nursing care facilities.
    c. nursing homes providing medical facilities for the elderly.
    d. residential housing for the elderly.

11. Basic VHDA services include all of the following *EXCEPT*
    a. administration of the federal Section 8 rent subsidy program.
    b. administration of the Virginia Residential Landlord and Tenant Act.
    c. Virginia Housing Fund loans.
    d. administration of some functions of the Virginia Housing Partnership Fund.

12. Who or what is paid first from a sale at foreclosure?
    a. The expenses of executing the trust, including commission, to the trustee
    b. All taxes, levies, and assessments with costs and interest, if they have priority over the deed of trust
    c. Any remaining debts and obligations secured by the deed of trust
    d. The owner

13. A deed of trust can be foreclosed on in Virginia in any of the ways listed *EXCEPT*
    a. decree of court (strict foreclosure).
    b. deed in lieu of foreclosure.
    c. sale by a trustee under the power of sale.
    d. bankruptcy sale.

14. With regard to advertising the date of sale on a foreclosure, the sale may take place
    a. no earlier than 30 days after the last advertisement.
    b. no earlier than 8 days after the first advertisement.
    c. no later than 8 days after the last advertisement.
    d. no later than 30 days after the first advertisement.

15. A program that has helped some homeowners in financial distress to modify their home loan to avoid foreclosure is called the
    a. Home Equity Conversion Mortgage (HECM).
    b. Federal Tax Credit program.
    c. New Good Faith Estimate (GFE) and Settlement Statement (HUD-1) forms.
    d. Home Affordable Modification Program (HAMP).

CHAPTER

7

Transfer of Title

■ **LEARNING OBJECTIVES**   *After successfully completing this chapter, you will be able to*

■ **describe** the requirements for a valid conveyance of title;

■ **explain** transfer of title by adverse possession and by will;

■ **review** the responsibilities of a settlement agent; and

■ **define** title examination and title insurance and the procedures involved.

■ KEY TERMS

90-day letter	present interest	testate
adverse possession	noncupative will	testator
chain of title	privity of estate	title examination
correction deed	recordation tax	title insurance
grantor tax	settlement agent	will
holographic will	specific power of attorney	
judgment	surety bond	

■ REQUIREMENTS FOR A VALID CONVEYANCE

In Virginia, the requirements for a valid deed are as follows:

■ Grantor who has the legal capacity to execute the deed
■ Grantee
■ Consideration
■ Granting clause

- Accurate legal description of the property
- Any relevant exceptions or reservations
- Signature of the grantor, sometimes with acknowledgment
- Delivery and acceptance of the deed

Virginia law allows the same person to be both the grantor and grantee in a deed.

■ **FOR EXAMPLE** An individual can convey the deed to his farm to himself and his grandson.

The grantee named to receive a deed to real property should be legally competent to receive the property. The grantee's full name should be used in preparing the deed. A deed to a nonexistent person is a valid conveyance to the intended but misnamed grantee if the intended grantee exists and the intention of the parties can be determined.

The grantor is presumed to have been competent at the time a deed was executed. The test of legal capacity is the party's mental ability to understand the nature and consequences of the transaction at the time it is entered into. The burden of proving incompetence is on the party who attacks the validity of the deed.

In Virginia, a conveyance of land by a minor is a valid transfer of title, unless it is repudiated by the minor after attaining majority. Repudiation may occur even though the grantee has already conveyed the property to another purchaser without notice that a minor was the grantor in the previous transaction.

Use of Power of Attorney

If a seller or buyer is unable to attend the closing, there are two options:

1. Prepare all papers to be signed in advance of the closing
2. Use a power of attorney

A power of attorney must be signed by the seller with the same formalities as a deed. Although a power of attorney can be general or specific, a **specific power of attorney** is strongly recommended to convey real property in Virginia. In reviewing a power of attorney, the licensee should have a lawyer verify that it specifically authorizes performance of all necessary acts and that the attorney-in-fact performs in accordance with the authority granted in the power of attorney.

Affidavits and other sworn statements cannot be signed by the attorney-in-fact. These must be signed by the principal prior to the closing. The deed or other instrument to be signed must indicate that it is being signed by an attorney-in-fact. Normally, this is accomplished by a recital in the body of the instrument or under the signature line.

If an institutional lender is making a new loan, the lender's permission should be obtained for a borrower to execute a power of attorney. The lender may not allow the use of an attorney-in-fact, especially if the loan is subject to truth-in-lending requirements.

A power of attorney must be recorded, and the recording fees are charged to the party using the attorney-in-fact. If the power of attorney is not recorded, it is as though the deed were unsigned by the party being represented by the attorney-in-fact.

■ TRANSFER TAXES AND FEES

Chapter 8 of Title 58.1 – Taxation, of the Code of Virginia, sets the tax on the transfer of property as levied on the seller and the purchaser individually. The seller pays a **grantor tax** and the purchaser pays a **recordation tax**. In some adjoining jurisdictions, the transaction is taxed as a whole and the tax liability is shared in some formula agreed on by the seller and the purchaser.

With certain exceptions, all deeds are subject to state and city or county recordation tax. The state recordation tax is currently $0.25 per $100 (or fraction of $100) of the consideration paid or the value of the property, whichever is greater. A more direct mathematical representation is $0.0025 \times$ the sales price. The county or city may charge up to one-third of that amount, which in the case of Fairfax County, for example, is an additional $0.0008 \times$ the sales price. County/city tax rates may differ.

Recordation taxes are usually paid by the buyer and collected at closing. Payment of these taxes is a prerequisite to having the deed recorded. There is also a transfer fee of $1.00 charged.

I N   P R A C T I C E   The state recordation tax is $0.25 per $100, or $0.0025 per $1. If the sales price of a home is $475,000, then the state recordation tax is $475,000 × 0.0025 = $1,187.50. For Fairfax County, the recordation tax is $475,000 × 0.0008 = $380. Recording fees are subject to change. Licensees should always be aware of the most current tax rates and fees.

In addition to the recordation taxes, all deeds are subject to a grantor's tax of $0.50 per $500 (or a fraction of $500) of the purchase price or the value of the grantor's equity in the property being transferred, in the case of assumption. (In many areas of Virginia, the rate is quoted as $1 per $1,000.) The grantor's tax is paid by the seller and is collected at closing and paid to the clerk of the county where the deed is recorded.

Congestion Relief Fee

As of July 1, 2013, a regional congestion relief fee is imposed on the recording of any deed or instrument conveying real property that is located in the Northern Virginia Region. The fee is paid by the seller (grantor) at the rate of $0.15 per $100 (or fraction thereof). Localities affected are the cities of Alexandria, Fairfax, Falls Church, Manassas, and Manassas Park, and the counties of Arlington, Fairfax, Loudoun, and Prince William.

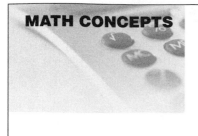

MATH CONCEPTS   **CALCULATING VIRGINIA TRANSFER TAXES**

A home is purchased in Fairfax County for $675,600. The state recordation tax rate is $0.25 and the Fairfax County tax rate is $0.08.

1. State and County or City Recordation Tax

$675,600 ÷ 100 = 6,756 recordation tax units

Purchaser will pay $1,689.00 in state recordation taxes (6,756 × $0.25 = $1,689.00) and $540.48 in county or city recordation tax (6,756 × $0.08 = $540.48)

2. Grantor Tax

$675,600 ÷ 500 = 1,351.2 grantor tax units

Round up to 1,352 grantor tax units

Seller's grantor tax is 1,352 grantor tax units × $0.50 = $676.00

Taxes and Fees on Mortgage Documents

Unless exempted, deeds of trust and mortgages are taxed on a sliding scale, according to the amount of the obligation (that is, the debt) that the instrument secures. If the amount is not ascertainable, the tax is based on the fair market value of the property, including the value of any improvements as of the date of the deed. Deeds of trust are also subject to city or county recordation taxes, clerk's fees, and any plat recordation fees. Deeds of trust that secure both construction loans and permanent loans are normally subject to tax.

For each document admitted to record, the clerk of court collects a transfer fee that is generally paid by the buyer. In addition to the transfer fee, the clerk of court collects a clerk fee for recording plats, powers of attorney, certificates of satisfaction, and release of judgments. The amount of the fee is usually based on the number of pages that must be recorded.

The buyer generally pays the fees to record the new items, and the seller pays for the release of the old items. The payment of fees may be negotiated between the parties.

■ ADVERSE POSSESSION

Establishing title to land by **adverse possession** is somewhat similar to an easement by prescription, which is described earlier in Chapter 3.

To establish title to land by adverse possession in Virginia, it is necessary to show actual, hostile, exclusive, visible, and continuous possession of property for the statutory period of 15 years. The possession by the defendant must be actual and continuous; that is, more than just a sporadic taking of timber or occasional camping is required. The adverse possession must be exclusive to constitute an ousting of the true owner.

When several persons enter upon land in succession, these possessions cannot be tacked to preserve the essential continuity unless there is a **privity of estate** between them. In other words, the intent to establish a continuous succession of adverse possessors must be proven.

Adverse possession cannot be claimed if the possession has been abandoned by the claimant during the required time period. The occupancy necessary to support a claim of title of adverse possession must be hostile and without the true owner's permission.

■ TRANSFER OF A DECEASED PERSON'S PROPERTY

When any person with title to real estate that may be inherited dies **testate**, that is, having executed a legal will, the real estate will pass according to the terms of the instrument.

In Virginia, circuit courts serve as probate courts. Normally there is a probate section in the clerk's office where wills, lists of heirs, affidavits, and other documents related to probate are located. A probate tax is charged on all estates exceeding $15,000 in value. As with other documents, a will index is located in the circuit courts.

IN PRACTICE When listing a property that is part of a decedent's estate, a licensee should establish that the rate of commission to be paid has been approved by the court handling the probate.

Until probate, the **will** is only the legal declaration of a person's intended disposition. A will may be revoked at any time after execution, while a deed cannot be revoked after it has been delivered to the grantee. The rule of construction in determining whether an instrument is a will or a contract is that if it passes a **present interest**, it is a deed or contract; but, if its rights or interests do not convey until the death of the maker, it is a testamentary paper, or will.

Legislation passed in 2013 allows landowners to name a beneficiary on their deeds, either on the initial filing or any subsequent revision. This allows a property to be transferred directly to heirs without going through the probate process and incurring recordation taxes.

Last Will and Testament

The person creating a will is called a testator. A **testator** can have only one last will and testament. A will may be set aside for fraud, undue influence, force, or coercion.

No person of unsound mind or under the age of 18 years is considered to be capable of making a valid will. Virginia law requires only testamentary capacity at the time the will is made; the testator's subsequent capacity is not relevant.

Neither the testator's poor health nor impaired intellect is sufficient, standing alone, to render a will invalid.

No will is valid unless it is in writing. A valid will must be signed by the testator or by some other person in the testator's presence and by the testator's direction in such a way as to make it clear that the name is intended as the testator's signature. A will is also valid that is wholly in the testator's handwriting (a **holographic will**) if the testator signs the will and acknowledges it in the presence of at least two competent witnesses who are both present at the same time. These witnesses also must sign the will in the presence of the testator. The testamentary intent must appear on the face of the paper itself. Virginia law is silent on the subject of oral or **nuncupative** (deathbed) **wills.**

IN PRACTICE   When representing the purchaser of property from a decedent's estate or in taking a listing of estate property, it is wise for a real estate licensee to request a certified copy of the will and determine whether the executor under the will has the power of sale. Where the executor does not have the power of sale, or in dealing with an intestate's property, all the heirs and their spouses must execute a deed as grantors conveying the property to the grantee.

■ SETTLEMENT AGENT

Real Estate Settlement Agents

The Real Estate Settlement Agents (RESA) act requires that persons who perform escrow, closing, or settlement services comply with consumer protection safeguards with respect to licensing, financial responsibility, and the handling of settlement funds.

RESA also provides specific language that is to be included in all contracts for the purchase of real estate containing not more than four residential dwelling units. The specific language is included here:

> Choice of Settlement Agent: Chapter 27.3 (§55.525.16 et seq.) of Title 55 of the Code of Virginia provides that the purchaser or borrower has the right to select the settlement agent to handle the closing of this transaction. The settlement agent's role in closing this transaction involves the coordination of numerous administrative and clerical functions relating to the collection of documents and the collection and disbursement of funds required to carry out the terms of the contract between the parties. If part of the purchase price is financed, the lender for the purchaser will instruct the settlement agent as to the signing and recording of loan documents and the disbursement of loan proceeds. No settlement agent can provide legal advice to any party to the transaction except a settlement agent who is engaged in the private practice of law in Virginia and who has been retained or engaged by a party to the transaction for the purpose of providing legal services to that party.

The provisions of Chapter 27.3 may not be varied by agreement, and rights conferred by this chapter may not be waived. In some cases, a builder may request the purchaser to use the builder's attorney because much of the preliminary work involved with the sale of a new property is already in the possesion of that attorney. However, the law is very clear that the seller may not require the use of a particular settlement agent as a condition of the sale of the property. The choice of settlement agent is left up to the purchaser or borrower.

Settlement agents cannot

- practice law, or
- provide legal advice unless they are practicing lawyers in Virginia.

A settlement agent who is an attorney practicing in Virginia may be retained by a party to the transaction for the purpose of providing legal services to that party.

A person licensed under Chapter 21 (§54.1-2100 et seq.) of Title 54.1, or such licensee's employees or independent contractors, may perform escrow, closing, or settlement services, as defined by RESA, to facilitate the settlement of a transaction in which the licensee is involved so long as the licensee, the licensee's employees, or independent contractors are not named as the settlement agent on the settlement statement and the licensee is otherwise not prohibited from performing such services by law or regulation.

The **settlement agent** will usually be either an attorney or a title company and must be registered with the Virginia State Bar, carry errors and omissions (E&O) or malpractice insurance at a minimum of $250,000, and maintain a **surety bond** of not less than $100,000.

In addition to the surety bond, a settlement agent is required to carry a blanket fidelity bond or employee dishonesty insurance policy covering persons employed by the settlement agent and providing a minimum of $100,000 in coverage. When the settlement agent has no employees except the owners, partners, shareholders, or members, the settlement agent may apply to the appropriate licensing authority for a waiver of this fidelity bond or employee dishonesty requirement.

If any interest is to be earned on funds deposited in connection with any escrow, settlement, or closing, this must be disclosed in the purchaser contract along with the future disposition of the interest earned. The settlement agent is provided a copy of the purchase agreement by either the buyer or seller. For more information, see the Code of Virginia, Title 6.1-2.19, at http://leg1.state.va.us/lis.htm.

Settlement Services

The escrow, closing, or settlement services include placing orders for title insurance, receiving and issuing receipts for money received from the parties, ordering loan checks and payoffs, ordering surveys and inspections, preparing settlement statements, determining that all closing documents conform to the parties' contract requirements, setting the closing appointment, following up with the parties to ensure that the transaction progresses to closing, ascertaining that the lender's instructions have been satisfied, conducting a closing conference at which the documents are executed, receiving and disbursing funds, completing form documents and instruments selected by and in accordance with instructions of the parties to the transaction, handling or arranging for the recording of documents, sending recorded documents to the lender, sending the recorded deed and the title policy to the buyer, and reporting federal income tax information for the real estate sale to the Internal Revenue Service (IRS) (§6.1-2.20). For further information about the IRS, visit www.irs.gov.

■ TITLE EXAMINATION

An important function of the settlement agent is to obtain a **title examination**. The seller should be asked to provide the settlement agent with any information specific to the title condition of the property, such as any unrealized deeds, existing title insurance policies, and any known unrecorded deed, lien, or encumbrance information. The seller is required to have marketable title at the time of settlement and must be given a reasonable time to correct any title defects found before settlement. If title defects are found, the seller should be formally notified and then take whatever actions are necessary to correct the defects.

The real estate licensee is not specifically involved with the title examination but can facilitate communication between the settlement agent and the seller or buyer.

In a title examination, the prospective seller's *chain of title* is developed by searching through the grantee index backward in time to some predetermined point to establish the source of title for each owner in the chain. Then, for each grantor in the chain of title, the examiner searches the grantor's index from the date the grantor acquired title to the date it was transferred to the next grantor in the chain. This process, called *adversing the title*, is done to determine whether any person not in the seller's direct chain of title might have some adverse claim or interest recorded against the property to be conveyed.

Finally, the examiner will search other indexes to determine whether there are any unrecorded claims against the property, such as judgment liens, mechanics' liens, or tax liens. While real estate licensees do not perform a title search in the normal course of taking a listing, they should alert the parties' attorneys in the event of even the slightest hint of title issues.

Title examinations may be classified as full or limited searches. In a *full search*, the seller's title must be established for at least 60 years. A *limited search* is a title examination that goes back fewer than 60 years. Limited searches are appropriate for some loan assumptions and second mortgage closings, unless the second mortgagee requires lender's title insurance.

A **chain of title** consists of consecutive terms of ownership; a gap in the chain could be caused by an unrecorded deed, a name change, an unadministered estate, a foreign divorce decree, or some other circumstance. Unless the missing link can be reconstructed from reliable sources, the defect could destroy the closing.

Errors, such as an erroneous legal description, a misspelled name, or an improper execution, in a prior recorded deed in the seller's chain of title must be corrected before the closing can proceed. Where possible, these problems can be cured by a **correction deed** from the same grantor to the same grantee; the correction deed must be recorded. A correction deed may not be used to change a greater estate to a lesser estate, nor can it be used to change the identity of the grantor altogether. It is the responsibility of the seller to locate the parties, then to correct the deed.

At a minimum, the title report should reveal

- title holder of record;
- legal description of property;
- existing lenders;
- other lienholders (such as mechanics' lienors, judgment lienors, and tax lienors);
- status of taxes;
- easements, covenants, and other restrictions;
- objections to marketability;
- other matters affecting title; and
- requirements for vesting marketable title in the purchaser.

■ TITLE INSURANCE

Settlement agents are required by Virginia law to advise purchasers and borrowers of the availability of owner **title insurance** and of the benefits of acquiring it. It is to the benefit of the purchaser to have title insurance because the premium paid is nominal compared with the potential cost an owner could incur in connection with a suit to quiet title or other litigation regarding a defect in title.

If the purchaser is obtaining a loan secured by a deed of trust on the property, the lender will require that a lender's title insurance policy be provided. This policy protects only the lender's interest and will diminish in protection as the loan is paid down.

The additional charge to obtain an owner's policy that protects the owner for the full value of the property is minimal compared with the amount of protection provided.

Title insurance is offered by many companies. The purchaser should contact the title insurance provider (usually through the settlement company) to obtain an advance copy of the types of policies, their costs, and options offered.

Full disclosure is required if the settlement agent has any ownership interest in the title insurance company offering title insurance on the transaction.

■ TITLE ISSUES

Judgments constitute liens against all real property that the defendant owns or subsequently acquires. If the seller denies being named in the judgment, and it is not certain that the judgment is against the seller, an affidavit to this effect may be sufficient to protect the purchaser.

Judgments against prior owners of property may remain as valid liens against the property despite the fact that the property has been subsequently conveyed. The purchaser should require that the seller satisfy all judgments against the property because they remain as liens against the property for 20 years and are subject to execution.

Unreleased Deed of Trust

A real estate licensee should be aware that it is not unusual for a title examiner to discover an unreleased deed of trust on the property. Most often, this is due to the failure of the lender or closer to have a certificate of satisfaction or deed of release signed by the beneficiary and recorded in a timely manner. Unreleased deeds of trust often go unnoticed until the seller attempts to sell the property. When the lender was a bank or mortgage company and the lien was in fact paid off, it is relatively easy to have a certificate of satisfaction executed and recorded prior to closing. However, if an individual or private lender was involved, these situations can cause delays in the closing, primarily owing to the problems associated with locating the individual.

Mechanics' or Materialmens' Liens

Reported mechanics' or materialmens' liens must be treated as adverse claims against the property. The purchaser should require that these liens be paid and satisfied of record or discharged by the filing of a proper bond at or prior to closing. Unreported liens are also of concern to the purchaser, who will take the property subject to all mechanics' and materialmen's liens for work or materials furnished within the last 90 days. For this reason, the purchaser should require that the seller provide an affidavit that there have been no improvements performed or materials supplied within the 90 days prior to the date of closing. This affidavit, commonly called a **90-day letter**, is required by all lenders and title insurance companies.

Mechanics' liens are generally not covered by standard title insurance. However, insurance carriers will provide this coverage for an additional premium.

■ WET SETTLEMENT ACT

The Wet Settlement Act applies to transactions involving purchase-money loans secured by first deeds of trust on real estate containing not more than four residential dwelling units. The act applies only to lenders regularly engaged in making loans secured by real estate.

A small change to the act made in 2011 clarifies that the definition of *settlement* applies only to the act and not to the use of the term in purchase agreements between buyer and seller.

At or before the loan closing, the lender must disburse the loan proceeds to the settlement agent. The lender may not charge or receive interest on the loan until disbursement of the loan funds and the loan closing have occurred.

The act requires the settlement agent or attorney to have the deed, deed of trust, and any other necessary documents recorded in time to disburse the settlement proceeds within two business days of settlement. A settlement agent or attorney may not disburse any loan funds prior to recording the deed of trust or other security instrument perfecting the lender's security instrument. As a result, the seller will not receive equity funds, and the real estate professional will not receive a commission check at the closing. Rather, all funds will be disbursed after the documents are recorded by the settlement agent.

IN PRACTICE   A seller is closing on the sale of a property in Virginia on Tuesday and expects to close on his new purchase in Maryland on Wednesday using the proceeds from the Tuesday closing in Virginia. He might not have access to the proceeds of Tuesday's Virginia closing in time for Wednesday's closing in Maryland because no disbursements can be made at the settlement table (closing) in Virginia until the transaction is recorded. The licensee should make sure that all parties are aware of the potential problem in time for special arrangements to be made.

CHAPTER 7 QUIZ

1. Which of the following would MOST likely invalidate a deed?
   a. Grantee's name misspelled
   b. Property description consisting of street address, city, and state
   c. Failure of all grantors to sign
   d. Failure of all grantees to sign

2. An heir was to have inherited real property under his uncle's will. However, the uncle sold the property shortly before he died. The heir now wants to have the sale rescinded on grounds of the uncle's incompetence. Will the heir win?
   a. Yes, any such pleading by a close relative will prevail in court.
   b. Yes, the grantor would have had to prove competence in court during his lifetime.
   c. No, a deed can be invalidated due to incompetence only during the grantor's lifetime.
   d. No, a person is presumed competent unless a court has ruled otherwise.

3. The seller in a transaction was called out of town on business the day before the closing. Any affidavits or sworn statements the seller is required to deliver at the closing must be signed by
   a. the seller.
   b. the seller's attorney-in-fact.
   c. the buyer's attorney-in-fact.
   d. the seller's real estate agent.

4. The seller is expected to pay which of the following?
   a. Recordation tax for recording of the deed
   b. Recordation tax for recording of the deed of trust
   c. Grantor tax of $0.50 per $500 of purchase price
   d. Transfer fee for each document admitted to record

5. All of the following are entitled to prevail on a claim of title by adverse possession EXCEPT
   a. a person who has been in possession of the property for 19 years.
   b. a person who held the property for 5 years after inheriting it from a parent, who was in adverse possession for 10 years.
   c. a person who has been entering an orchard and taking apples every October since 1972.
   d. a person who has erected a stall on and has been using a neighbor's property to sell produce for 20 years without permission.

6. An elderly woman was very ill, and she wrote a will in her own handwriting, leaving all her property to her niece. Three witnesses heard her say, "This is my will." The witnesses watched the woman's friend sign the woman's name to the document because she was too exhausted to do it herself. "That's as good as my signature," she said weakly. The witnesses signed the will. What is the status of this document?
   a. The will is invalid because Virginia does not recognize holographic wills.
   b. The will is valid.
   c. The will is invalid because *she* did not sign it herself.
   d. The will is valid, but cannot be enforced because it is a nuncupative will.

7. When is the seller of real property required to have marketable title?
   a. At the time the listing is taken
   b. When a sales contract is signed
   c. By the time the buyer's loan is approved
   d. At closing

8. A buyer is purchasing property from a seller. Prior to closing, certain defects are found in the title. What is the status of the sales contract between these parties?

    a. It is automatically rescinded.

    b. Because the seller has a reasonable time to correct defects, the contract is still in effect.

    c. The buyer may, at her option, cancel the contract and recover the earnest money.

    d. The contract is in force, and the buyer must close the transaction and accept the transfer as long as the defects are curable.

9. According to Real Estate Settlement Agents (RESA) law, the selection of a settlement agent is made by

    a. the seller.

    b. the buyer.

    c. either the buyer or the seller.

    d. either the buyer's or the seller's agent.

10. At the time of taking a listing, the listing agent will find it helpful to ask to see all documents concerning the property that the seller has available in order to do all of the following *EXCEPT*

    a. find out about unrecorded deeds.

    b. verify deed of trust loan numbers and payment status.

    c. learn of any liens that may not be recorded.

    d. determine whether a seller has marketable title at the time a property is held out for sale.

11. A full title search goes back how many years?

    a. 20

    b. 40

    c. 60

    d. 80

12. Which of the following changes may *NOT* be accomplished by using a correction deed?

    a. A change from a fee simple to a life estate

    b. Correction of an erroneous legal description

    c. Respelling of a misspelled name

    d. Correcting the signature on an improperly executed deed

13. In cases where title must be cleared by having correction deeds signed, who is responsible for locating the parties who must sign?

    a. The buyer

    b. The seller

    c. The settlement attorney

    d. The real estate licensee who represents the owner

14. A buyer has recently purchased a property from a seller. The buyer has reason to believe that there is an outstanding judgment lien against the seller. The buyer

    a. has no need to worry because the property has been conveyed.

    b. has no need to worry because he was not named in the judgment.

    c. should be worried because judgment liens remain against the property.

    d. should be worried because the seller has really bad credit.

15. In preparing for the settlement on a sale of property, it was discovered that an unreleased deed of trust is still shown on the county records. This *MOST* likely occurred because

    a. the seller never paid off the deed of trust.

    b. the lender neglected to have a deed of release signed and recorded.

    c. the original settlement attorney absconded with the funds.

    d. the seller still owes for county property taxes.

CHAPTER 8

Virginia's Real Estate License Law

LEARNING OBJECTIVES

After successfully completing this chapter, you will be able to

- **define** Real Estate Board and important statutory words and phrases;
- **list** the requirements for licensure;
- **describe** the continuing education requirements for license renewal;
- **review** the rights and responsibilities of a broker; and
- **discuss** the REB Standards of Conduct.

KEY TERMS

actively engaged	consent to suits and	license by reciprocity
bait and switch	services	place of business
active license	continuing education	post-licensing education
concurrent license	inactive license	referral agent
conflict of interest	Informal Fact-Finding	summary and
consent order	Conference (IFFC)	recommendation
	institutional advertising	

CODE OF VIRGINIA AND VIRGINIA ADMINISTRATIVE CODE (VAC)

The Code of Virginia 54.1, Chapter 21, is the section of the statute that governs the practice of real estate professionals. The purpose of the law is to protect the public interest against fraud, misrepresentation, dishonesty, and incompetence in real estate transactions.

127

The law designates the Real Estate Board (REB) as the authority with the power to enforce, amend, and promulgate rules and regulations for implementing the law.

References are made in this chapter to both the Code of Virginia statutes under Title 54.1, Chapter 21, and to Rules and Regulations under the Virginia Administrative Code (VAC), Agency 135. The most recent update of the Regulations is April 1, 2008. A copy of the regulations can be found online or ordered from the DPOR office at 9960 Mayland Drive, Suite 102, Richmond, VA, 23233.

■ DEFINITIONS

Certain words and phrases are used throughout both the License Law and the Rules and Regulations of the REB. These words and phrases have specific, statutory meanings separate and apart from any definition they might have outside the real estate profession. Several of these definitions were addressed in Chapter 1 and are repeated here for emphasis.

- *Active*—Any broker or salesperson under the supervision of a principal or supervising broker performing real estate brokerage activities.
- *Actively engaged*—A broker or salesperson having active licensure with a licensed real estate firm or sole proprietorship and active for an average of at least 40 hours per week. The REB may waive the 40-hour-per-week requirement at its discretion.
- *Associate broker*—Any individual holding a broker's license other than the one designated as the principal broker.
- *Client*—An individual who has entered into a brokerage relationship with a licensee.
- *Customer*—An individual who has not entered into a brokerage relationship with a licensee but for whom a licensee may perform ministerial acts.
- *Firm*—Any sole proprietorship (non-broker-owner), partnership, association, limited liability company (LLC), or corporation, other than a sole proprietorship (principal-broker-owned), that is required by regulation to obtain a separate brokerage firm license. The firm's licensed name may be any assumed or fictitious name properly filed with the board.
- *Inactive status*—Any broker or salesperson who is not under the supervision of a principal broker or supervising broker, who is not affiliated with a firm or sole proprietorship, or who is not performing any real estate activities.
- *Independent contractor*—A licensee who acts for or represents a client other than as a standard agent and whose duties and obligations are governed by a written contract between licensee and the client.
- *Licensee*—Any person, partnership, association, corporation, or LLC that holds a license issued by the REB to act as a real estate broker or real estate salesperson.
- *Limited service agent*—A licensee who acts for or represents a client pursuant to a brokerage agreement that provides that the limited service agent will not provide one or more of the duties of a standard agent.
- *Principal broker*—The individual broker designated by each firm to ensure compliance with Chapter 21 of Title 54.1 of the Code of Virginia and to receive all communications and notices from the REB that may affect the

firm and/or its licensees. In the case of a sole proprietorship, the licensed broker who is the sole proprietor has the responsibilities of the principal broker. The principal broker shall have responsibility for the activities of the firm and all of its licensees.

- *Principal to a transaction*—Any party to a real estate transaction in the capacity of a seller, buyer, lessee or lessor, optionor or optionee, or licensor or licensee. The listing and selling brokers are not, by virtue of their brokerage relationship, principals to the transaction.
- *Real estate*—As defined in the Virginia law, real estate includes condominiums, leaseholds, time-sharing, and any other interest in real property. Ownership of a cooperative apartment is also considered real estate ownership, even though the shares held by members of the co-op are construed as personal property.
- *Sole proprietor*—Any individual, not a corporation, who is trading under her own name or under a fictitious or assumed name, as provided by the regulations. A licensed broker who is a sole proprietor shall have the same responsibilities as a principal broker. A sole proprietor who is not licensed must designate a licensed broker to perform the duties of a principal broker.
- *Standard agent*—A licensee who acts for or represents a client in an agency relationship. A standard agent shall have the obligations as provided in Article 3 of Chapter 21 of Title 54.1 of the Code of Virginia.
- *Supervising broker*   May be either the principal broker or an individual broker designated by the principal broker to supervise the provision of real estate brokerage services by associate brokers and salespersons assigned to an office.

■ THE REAL ESTATE BOARD (REB) (§54.1-2104, 2105)

The Virginia Real Estate Board (REB) is 1 of 19 boards that regulate more than 30 occupations and professions as part of the Department of Professional and Occupational Regulation (DPOR). The Department of Professional and Occupational Regulation's (DPOR's) mission is to serve and protect the public through

- licensure of qualified individuals and businesses in professions that, if not regulated, may harm the public's health, safety, and welfare; and
- enforcement of laws pertaining to professional conduct.

The REB is composed of nine members. Seven members may be either brokers or salespersons with at least five consecutive years' experience immediately prior to appointment, and two are citizen (consumer) members. Appointments are made by the governor for a term of four years. Sitting members may be reappointed for one additional four-year term. Members of the REB select the chairperson.

REB Authority

The REB, by statute, may do all things necessary and convenient for carrying into effect the provisions of the law. REB's authority includes

- issuing and renewing real estate licenses;
- enforcing the license law;

- taking disciplinary action for violations of license law or rules and regulations by
  - suspending or revoking a license,
  - levying fines, or
  - denying license renewal;
- establishing requirements for real estate licensing;
- approving schools for teaching authorized courses for real estate brokers and salespersons;
- determining license fees; and
- waiving all or part of the prelicensing requirements if an applicant for licensure is currently licensed in another state or the District of Columbia.

In addition to administering the real estate license law, the REB has the responsibility of administering the Virginia Fair Housing Act and the Virginia Real Estate Transaction Recovery Fund. The Virginia Condominium Act, the Virginia Time-Share Act, the Virginia Cooperative Act, and the Virginia Property Owners Association Act are now administered by the Common Interest Community (CIC) Board discussed in Chapter 1.

The REB also sends out notices from time to time regarding important state issues or services, such as the Broker Price Opinion Guidance Document that was approved in 2009. There are some aspects of real estate practice with which the REB does not become involved. For example, the REB does not

- arbitrate disputes between salespersons and brokers;
- become involved in disputes between brokers;
- establish commission rates or commission splits; or
- standardize listing agreements, sales contacts, or many other forms used in the industry although from time to time the REB may be charged with development of specific forms, such as the disclosure forms required by the Virginia Residential Property Disclosure Act.

The REB could become involved in any of these matters in case of a violation of the license law or the rules and regulations.

The Real Estate Board newsletter, *VREB Speaking*, is published four times a year and is available online at www.dpor.virginia.gov/boards/real-estate/. It is a valuable source of current information from the REB.

■ WHO MUST HAVE A LICENSE? (§54.1-2106.1; 18 VAC 135-20-20)

Any person, firm, partnership, association, LLC, corporation, or sole proprietorship (broker-owned or non-broker-owned) who, for a fee, commission, or other valuable consideration, performs an act of real estate brokerage for others, is required by Virginia law to be a licensed real estate broker or salesperson. The phrase *act of real estate brokerage* includes selling or offering real estate for sale; buying or offering to buy real estate; negotiating the purchase or exchange of real estate; and renting, leasing, or negotiating a lease for real estate. A single performance of any one of these acts requires a real estate license.

A separate firm license is required for business entities, such as

- sole proprietorships (non-broker-owned),

- partnerships,
- associations,
- limited liability companies (LLCs), and
- corporations.

This firm license is separate and distinct from the broker licenses required of each partner, associate, LLC manager, or corporate officer of these business entities who actively participate in brokerage activities. A broker-owned sole proprietorship is not required to obtain a separate firm license unless operating under a fictitious name.

If the REB is aware of someone who is engaging in acts of real estate brokerage without a license, it will investigate the matter. If the suspicion is true, the REB may issue a cease and desist order from acting as a real estate broker and impose a civil penalty for up to $1,000 for each transaction or the commission received, whichever is greater. The REB may also refer the matter to the Commonwealth attorney for further action. Operating without a license is considered to be a Class 1 misdemeanor with a penalty of up to $1,000 per violation. A third or subsequent violation within a single three-year period constitutes a Class 6 felony. The civil penalties against one person or business entity cannot exceed $10,000 per year. The Department of Professional and Occupational Regulation (DPOR) also has the authority to investigate unlicensed activity and to enforce licensure and regulatory provisions of Title 54.1 by instituting proceedings in general district or circuit courts.

■ REQUIREMENTS FOR LICENSURE (18 VAC 135-20-30 THROUGH 135-20-60)

The following general requirements apply to any person seeking licensure either as a salesperson or broker. The applicant must

- be at least 18 years old;
- have, at a minimum, a high school diploma or its equivalent;
- if licensed in another jurisdiction, be in good standing in every jurisdiction where licensed;
- have a good reputation for honesty, truthfulness, and fair dealing and be competent to transact real estate business in such a manner as to safeguard the public interest;
- not have been found guilty of violating the fair housing laws of Virginia or any other jurisdiction;
- meet the current educational requirements by achieving a passing grade in all required courses before sitting for the licensing exam and applying for licensure;
- pass a written license examination approved by the REB within 12 months prior to applying for a license and follow all rules established by the REB or the testing service regarding the conduct of license applicants, including any written or verbal instructions communicated prior to the examination date or at the test site;
- be in good standing and not have had a real estate license suspended, revoked, or surrendered in connection with a disciplinary action, or been the subject of disciplinary action in any jurisdiction;

- not have been convicted, in any jurisdiction, for a misdemeanor involving moral turpitude, sexual offense, drug distribution, physical injury, or any felony (a plea of nolo contendere [no contest] is considered a conviction); and
- follow all rules established by the REB with regard to conduct at the examination.

All new real estate salesperson and broker license applicants must submit a set of fingerprints to the Virginia Central Criminal Records Exchange (CCRE). PSI Exams, Inc. (PSI), the Board's license examination provider, will electronically fingerprint license applicants at one of the PSI's testing locations.

The Licensing Examination

Once a license applicant has successfully completed the educational requirements, the applicant's next step is to take and pass an examination administered by the REB or a designated testing service. In Virginia, real estate licensing examinations are prepared by PSI Examination Services.

Applicants must obtain approval from the REB prior to taking the exam. The application is sent to PSI. When PSI receives the application and the required application fee and registers the applicant into the system, the applicant may schedule the examination.

The examination consists of two portions—the state (45 minutes) and the national (105 minutes). The fee is $60.50. The passing score is 70% for the national portion and 75% for the state portion.

The examination is administered by computer, and applicants will know the results as soon as they have completed the exam. If the applicant passes, successful notification appears on the computer screen. License application forms for submittal to the REB will be available at the test center. If the applicant does not pass, unsuccessful notification appears on the screen. Registration forms for submittal to PSI to retake the examination will be available at the test center. There is no prescribed waiting period. The retake fee is $60.50. If the applicant fails one portion of the exam (state or national) that portion must be retaken and passed. All license applications must be received by the DPOR within one year of passing the exam. Exam results are confidential and are reported only to the applicant and to the DPOR.

More information and test application forms may be found at https://candidate.psiexams.com.

An applicant for a broker's license must meet additional educational requirements and must have been **actively engaged** as a real estate salesperson for 36 of the previous 48 months. Note that the definition of actively engaged means an average of 40 hours per week. The specific licensing requirements for a broker, salesperson, and reciprocal licenses are discussed later in this chapter.

If a license applicant has had a real estate license suspended, revoked, or surrendered in connection with a disciplinary action or has been subject to disciplinary action in any jurisdiction, the applicant must include a detailed explanation of the circumstances that caused the action along with application for licensure.

If an applicant has been convicted of a misdemeanor involving moral turpitude, sexual offense, drug distribution, physical injury, or any other felony, the following must be submitted with the license application:

■ An official FBI record, the original state police criminal record, and certified copies of court papers relative to the conviction

■ A written account of the part that the individual played in the offense and the current status or resolution of the final conviction. If a prospective licensee is concerned about becoming licensed due to a past criminal conviction, the applicant must first meet the educational and testing requirements for licensure. The documentation is submitted with the license application.

All initial applications for licensure must be made within 12 months of the examination date. Failure to apply within this time period will require retaking the exam.

An applicant for licensure as a real estate salesperson must, in addition to the general requirements discussed above, have successfully completed a *Principles of Real Estate* or similar course approved by the REB. The course must contain four semester credit hours or a minimum of 60 classroom, correspondence, or other distance learning instruction hours prior to making application for the examination.

Broker License Requirements

Applicants for a real estate broker's license must meet the following requirements in addition to meeting the salesperson licensing requirements. An applicant must have

■ been actively engaged as a real estate salesperson for 36 of the 48 months immediately preceding the date of application for licensure as a real estate broker, and

■ successfully completed 12 classroom or correspondence semester credit hours (four 45-hour courses, or 180 classroom hours) of study approved by the REB in such subjects as brokerage, real estate law, real estate investments, real estate finance, and real estate appraisal, or related approved subjects prior to the licensing examination. All applicants are required to complete the 45-hour brokerage course.

Brokers who are active in more than one legal entity, that is, who work for more than one brokerage firm, may apply for **concurrent licenses**. Concurrent licenses will be issued to brokers who provide written statements verifying that written notice of the applicant's concurrent status has been provided to the principal broker of each firm with which the applicant is or will be associated.

Concurrent licensure does not refer to persons holding licenses in multiple states.

A successful real estate broker often has offices in several different markets. When a broker maintains multiple offices within Virginia, a branch office license must be issued for each branch office. The application form must include the name of the firm, the location of the branch office, and the name of the branch office's supervising broker. The branch office license is maintained at the branch office. In addition, a roster of every salesperson and broker assigned to the branch shall be available to the public in each office. Typically, this roster is posted in the office lobby.

■ ACTIVE AND INACTIVE STATUS

An **active license** means that the licensee is affiliated with or employed by a broker. The licensee's broker must certify her license application and agrees to be responsible for the licensee's brokerage activities. When the REB has approved the application, the license will be issued and sent to the principal broker. The licensee is now considered to have active status—licensed to engage in real estate activities—and receives a pocket card as evidence of status as a broker or salesperson. The principal broker is responsible for maintaining the licenses of every salesperson and broker (affiliated with or employed by the brokerage entity) at the main office of the firm.

Alternatively, an individual may satisfy all the licensing requirements and pass the license examination but choose to apply for **inactive license** status. Although the person has an inactive license, he is not affiliated with or employed by a broker and may not engage in acts of brokerage or earn compensation, including referral fees. The license of an inactive licensee is maintained by the REB.

Active to Inactive Status   Any licensee may request that his license be placed on inactive status, which means that the licensee is no longer affiliated with or employed by any broker.

If a licensee changes from active to inactive status, it is the responsibility of the individual licensee to make application for the change and to request that the broker return the actual license. The REB, on receipt of the change of status application, notifies the former broker of the change request. If the broker has not yet returned the license of the individual involved in the change, the broker must do so by certified mail so that it is received by the REB within 10 days of the date of notification.

No licensees shall engage in acts of real estate brokerage or earn compensation while their licenses are on inactive status.

Inactive to Active Status   When an inactive licensee wishes to activate a license and affiliate with a broker, proper application must be made to have the license activated. This is accomplished by filling out an application form, then having the broker certify the application and mail the form with the proper fees to the REB. If a licensee has been on inactive status for three years or more, the licensee must meet educational requirements in effect at that time to be reinstated to active status. If the licensee was engaged in a real estate-related field while inactive and can demonstrate to the REB that the knowledge of real estate has been retained, the REB may waive the education requirements. If the licensee was on inactive status at the time the license was renewed, the licensee must submit evidence of successful completion of the required 16 hours of continuing education during the 24 months preceding reactivation.

Referral Agents

A **referral agent** is a real estate licensee who does not engage in real estate activities, such as listing and selling property. As the title implies, a referral agent refers prospective buyers or sellers to the broker with whom the agent is affiliated. If a sale results from the referral, the broker may pay the licensee a fee for the referral. The referral agent's license is displayed either in the referral office or in the main office of the broker with whom the agent is affiliated. The REB considers a person acting in the capacity of a referral agent to be active, not inactive. A referral agent will be required to complete the mandatory 16 hours of continuing education within each two-year licensing cycle.

Licensees and Professional Organizations

Licensees may become members of professional real estate organizations, such as the National Association of REALTORS® (NAR) and its state and local affiliates. However, only a duly licensed person or entity is authorized to engage in acts of real estate brokerage in Virginia.

IN PRACTICE Membership by licensed brokers in most local real estate associations affiliated with NAR typically requires all licensees affiliated with the broker to maintain active membership in the REALTORS® association. A referral company is typically a firm in which the principal broker and the affiliated licensees are not members of a REALTORS® association.

Transfer of License

In March 2013, the DPOR initiated a streamlined transfer process that allows licensees to begin working with a new firm on the day the agent and new broker submit a completed application to DPOR. Under this process, the transferring licensee must certify that the licensee's current firm has been notified. The new broker must

- affirm that verification has been made and that the transferring agent's license is active (see www.dpor.virginia.gov/licenselookup/),
- agree to assume supervisory responsibility for the transferring licensee, effective on the date of the transfer application, and
- affirm that the licensee is of good character and competent to practice real estate.

The streamlined transfer application and guidance document are available at www.dpor.virginia.gov/boards/real-estate/.

■ LICENSURE BY RECIPROCITY (18 VAC 135-20-60)

A person who holds a real estate license issued by another state may apply to the REB for a **license by reciprocity**. Applicants may obtain a Virginia real estate license by reciprocity if they

- are at least 18 years old;
- have, at a minimum, a high school diploma or its equivalent;
- have received the salesperson's or broker's license by passing a written licensing examination that is substantially equivalent to Virginia's examination;
- pass the Virginia license examination;

- are in good standing as a licensed broker or salesperson in their state and have not been subject to suspension, revocation, or surrender of their license in connection with a disciplinary proceeding;
- (for a salesperson's license) have been actively engaged in real estate practice for 12 of the preceding 36 months or have met educational requirements substantially equivalent to Virginia's;
- (for a broker's license) have been licensed as a real estate broker and actively engaged as a broker or salesperson for 36 of the 48 months immediately prior to application; and
- satisfy the reputation and criminal record requirements demanded of licensees in Virginia.

One additional requirement for nonresidents is that they file an irrevocable **consent to suits and services**. A consent to suits and services is a binding legal agreement that allows the Director of the DPOR to accept service of any legal process or pleading on the nonresident licensee's behalf.

The service of legal documents on the director is as valid and binding on the licensee as if service had been made on the licensee in person (§54.1-2111).

■ **FOR EXAMPLE**   An individual is licensed in Maryland and wishes to also be licensed in Virginia. In case his actions result in potential harm to a member of the public, it will be necessary for the aggrieved party to be able to file a suit against him. The consent to suits and services form authorizes the director of the DPOR to accept notice of the suit on his behalf. Otherwise, he might be able to legally avoid having court action taken against him.

■ LICENSURE OF BUSINESS ENTITIES (18 VAC 135-20-45)

A salesperson or associate broker may apply for a salesperson's license as a business entity. This business license is in addition to the individual license. The individual(s) participating under this concept still operates under the supervision of a principal broker. This concept is in response to the practice of several salespersons or associate brokers operating as a team or as an individual operating under her own business entity within the brokerage firm or sole proprietorship (broker-owned).

This business entity may take any form or name as long as the entity is authorized to do business in accordance with the requirements of Code of Virginia, §§59.1-69 through 59.1-76, which address transacting businesses under an assumed name. Every member or owner under this type of entity who actively participates in the brokerage business must be licensed as either a salesperson or broker.

Business entity license holders are reminded that all advertising must be under the direct supervision of the principal or supervising broker and in the name of the firm. The firm's licensed name must be clearly and legibly displayed on all advertising. Disclosure requirements include advertising by the firm that contains the firm's licensed name and address or advertising by a licensee that must contain the licensee's name, the name of the firm where the licensee is affiliated, and the firm's address.

■ **F O R   E X A M P L E**   Two salespersons are active with a brokerage, which holds a firm license. The salespersons wish to form a corporation and apply for a salesperson license as a business entity while still active with the brokerage. They form their corporation and meet the requirements for operating under a fictitious name. A separate salesperson license as a business entity is issued by the REB. Members of the new business entity still maintain their individual salesperson licenses and are under the supervision of their principal broker.

■ RENEWAL OF LICENSES (18 VAC 135-20-90 THROUGH 135-20-140)

The real estate licenses of salespersons, brokers, and firms expire every two years, on the last day of the month in which the license was issued. For a licensee to continue professional real estate activities, the license must be renewed. Renewal requirements apply to active and inactive licensees alike.

The REB reserves the right to deny the renewal or reinstatement of any license for the same reasons that it would deny initial licensure or discipline a current licensee, or failure to pay imposed monetary penalties.

The REB mails renewal notices, usually to each licensee at the last known home address of that individual. Renewal notices for firms are mailed to the last known business address. Failure to receive a notice of renewal does not relieve the licensee of the responsibility to renew.

The applicant for renewal completes the application form and returns it to the REB, along with the required fee and any other documentation that may be required. The application form and fees must be received by the REB prior to the expiration date that appears on the license. If the licensee does not renew his license prior to expiration, the licensee must apply to have the license reinstated. Applicants for reinstatement of an active license must have completed the required continuing education hours.

The regulations allow for reinstatement of a license up to one year following expiration. If the application to reinstate is received within 30 days of expiration, there is no monetary penalty. However, from the 31st day up to one year, application for reinstatement is subject to the current reinstatement fee. The reinstatement fee is a flat fee and is not in addition to the normal renewal fees.

After 12 months, reinstatement is not possible under any circumstances, and the licensee must meet all educational and examination requirements in effect at that time and apply for licensure as a new applicant.

Once the license has expired, the licensee may not engage in any acts of real estate brokerage until the license has been reinstated. Licensees who engage in acts of real estate brokerage after their licenses have expired are legally subject to the penalties associated with operating without a license, including during the reinstatement period.

Continuing Education Requirements

As a condition of renewing their licenses, all active real estate brokers and salespersons, whether or not they are Virginia residents, must complete one or more continuing education courses, totaling at least 16 hours during each licensing term for salespersons and 24 hours during each licensing term for brokers. Licensees who are called to active duty in the United States Armed Forces must complete the continuing education requirement within six months of their release. Virginia agency law was changed in 2012, requiring all licensees to take a three-hour course in residential standard agency prior to July 1, 2014. This requirement has now expired.

The course or courses must be provided by an accredited university, college, community college, or other accredited institution of higher learning, or by an approved proprietary school, that is, a privately owned school, real estate professional association, or a related entity approved by the REB. The courses may be taken by correspondence or by other distance learning instruction.

Eight of the 16 hours must include the subjects of ethics and standards of conduct (three hours), fair housing (two hours), legal updates and emerging trends, real estate agency, and real estate contracts (all one hour each). The remaining eight hours shall be on other approved subjects. Licensees from other jurisdictions may substitute continuing education completed in their jurisdictions for the remaining eight hours. Approved subjects include, but are not limited to,

- property rights,
- contracts,
- deeds,
- mortgages and deeds of trust,
- types of mortgages,
- leases,
- liens,
- real property and title insurance,
- investment,
- taxes in real estate,
- real estate financing,
- brokerage and agency contract responsibilities,
- real property management,
- search, examination, and registration of title,
- title closing,
- appraisal of real property,
- planning subdivision developments and condominiums,
- regulatory statutes,
- housing legislation,
- fair housing,
- REB regulations,
- land use,
- business law,
- real estate economics,
- real estate investments,
- federal real estate law,

- commercial real estate,
- Americans with Disabilities Act,
- environmental issues impacting real estate,
- building codes and design,
- local laws and zoning ordinances,
- escrow requirements,
- ethics and standards of conduct, and
- common interest ownership.

Post-Licensing Education

Post-licensing education (PL or PLE) is proscribed by the Real Estate Board as that education required to obtain the first renewal of a real estate salesperson license. New real estate salespersons must complete the 30-hour post-license education curriculum within one year of obtaining the salesperson license. If a new salesperson fails to complete this 30-hour post-license education requirement within one year of initial licensure, then the Board will automatically place the license on inactive status. A licensee cannot practice real estate in Virginia with an inactive license. A new salesperson licensee can activate an inactive license only by

- completing the 30-hour post-license education requirement, and
- filling out and submitting an Activate/Transfer Application form with a $60 fee to the Board.

Effective January 1, 2014, a new single-track PL system is in place that replaces the original three-track PL system. All 30 hours must be completed under the new PL system within one calendar year of license issuance date. The specific courses and number of hours are as follows:

- Fair Housing, ADA, and Civil Rights (two hours)
- Real Estate Law and Regulations (eight hours)
- Ethics and Standards of Conduct (three hours)
- Current Industry Issues and Trends (two hours)
- Agency Law (three hours)
- Contract Writing (six hours)
- Risk Management (three hours)
- Escrow Requirements (three hours)

The 30 hours will count as credit toward license renewal as long as the eight mandatory hours for ethics and standards of conduct, fair housing, legal update, agency, and contracts are included.

Continuing education (CE or CED) is proscribed by the Real Estate Board as that education required to obtain the second and all subsequent renewals of a real estate license. All brokers to whom active licenses have been issued by the board are required to satisfactorily complete courses of not less than 24 hours of classroom or correspondence or other distance learning instruction during each licensing term. Of the total 24 hours, the curriculum must include

- a minimum of eight required hours to include at least three hours of ethics and standards of conduct, two hours of fair housing, and the remaining three hours of legal updates and emerging trends, real estate agency, and real estate contracts;

■ a minimum of eight hours of courses relating to supervision and management of real estate agents and the management of real estate brokerage firms as are approved by the board; and

■ eight hours of general elective courses as are approved by the board.

Legislation gives the REB the ability to require, by regulation, CE courses in response to changes in the market on a rapid basis. These courses fall in the electives category with no increase in overall hours required. An example is the required course in Residential Standard Agency.

Licensees are responsible for retaining proof of completed continuing education for three years. A certificate of course completion issued by the school and containing the hours of credit completed is adequate proof of course completion. Failure by the licensee to provide course completion certification as directed by the REB will result in the license not being renewed and/or disciplinary action.

The REB requires that each school establish and maintain a record of continuing education for each student for a minimum of five years.

Any person who is active at the time of license renewal must complete the required course or courses as a condition of renewal. The courses must be completed prior to the date the license expires. An active licensee who does not complete the continuing education requirement prior to license expiration may complete the courses during the period of time allowed for license reinstatement (one year) but cannot reinstate the license until the continuing education courses are completed. Referral agents are considered active and therefore must complete the courses as a condition of renewal.

Any person who is inactive at the time of license renewal may renew the inactive license and is not required to complete the courses as a condition of renewal. However, when that licensee chooses to activate the license, she must document that the required continuing education courses have been completed within the past 24 months.

■ EXEMPTIONS FROM LICENSURE (§54.1-2103)

The law recognizes that under certain circumstances, individuals or business operations engaging in what could be considered an act of real estate brokerage may be entitled to exemption from the requirements of licensure. Those conditions include, but are not limited to, the following:

■ Owners, lessors, and their employees dealing with their own property
■ Persons acting as attorneys-in-fact under a power of attorney for final consummation of contracts for sale, lease, or exchange of real estate
■ Attorneys at law in the performance of duties as an attorney at law to include the sale of real estate, condemnation proceedings, and so forth
■ Receivers, trustees in bankruptcy, administrators, executors, or other persons acting under court order

- Trustees under trust agreements, deeds of trust, or wills or their employees
- Corporations managing rental housing when officers, directors, and members in the ownership corporation and the management corporation are the same persons and the management corporation manages no property for others
- Any existing tenant of a residential dwelling who refers a prospective tenant to the owner of the unit or to the owner's agent or employee and receives, or is offered, a referral fee from the owner, agent, or employee
- Auctioneers when selling real estate at public auction when employed by the owner (an auctioneer cannot advertise that he is authorized to sell real estate)
- Salaried residential property managers
- Appraisers, mortgage bankers, and loan officers in the normal practice of their profession

All real estate licensees are always required to comply with the REB regulations, even though they also may be in one of the exempt categories.

License Application and Renewal Fees

The statute allows for the collection of fees associated with the issuance and renewal of licenses. The REB has the authority to set these charges. The purpose of these fees is to help defray the cost of administering the license law and to fund services provided by the REB to the real estate community throughout Virginia. The fee structure as of 2014 is shown in Figure 8.1.

FIGURE 8.1

Licensing Fees (18 VAC 135-20-80; 135-20-120)

Type of License	Application Fee	Renewal Fee
Salesperson by education and examination	$170*	$65
Salesperson's or associate broker's license as a business entity	$210*	$90
Broker by education and examination	$210*	$80
Broker concurrent license	$140	$80
Firm license	$250	$160
Branch office license	$190	$90
Transfer application	$60	n/a
Activate application	$60	n/a

*Each new licensee, whether salesperson or broker, must pay $20 into the Transaction Recovery Fund.

■ BROKERAGES (18 VAC 135-20-160 THROUGH 135-20-170)

Name and Place of Business

There may be only one principal broker for each firm, regardless of the number of agents affiliated with that firm or the number of offices the firm operates.

A brokerage business may be known by any name that identifies the owner or owners, or it may use an assumed or fictitious name. If the firm chooses to operate under an assumed or fictitious name, the application for licensure of the firm must be accompanied by a certificate of ownership that has been filed with the clerk of the court in the jurisdiction in which the business operates. This fictitious or assumed name is the name by which the business will be known to the public.

Every licensed broker who is a resident of Virginia must maintain a place of business within the commonwealth. A **place of business** is defined as one where the business of real estate brokerage is normally transacted and where business calls can be directed and received. A place of business may be located in a private residence only if the business area is separate and distinct from the living quarters and is accessible to the public.

Office Supervision

Each place of business or branch office must be supervised by a supervising broker who is responsible for exercising reasonable and adequate supervision of the provision of real estate brokerage services by the associate brokers and salespersons assigned to that office. Two important factors are

- the availability of the supervising broker to review and discuss contracts, brokerage agreements, and advertising; and
- the availability of training and written procedures and policies providing clear guidance in areas specified by the REB.

The current emphasis is on the ability of the supervising broker to provide adequate supervision and training of those assigned to an office, rather than a physical presence in a specific location.

Death or Disability of Broker

New legislation in 2014 clarified the confusion over who would assume the responsibility of running a brokerage firm on the death or disability of the principal broker. The Real Estate Board is to notify brokers of their ability to designate an agent to run the firm for 180 days following the death or disabling of the broker. This agent, in order of priority, should be

- the broker's personal representative,
- the person holding power of attorney,
- the broker's executor,
- an adult family member of the broker, or
- an employee of the broker.

If the deceased was a sole proprietor or the only broker in the firm, two things happen by operation of law:

- All listings are terminated.
- The licenses of any licensees active with the broker or firm must be returned to the REB because there is no longer a broker to be responsible for licensees who are not allowed to operate in their own names.

If the principal broker of a large real estate firm dies, the officers of the firm designate a new principal broker and immediately file the appropriate form with REB naming the new principal broker.

Broker Audit Requirement

As of January 1, 2013, every principal and supervising broker is required to conduct a self-audit at least once during each firm (or sole proprietor) license term to ensure compliance with Virginia Real Estate Board regulations. The audit must be recorded on the Firm/Sole Proprietor Audit Form, which can be found on the Real Estate Board's website at www.dpor.virginia.gov/Boards/Real-Estate. The completed form must be signed by the principal or supervising broker and kept on file at the firm. The audit form does not have to be submitted to the Real Estate Board but must be available if requested by the board.

Office Signage

The broker may display a sign at his office(s). Any sign must state the name by which the brokerage is known to the public, that is, the name that appears on the license issued by the REB, and the words *real estate*, *realty*, or the name of a generally recognized organization of real estate professionals. The signs must indicate clearly that the business being conducted is real estate brokerage.

Change of Location, Name, or Ownership

In the event the broker's main office changes location or the name of the brokerage changes, it is the principal broker's responsibility to advise the REB of the change within 30 days. The REB will issue new licenses for the remainder of the license period. This is necessary because the broker's name and business address appear on individual licenses.

If the location of a branch office changes, only the branch office license needs to be returned.

Salespersons and individual brokers are responsible for keeping the REB informed of their current home addresses and of any changes in their names or addresses within 30 days of the change.

Transfer or Termination of Active Status

When a salesperson or broker is discharged or in any way terminates active status, the principal broker must sign and note the date of termination on the license and return it by certified mail to the board so that it will be received within 10 calendar days of the date of termination or status change. If the principal broker is discharged or terminates active status, the firm must notify the board and return the license by certified mail within three business days of termination.

Any licensee may transfer from one licensed real estate firm to another by completing and submitting to the board a transfer application signed by the new supervising broker along with the accompanying transfer fee (see Figure 8.1).

All licenses are the property of the REB. All licenses must be returned to the REB on termination of the licensee, termination of the business entity, death of a licensee, status change, or change of name or address.

■ BROKER ESCROW ACCOUNTS (§54.1-2108; 18 VAC 135-20-180)

Any broker who holds money belonging to others pending consummation or termination of a real estate transaction must maintain an escrow account solely for those funds. There is, however, no requirement that a broker hold a buyer's earnest money deposit in the case of a sales transaction. In this situation, the money may be held by a settlement agent, an attorney, or even a seller. Who holds the earnest money deposit is a matter to be negotiated in the sales contract.

Other funds that require an escrow account include down payments, rental payments, security deposits, money from buyers or sellers for payment of settlement expenses, money advanced by the broker's client or expended on behalf of the client, and other funds received on behalf of the client or other person unless otherwise agreed in writing. If a fund is to be deposited in an escrow account, it must be deposited by the fifth business banking day following ratification of the sales contract or receipt of the lease unless otherwise agreed in writing.

IN PRACTICE A business banking day can be described as Monday through Friday with the exception of legal holidays as defined by the Federal Reserve Bank. Though many banks offer Saturday and even Sunday hours of operation, the Federal Reserve Bank is closed on weekends and legal federal holidays. A list of banking holidays is available at www.federalreserve.gov/aboutthefed/k8.htm.

Establishing and Maintaining an Escrow Account

Each account established shall be opened and maintained in a federally insured depository in Virginia. When the account is opened, it must be made clear to the financial institution that the account is an escrow account. Each account—and all checks, deposit slips, and bank statements relating to it—must be labeled *escrow* as part of the account name. The designation of the account as an escrow account precludes attachment of the funds by the broker's creditors. It also puts the financial institution on notice that this account contains funds that belong to people other than the broker who opened the account.

The principal broker will, and the supervising broker may, be held responsible for these accounts. The balance in the escrow account must at all times be sufficient to account for funds designated to be held by the firm.

Once deposited, no funds may be removed from the escrow account until the transaction is consummated unless agreed to, in writing, by all principals to the transaction. In the event that the transaction is not consummated, the broker or supervising broker must hold funds in escrow until

- consummation of transaction (i.e., settlement);
- all principals to the transaction agree, in writing, to the disposition;
- a court orders disbursement; or
- the broker can determine, in accordance with the specific terms of the contract, exactly who is the rightful recipient of the funds.

Broker Disbursal Options If the broker decides to distribute the funds according to the terms of the contract, she must first give written notice to the principal to the transaction who is not to receive the funds. Notice may be either hand-delivered or delivered by certified mail with return receipt requested, addressed to the notice address set forth in the contract, or to the last known address of the recipient including a statement that reads that "payment will be made unless a written protest is received within 30 days of delivery of the notice."

If the payment is to be made within 90 days of the date of the nonconsummation of the contract, notice may be sent by receiptable email or fax, if such information is provided in the contract.

No broker is required to make such determination, nor is a broker deemed to have violated any obligations to a client by making the determination.

Any money in the escrow account that will ultimately belong to the broker may be left in the account and not be considered commingling, provided that these funds are clearly identified in the account records and that these funds are removed from the account at periodic intervals of not more than six months. Withdrawals from the escrow account for payment of commissions shall be paid to the firm by a check drawn on the escrow account.

If necessary, the broker may use a nominal amount of personal funds to establish or maintain the escrow account and not be guilty of commingling, provided that any funds so used are clearly identified in the account records.

There is no legal requirement that escrow funds be held in an interest-bearing account. If the escrow account does earn interest, the broker must disclose, in writing, to all parties involved exactly how any earned interest will be disbursed. Such disclosure shall be made at the time the contract or lease is written.

Property Management

Brokers acting as property managers need to maintain escrow accounts. They will be receiving monies as security deposits that will ultimately be returned to tenants. They also receive rental money that belongs to the property owner. Brokers who manage several different properties should establish separate accounts for each property, even if the properties are owned by the same person. A broker cannot use funds from one property for another or disburse monies from an escrow or property management escrow account unless there is sufficient money on deposit in the account.

■ RECORD KEEPING AND ESCROW FUNDS (§54.1-2108; 18 VAC 135-20-185)

The broker must maintain a bookkeeping system that accurately and clearly discloses full compliance with the requirements of these regulations. The records must include the following information:

- The source of the funds
- The date the funds were received
- The date the funds were deposited
- Where the funds were deposited

- The date money was disbursed from the account
- The name of the person or persons who received the money

Escrow account records must be maintained for three years from date of consummation or termination of the transaction.

Improper Record Keeping and Maintenance of Escrow Funds

Actions that constitute improper record keeping and maintenance of escrow funds by the principal or supervising broker include

- accepting any note, nonnegotiable instrument (such as a promissory note or postdated check), or anything of value not readily negotiable (such as jewelry), as a deposit on a contract, offer to purchase, or lease, without acknowledging its acceptance in the agreement;
- commingling any person's funds with the personal or business funds of a principal or supervising broker or his employees or any licensee with his own funds or those of his corporation, firm, or association;
- failure to deposit escrow funds in accounts designated to receive escrow funds within five business banking days of ratification of the sales contract;
- failure to have sufficient balances in an escrow account at all times;
- failure of the principal broker to report to the Real Estate Board within three business days of any circumstance where it is believed that the improper conduct of a licensee has caused an insufficient balance in an escrow account;
- failing to retain a complete and legible copy of each disclosure of a brokerage relationship, executed contract, listing or buyer agency agreement, closing statement, and other material documents related to a real estate transaction in the broker's control or possession for a period of three years from the date of the closing or ratification (if the transaction fails to close);
- failing to maintain, for a period of three years from the date of the closing or termination of a lease of the licensee's or conclusion of a licensee's involvement in a lease, a complete and accurate record of monies received and disbursed on behalf of others; and
- failing to account for or remit, within a reasonable time, any funds coming into the licensee's possession that belongs to others.

The mismanagement of escrow funds is the basis of many complaints filed with the REB. If the REB has reason to believe that a broker is unable to properly protect escrow funds, for whatever reason, it may petition the court to intercede. The court may bar the licensee from any further activity with the escrow account and may take whatever other actions are necessary to protect the funds. The court may appoint a receiver to manage the funds, pending a complete investigation by the REB. It is the court that makes the appointment, not the REB.

If, as a result of the investigation, it is determined that the licensee has been at fault or has mismanaged the escrow funds, the licensee must pay the costs of the receiver. If the licensee has no funds to pay the receiver, the receiver will be paid from any monies in the escrow account that would normally be due the licensee. If no such funds are available, the REB shall determine whether the receiver will be paid from the Transaction Recovery Fund.

If the investigation determines that the licensee is not at fault, the receiver will be paid from the funds of the REB.

◼ ADVERTISING (18 VAC 135-20-190)

REB regulations define *advertising* as all forms of representation, promotion, and solicitation related to real estate activity that is disseminated by any means to consumers. **Institutional advertising** is advertising where no specific real property is identified, for example, an ad placed by a real estate firm to solicit new agents.

All advertising must be under the direct supervision of the principal or supervising broker and in the name of the firm. The firm's licensed name must be clearly and legibly displayed on all advertising. Disclosure requirements include advertising by the firm that contains the firm's licensed name and address or advertising by a licensee that must contain the licensee's name, the name of the firm where the licensee is active, and the firm's address.

Activities that are prohibited include

- implying that property listed by the licensee's firm is actually for sale or rent by the owner or any unlicensed person;
- failing to include a notice that the owner is a real estate licensee if the licensee has any ownership interest in the property and is not using the services of a licensed real estate entity;
- failing to include the firm's licensed name on any sign outside each place of business;
- failing to obtain written consent from the principals involved before advertising a specific property; and
- failing to identify the type of services offered when advertising a property not actually listed by the person making the advertisement.

Online Advertising

Disclosure in the context of online advertising includes the name of the firm, the city and state where the firm's main office is located, and the jurisdiction in which the firm holds a license. In the case of advertising by a licensee, the name of the licensee, the name of the firm, the city and state where the licensee's office is located, and the jurisdiction in which the licensee holds a license must be clearly visible.

Online advertising for the purpose of any licensed activity that appears as a separate unit (for example, email and webpages) must contain the following disclosures:

- *Webpage.* Either a firm or licensee webpage must contain disclosure or a link to disclosure on the viewable page.
- *Email, newsgroups, discussion lists, and bulletin boards.* These must include disclosure at the beginning or end of each message.
- *Instant message.* Disclosure is not required if the licensee has provided disclosure previously in another format.
- *Chat.* Disclosure is required prior to providing, or offering to provide, real estate services during the chat session.
- *Voice Over Internet Protocol (VoIP).* Disclosure is required prior to advertising, or the disclosure text must be clearly visible on the same webpage.
- *Banner ads.* A link to disclosure is required if disclosure is not included on the banner.

False Advertising

Legislation passed in 2013 clarified that licensed real estate brokers or salesperson are not liable for false advertising when relying on public records or information from a third party. This includes any civil action or regulatory action brought under the real estate licensing laws.

THE VIRGINIA REAL ESTATE TRANSACTION RECOVERY FUND (§54.1-2112 ET SEQ.)

This was covered in detail in Chapter 1. The significant issue for a licensee is that payment from the fund causes the licensee's license to be immediately revoked. The respondent may also be subject to other disciplinary action by the REB. The licensee may not apply for a new license until the fund has been repaid in full, plus interest at the judgment rate of interest from the date of payment from the fund.

Repayment to the fund does not guarantee that the license will be reissued. The REB may take disciplinary action against a licensee for a disciplinable violation whether or not the fund has been reimbursed.

STANDARDS OF PRACTICE AND CONDUCT

Part IV of the REB regulations establishes certain required standards of professional behavior expected of all real estate licensees in Virginia.

Disclosure of Interest (18 VAC 135-20-210)

If a licensee has any family, business, or financial relationship with any of the principals to the contract, all parties to the contract must be informed of the relationship in writing in the offer to purchase or lease. This requirement applies to any licensee who could be considered an *interested party* to the transaction.

Disclosure of Brokerage Relationships (18 VAC 135-20-220)

Unless disclosure has been made previously, a licensee must disclose the party he represents to an actual or prospective buyer or seller who is not the client of the licensee and who is not represented by another licensee. In the case of both buyers and sellers, the disclosure must be made when "substantive discussions about specific property" take place. The written disclosure must be provided "at the earliest practical time, but in no event later than the time specific real estate assistance is first provided."

The disclosure must advise prospective buyers, sellers, landlords, or tenants of the duties of real estate brokers and salespersons under Virginia law, and it must encourage them to obtain relevant information from other sources.

A licensee who is acting as a dual or designated representative must obtain the written consent of all parties "at the earliest practical time." The disclosure may be made in conjunction with other required disclosures if it is conspicuous, printed in bold lettering, all capitals, underlined, or within a separate box.

IN PRACTICE   The REB's regulations do not contain a list of specific events that trigger the disclosure requirement. Common sense should tell the licensee when disclosure is required: If in doubt, disclose.

Provision of Records to the Board (18 VAC 135-20-240, 250)

A licensee must produce any document, book, or record concerning a real estate transaction in which the licensee was involved, or was required to maintain records, within 10 days from the request by the REB. Any other inquiries made by the board must be responded to within 21 days.

Unworthiness and Incompetence (18 VAC 135-20-260)

Actions that constitute unworthy and incompetent conduct include the following:

- Obtaining a license by false or fraudulent representation—for example, providing false information in the license application or cheating on the license examination. It is also improper for a currently licensed real estate salesperson to sit for the salesperson's licensing examination, or for a currently licensed broker to sit for the broker's examination (of course, a qualified, licensed salesperson may sit for the broker's exam).
- Holding more than one license as a real estate broker or salesperson in Virginia, unless permitted to do so by law. Only brokers may hold more than one Virginia license.
- Having been finally convicted or found guilty of a misdemeanor involving moral turpitude, sexual offense, drug distribution, physical injury, or any felony. Any plea of nolo contendere is considered a conviction.
- Failing to inform the board in writing within 30 days of pleading guilty or nolo contendere or being convicted or found guilty of any convictions as previously stated.
- Having had a license suspended, revoked, or surrendered in connection with a disciplinary action.
- Having been found guilty of violating the Virginia Fair Housing Act or any other local, state, or federal fair housing laws.
- Failing to act in such a manner as to safeguard the interests of the public or otherwise engaging in improper, fraudulent, or dishonest conduct.

Conflict of Interest (18 VAC 135-20-270)

Actions constituting a **conflict of interest** include the following:

- Being active with or receiving compensation from a real estate broker other than the licensee's principal broker without the written consent of the principal broker.
- Acting for more than one party in a transaction without the written consent of all principals for whom the licensee acts. Dual agency is not illegal in Virginia, provided that the principals to the transaction know it and agree to it in writing.
- Acting as a standard agent or independent contractor for any client in a real estate transaction outside the licensee's brokerage firm or sole proprietorship. All of a licensee's, salesperson's, or associate broker's acts of real estate brokerage must be conducted in the name of the employing broker.

Improper Brokerage Commission (18 VAC 135-20-280)

Brokers may pay commissions or fees to any licensees affiliated with their firm. Brokers also may pay commissions or fees to other brokers (or firms), regardless of where those brokers are located.

Salespersons and associate brokers may receive compensation only from the licensee's principal broker at the time of the transaction.

The performance of all real estate acts or the use of information gained as a result of such performance must be done with the consent of the principal broker. No licensee may act as an employee of a real estate settlement services company or provide real estate settlement services to clients or customers of the firm without the written consent of the broker.

Licensees are prohibited from receiving kickbacks from a third party who provides services or goods necessary to fulfill a contract, such as an appraiser, a home inspector, or a surveyor, when one of the principals to the contract is paying for the services unless full written disclosure is made to the principal. The principals must be informed, in writing, of any *finder's fees* or commissions paid to the licensee.

Licensees should be careful not to interpret the foregoing as a license to accept kickbacks as long as the principals are informed, in writing, of any finder's fees or commissions paid to the licensee. Additionally, licensees are reminded that all commissions and/or fees are required to be paid directly to the broker first. No licensee may receive a commission or fee from anyone other than the licensee's principal broker.

A listing contract or lease that provides for a net return to the seller/lessor is not allowed in Virginia (see Chapter 2).

Finally, no licensee may charge money or other valuable consideration to, or accept or receive money or valuable consideration from, any person or entity other than the licensee's principal for expenditures made on the principal's behalf without the written consent of the principal.

IN PRACTICE   When recommending services or third-party vendors, such as lenders, appraisers, or home inspectors, licensees should be careful to offer clients and customers options for services or vendors from which to choose. This will avoid the appearance that the licensee is steering the client or customer to any one service or vendor for personal gain. A choice of three options is recommended.

Similarly, a licensee may not personally pay for services required by the terms of a real estate contract without written disclosure of the payment to the principals. For example, a buyer might be short of the cash needed to pay for a survey of the property. If the licensee agrees to pay for the survey personally, there could be accusations later that the survey was inferior or not done by a competent professional surveyor unless all of the principals agree to the arrangement. The licensee has a personal interest in the transaction being completed; offering to pay for one of the steps necessary for completion could appear to be self-serving.

Improper Dealing (18 VAC 135-20-290)

Actions that constitute improper dealing include

- entering into a brokerage relationship that does not have a specific, definite termination date (most listing and buyer representation agreements include a blank space in which the date may be inserted);
- offering property for sale or lease without the owner's knowledge and consent or on terms other than those authorized by the owner;
- placing any sign on any property without permission (this regulation could include the placement of directional signs on the property of someone other than the seller); and
- advertising property for sale, rent, or lease in any newspaper, periodical, or sign without including in the advertisement the name of the firm or sole proprietorship.

Misrepresentations and Omissions (18 VAC 135-20-300)

The regulations prohibit specific actions as misrepresentations or omissions. They are

- using bait and switch tactics by advertising or by offering real property for sale or rent with the intent not to sell or rent at the price or terms advertised, unless the advertisement or offer clearly states that the property advertised is limited in specific quantity and the licensee or registrant did in fact have at least that quantity for sale or rent;
- failing to disclose material information related to the property that is reasonably available to the licensee—a dual representative may not disclose confidential information to either client;
- failing to promptly present every written offer, rejection, or counteroffer to the buyer and seller;
- failing to include the complete terms and conditions of the real estate transaction in any offer to purchase or rent, including identification of all those holding any deposits;
- knowingly making any false statement or report, or willfully misstating the value of any land, property, or security for the purpose of influencing a lender regarding applications, advance discounts, purchase agreements, repurchase agreements, commitments of loans, or to change the terms or time limits for any of these items without the written consent of the principals;
- making any misrepresentation; and
- making a false promise through agents, salespersons, advertising, or other means.

Delivery of Instruments (18 VAC 135-20-310)

Actions constituting improper delivery of instruments include

- failing to promptly deliver complete and legible copies of any written listings, offers to lease, offers to purchase, counteroffers, addenda, and ratified agreements to each party in a transaction—individuals who sign their name to a document are entitled to a copy;
- failing to provide timely, written notice of any material change in the transaction to all parties;

- failing to deliver a complete and accurate statement of money received and disbursed by the licensee, duly signed and certified by the principal or supervising broker (or the broker's authorized agent), to the seller and buyer at the time a real estate transaction is completed. However, if the transaction is closed by a settlement agent other than the licensee (or the licensee's broker) and if the financial disclosure is provided on the applicable settlement statement, the licensee is not required to provide a separate statement of receipts and disbursements; and
- refusing or failing without just cause to surrender any document or instrument to the rightful owner on demand.

Principal and Supervising Broker's Responsibility for Licensees (18 VAC 135-20-330)

A principal or supervising broker is liable for the unlawful acts of a real estate salesperson, employee, partner, or affiliate of a principal or supervising broker only if the REB finds that the principal or supervising broker knew or should have known of the unlawful act or violation.

Effect of Disciplinary Action on Subordinate Licensees (18 VAC 135-20-345)

If a principal broker's or sole proprietor's license is revoked or suspended, or if renewal is denied, the licenses of any and all individuals affiliated with or employed by the affected firm are automatically ordered returned to the REB until such time as they are reissued on the written request of another sole proprietor or principal broker. That is, affiliated licensees must either transfer or become inactive.

■ COMPLAINT PROCEDURE

The Compliance & Investigations Division of the Department of Professional and Occupational Regulation (the Department) reviews complaints to determine whether the Department is authorized to process the complaint. The Department will only process complaints against individuals or businesses that are subject to the laws or regulations of regulatory boards within the Department.

This section of DPOR is responsible for the receipt, processing, and analysis of all complaints coming into the Department regarding real estate regulants. Upon review, the Complaint Analysis and Resolution Section may close the file, investigate the complaint, resolve the matter by a consent order, or refer the case to Alternative Dispute Resolution or Investigations for further action.

Complaints must be in writing; forms for filing a complaint are available online at www.dpor.virginia.gov/Report-Licensee/.

Possible Solutions/Options

A complaint can be handled in a variety of ways:

- Investigation
- Informal resolution through a Compliance or Consent Order

- Alternate dispute resolution (uses conciliation and mediation)
- Adjudication

A complaint may be

- closed;
- resolved by Complaint Analysis and Resolution through a Compliance or Consent Order;
- referred to staff for technical review regarding violations and/or offering a Consent Order; or
- referred to Adjudication Division for an **Informal Fact-Finding Conference (IFFC)**.

The Adjudication Section

The Adjudication Section reviews files referred from Complaint Analysis & Resolution or Field Investigations that there is probable cause of a violation of the Board's regulations and/or laws. The Adjudication Section is responsible for conducting IFFCs, which includes scheduling the IFFC, sending the Notice, presenting the IFFC, and providing support to the Presiding Officer or Board member at the IFFC in preparing the Summary.

The Informal Fact-Finding Conference (IFFC)

The IFFC is a hearing conducted at the offices of DPOR; it is presided over by an REB member and supported by DPOR staff.

The presiding board member

- listens to the testimony of participants,
- asks questions,
- reviews additional information presented,
- leaves the record open for additional evidence to be presented or collected,
- maintains control of the conference by avoiding an adversarial proceeding, and
- remains neutral.

After considering the testimony and evidence, the presiding board member will offer a **consent order** or prepare a **summary and recommendation**.

The regulant accepts responsibility without contest (no appeal possible) and submits to the judgment recommended by the presiding board member. The Consent Order is presented at the full board meeting for approval. The board may

- accept the consent order as presented,
- reject the consent order,
- make a counteroffer, and
- remand it to an IFFC.

The presiding board member can recommend the following:

- Probation
- Revocation
- Suspension
- Denial of renewal

- Fines
- Any other remedy granted by statute or regulations (e.g., education, examination, or reprimand)

Complaints not resolved or closed are referred to Adjudication Section for an IFFC.

REB Board Meetings

It is important to note that all disciplinary decisions come before the full REB for review and approval. REB scheduled meetings (there are approximately eight per year) are open to the public. IFFC participants are afforded an opportunity to address the full board at these meetings and may speak for five minutes, but no new evidence may be presented. The board carefully considers the IFFC Summary and Recommendation, which outlines thoughts, analysis, and credibility issues and makes its final decision.

The possible outcomes are the following:

- IFFC Summary and Recommendation: accept, reject, or modify violations and/or sanctions
- Consent Order: accept, make counteroffer, ask for exhibits, or request an IFFC (if one has not been held)

If the REB finds the licensee guilty, it may impose a monetary penalty of up to $2,500 for each violation. The REB may also suspend, revoke, or deny renewal of the respondent's license. The REB's decision is final although the licensee may appeal the decision through the Court of Appeals. In all of these proceedings, the accused has the right to be represented by legal counsel.

There are two instances in which disciplinary action may be taken against a licensee, and a license may be suspended or revoked without review or a hearing:

- If a licensee does not pay the assessment to the Transaction Recovery Fund, his license will be automatically suspended.
- If a payment is made from the Transaction Recovery Fund, the license of the respondent will be automatically revoked.

CHAPTER 8 QUIZ

1. Which of the following is an accurate description of the Real Estate Board?
   a. Seven members: six licensees and one consumer
   b. Seven members: five licensees and two consumers
   c. Nine members: either licensed brokers or salespersons
   d. Nine members: seven licensees and two consumers

2. The Real Estate Board's authority includes all of the following *EXCEPT*
   a. issuing and renewing real estate licenses.
   b. enforcing license law.
   c. administering the Virginia Real Estate Transaction Fund.
   d. administering the Virginia Property Owners Association Act.

3. A licensee who acts for a client pursuant to a brokerage agreement that specifies what duties of a standard agent will *NOT* be done is a
   a. dual standard agent.
   b. designated standard agent.
   c. limited service agent.
   d. independent contractor.

4. A licensee was out of town on vacation. When she returned on October 10, she found her license renewal notice and realized that her license had expired on July 31. If she wants to remain licensed, she must
   a. reapply for a new license as a new applicant.
   b. meet the current educational requirements.
   c. apply for reinstatement of her license and pay the current reinstatement fee.
   d. apply to have her license placed on inactive status.

5. How often are real estate licenses renewed in Virginia?
   a. Annually, in the month issued
   b. Every two years, in the month of the licensee's birthday
   c. On June 30 of each even-numbered year
   d. Biennially, on the last day of the month in which issued

6. All of the following statements are correct regarding an active licensed broker who has been licensed in Virginia since 1975 *EXCEPT*
   a. the broker may be licensed in more than one legal real estate entity.
   b. the broker is exempt from the continuing education requirements on the basis of having been licensed for more than 15 years.
   c. the broker may contract to be a property manager.
   d. the broker's office may be located in her home under certain circumstances.

7. If a broker establishes an account to hold money belonging to others, which of the following is *TRUE*?
   a. All checks, deposit slips, and bank statements must include the word *escrow* as part of the account name.
   b. Accounts may be labeled either *trust* or *escrow*.
   c. The account cannot be in the same bank as the broker's personal checking account.
   d. An individual account is required for each transaction.

8. Earnest money deposits may be distributed from the broker's escrow account in any of the following situations *EXCEPT*
   a. at settlement on the property.
   b. when all parties to the transaction agree to disbursement.
   c. when requested by one party's attorney.
   d. when the broker determines distribution according to the contract.

9. A broker manages three properties for the same owner. One property is in need of emergency repairs, but there is not enough money in the management account to cover the cost. The broker borrows money from the escrow account of one of the other properties to make the repairs. Which of the following is *TRUE*?

   a. The broker has acted properly by safeguarding the client's interest.
   b. Such action is proper because all properties are owned by the same person.
   c. The broker is in violation of regulations for improperly handling escrow funds.
   d. The broker must use personal funds for repairs if there is not enough money in the management account.

10. What must appear on all For Sale signs placed on property by a broker?

    a. The broker's phone number
    b. The name of the person who listed the property
    c. The selling price of the property
    d. The name of the broker

11. A broker created her own webpage to advertise her listings for sale. Online disclosure requirements require that she include on each page her

    a. full name and address.
    b. name and her firm's name.
    c. name and her firm's name and address.
    d. name, her firm's name and address, and the jurisdiction in which her firm is licensed.

12. A broker is convicted on May 1 of possession and distribution of a controlled substance. Both the crime and the conviction took place in the state of Maryland. On June 15, the broker calls the REB and leaves a message informing the REB of the conviction. Based on these facts, which of the following is *TRUE*?

    a. The broker has properly informed the REB within 60 days after the conviction, and the broker's license may be renewed.
    b. Both the conviction and the broker's failure to notify the REB within 30 days violate REB regulations.
    c. Because the conviction did not occur in Virginia, it is not evidence of unworthy conduct.
    d. The conviction is evidence of both improper dealing and fraud.

13. Several weeks after a closing, an associate broker received a thank-you letter and a nice bonus check from the seller of the house. The associate broker cashed the check because he felt it was earned. In this situation, which of the following is *TRUE*?

    a. The associate broker may accept the bonus because he is licensed as an associate broker.
    b. Accepting the money is allowed if more than 30 days have elapsed since the closing.
    c. The associate broker may accept the money if his broker permits him to do so.
    d. Accepting the money is a violation of REB regulations.

14. Under the terms of a sales contract, the seller is required to provide a termite certificate. The seller requests that the salesperson order one. The salesperson does so, knowing she will receive a referral fee from the pest control company. Is this a violation of the license law?

    a. No, if the fee is less than $25
    b. No, if the fee is disclosed in writing to the parties to the contract
    c. Yes, a salesperson may not receive a referral fee
    d. Yes, special fees may be paid to the salesperson only by the seller

15. An airline pilot told a broker about some friends who were looking for a new home. The broker contacted the friends and eventually sold them a house. When may the broker pay the pilot for the valuable lead?

    a. As soon as a valid sales contract is signed by the parties
    b. Only after the sale closes
    c. After the funds are released from escrow
    d. Never because the broker may not pay the pilot for the lead

16. When a sole proprietor has her license suspended for two years, what effect does this have on the associate brokers and salespeople affiliated with the proprietor?

    a. The affiliates' licenses will be revoked, subject to reinstatement after one year.
    b. The affiliates' licenses will be also be suspended for a two-year period.
    c. The suspension has no effect on the affiliates.
    d. The affiliates' licenses must be returned to the REB.

17. When a salesperson is alleged to have violated the license law, possibly resulting in disciplinary action, which of the following statements is TRUE?

    a. An investigation will be conducted by the REB.
    b. The salesperson is entitled to a jury trial before any action can be taken.
    c. The salesperson's license will be temporarily suspended until the REB can schedule a formal hearing.
    d. The employing broker also is charged with the same violation.

18. A licensee in Virginia made a buyer referral to a licensee in Texas. Upon the closing of the sale in Texas, she receives a referral fee in the form of a check from the Texas broker for $2,500. Which is TRUE?

    a. She can deposit the check.
    b. She must give the check to her broker, even if it is made payable to her.
    c. She cannot receive a referral fee because she is not licensed in Texas.
    d. She can cash the check and give her broker his share of their mutual commission split.

19. A broker advertises a property for sale but has no intention of accepting an offer at the price or terms listed. This is called

    a. caveat emptor.
    b. bait and switch.
    c. nolo contendere.
    d. steering.

20. If the REB finds a licensee guilty of violating license law, it may impose any of the following EXCEPT

    a. monetary penalty up to $5,000.
    b. suspend the license.
    c. revoke the license.
    d. deny renewal of the license.

CHAPTER 9

Leasing Real Estate in Virginia

■ **LEARNING OBJECTIVES**   *After successfully completing this chapter, you will be able to*

■ **review** the general principles of leasing real estate in Virginia;

■ **describe** the obligations and remedies that apply to a landlord under the Virginia Residential Landlord and Tenant Act; and

■ **describe** the obligations and remedies that apply to a tenant under the Virginia Residential Landlord and Tenant Act.

■ KEY TERMS

distress warrant	retaliation	security deposit
eviction	reasonable	unlawful detainer action
pay or quit notice	accommodation	
prepaid rent	reasonable modification	

Leases and landlord–tenant relationships are governed by Title 55 – Property and Conveyances in Chapter 13 – Landlord and Tenant of the Code of Virginia. Chapter 13 (§§55-217 through 55-248) covers general leasing principles under the Virginia Landlord Tenant Act (VLTA). Chapter 13.2 deals specifically with the Virginia Residential Landlord and Tenant Act (VRLTA) (§§248.2 through 248.40). Chapter 13.3 covers manufactured home rentals.

This first part of this chapter on leasing covers general leasing principles that are covered under the VLTA. The rest of the chapter covers the six articles of VRLTA.

For more information on leasing in Virginia, refer to Virginia General Assembly Legislative Information System, Code of Virginia, Title 55, Chapter 13 at http://leg1.state.va.us.

■ GENERAL LEASING PRINCIPLES

Fair Housing

One of the most important aspects of the landlord-tenant relationship is to uphold all provisions of both federal and state fair housing acts. The majority of fair housing complaints come from rental situations. Fair housing will be covered in detail in Chapter 10, but the following brief checklists may be helpful for all new landlords.

Landlords may

- ask qualifying questions, as long the same questions are asked of all applicants;
- check references of prospective tenants;
- verify the prospective tenant's ability to pay the stated rent;
- develop rules to be followed by all tenants, taking care that none are discriminatory; and
- require that any modifications made for a tenant with a disability be restored to the original condition if the modification would affect the value of the property.

Landlords may not

- refuse to rent to anyone based on discrimination against any of the protected classes (race, color, religion, national origin, sex, elderliness, familial status, or handicap) ;
- apply different rules, deposits, or amount of rent to different tenants;
- make false statements about the availability of any unit;
- refuse to make reasonable modifications or accommodations for a tenant with a disability;
- intimidate or retaliate against a tenant who makes a complaint; or
- advertise in any way that shows potential discrimination.

The handicap provision of fair housing law is more often referred to today as a person with a disability. The law requires the landlord to provide reasonable modifications and reasonable accommodations that may be required in order for the person with a disability to be able to enjoy the full use of the housing.

Reasonable Modifications

Reasonable modifications are those that affect the physical features of a property. Depending on the type of disability, the tenant might require a ramp at the entrance, widening of doorways, grab bars in kitchen and bathroom, lowered electrical outlets, or removal of carpet. The tenant is responsible for paying for the modifications and can be required to restore the property to its original condition when the lease is terminated if it actually affects the value of the property. The landlord is not required to make unreasonable modifications, such as installing an elevator or completely redoing a kitchen. If the modifications are substantial, the landlord can require the tenant to pay into an interest-bearing escrow account in an amount sufficient to restore the property. No additional security deposit may be charged.

Reasonable Accommodations

Reasonable accommodations are changes to existing rules and procedures that may be needed in order for the tenant to enjoy full use of the dwelling place, such as a requirement that all tenants come to the second floor rental office to personally sign the lease. To meet the needs of a person with a disability, it may be necessary to agree to meet on the first floor or hand-deliver the lease to a place of the tenant's choosing.

Other examples of reasonable accommodations include

- allowing service animals in a no-pets policy building,
- providing accessible parking near the unit for the person with a disability, and
- having lease documents available in Braille or audio format.

Sale of Rental Property

When property that is currently being rented is sold, the new owner stands in the same legal relationship to the lessee as did the previous owner. Likewise, the lessee may have the same benefits of the lease as were enjoyed with the previous owner "except the benefit of any warranty in deed or law" (§55-218).

Unless specifically stated otherwise in the lease, the tenant retains the same rights and privileges when the rental property is sold. If the new owner is another investor, an existing lease is generally a plus. However, if the new owners want to move in, they will either have to wait until the lease terminates or make special arrangements with the existing tenants.

Nonresident Agents

A nonresident of Virginia who owns real property consisting of four or more rental units (whether residential or commercial) must appoint a Virginia resident as agent for the purpose of receiving any notices, service of process, or other legal paper that would otherwise have been served on the owner. If an agent is not appointed, or if the one appointed cannot be found, the secretary of the Commonwealth serves as agent. The secretary forwards any papers to be served on the owner to the owner's home address (§55-218.1).

Termination of Lease

Virginia law requires different notice periods, depending on the length of the lease being terminated. The notice periods are

- a three-month notice to terminate a year-to-year lease,
- a 30-day notice to terminate a month-to-month lease, or
- a 120-day written notice to terminate a month-to-month lease, where the termination is due to rehabilitation of the property or a change in the property's use (such as conversion to a condominium).

If a definite termination date has been established, no notice is required (§55-222).

Tenant Holdover

A tenant who, through no fault of his own, is unable to vacate the premises at the end of the lease term is not legally held to another full term of the lease. Rather, the tenant is liable to the lessor only for use and occupation of the premises and for any loss or damage suffered by the lessor. There may, however, be further legal issues (§55-223).

2011 Additions to Article 13 – §55-225

In 2011, the General Assembly passed legislation expanding §55-225.9 and §55-225.10 and also added four new sections as follows. These changes are also reflected in the Virginia Residential Landlord and Tenant Act.

§55-225.9   Where a mold condition exists, the landlord may require the tenant to temporarily vacate the dwelling to a comparable dwelling unit or hotel room at the landlord's expense. (The tenant is still responsible for payment of rent.)

§55-225.10   The landlord shall give written notice to the tenant of any mortgage default, acceleration, or notice of foreclosure on the dwelling unit within five business days after such notice is received by the landlord. If such notice is not provided, the tenant shall have the right to terminate the rental agreement with written notice at least five days prior to the date of termination. This requirement for disclosure also applies for any dwelling units being offered for rent.

§55-225.11   If the landlord has actual knowledge of the existence of defective drywall within the unit, written disclosure must be given to any prospective tenant. A tenant may terminate the lease agreement within 60 days of discovery of defective drywall with written notice to be effective 15 days from the mailing of the notice or the date through which rent has been paid, whichever is later. In no event shall the termination exceed one month from the date of mailing.

§55-225.12   This rather lengthy section deals with a tenant's assertion that conditions exist on the leased premises that constitute a fire hazard or serious threat to the life, health, or safety of occupants. The assertion is filed in a general district court and the forms of relief are listed in subsection C. The tenant must show the court that written notice has been served to the landlord who has not remedied the situation, that rent has been paid to the court, and that the condition was not caused by the tenant.

§55-225.13   If there is a material noncompliance by the landlord with the rental agreement or any condition materially affecting health and safety, the tenant may serve written notice to the landlord specifying the breach and setting a termination date not less than 30 days after receipt of the notice if the breach is not remedied within 21 days.

§55-225.14   This section stipulates the requirements for a tenant to pay rent into a court escrow account when a continuance of a the tenant's case is requested.

Destruction of Premises

In some states, if the improvements on leased land are destroyed, the lessee is still bound by the terms of the lease and must continue paying full rent. Virginia has repealed this common-law doctrine. Tenants who are not at fault in the destruction of the improvements are entitled to a reduction in the amount of rent until the improvements are rebuilt and the tenants' previous use of the property can be restored (§55-226).

Seizure of Tenant Property

Goods belonging to a tenant may be seized for nonpayment of rent for up to five years after the rent is due, whether or not the lease has ended. The seizure is made by a sheriff or other officer, based on a warrant issued by a judge or magistrate. The warrant is based on a petition from the lessor. The lessor's petition must show (1) the grounds for believing that the rent is due and (2) the exact amount owed. The lessor must post a bond.

A copy of the **distress warrant** (the order of seizure) is given to each defendant, along with a copy of the bond. The goods subject to seizure may include anything on the premises belonging to the tenant (including any assignees' or subtenants' goods) or goods that have been removed within the 30 days prior to seizure. If any of the goods seized are subject to a prior lien, the lessor's proceeds may be based only on the interest the tenant actually had in the personal property. Any sublessee is liable only to the extent that money is owed to the original tenant.

The seizure of a tenant's property arises from enforcing a landlord's lien, which is a statutory right. The landlord's lien relates back to the beginning of the tenancy, not merely to the time the rent became delinquent.

If seizure of the tenant's property is made for rent due and any irregularity or unlawful act is performed during the proceeding by or for the landlord, the tenant may sue to recover damages from the landlord. However, the distress warrant itself is still lawful, and the tenant still owes the rent, despite any improper enforcement actions (§§55-230 through 55-236).

Prevention of Forfeiture

If a tenant who has been served with a **pay or quit notice** pays the arrears before his case comes to trial, the tenant will hold the tenancy just as he did before the proceedings began, without a new lease or conveyance. This could be looked upon as a type of right of redemption, similar to a debtor's right to recover property prior to a foreclosure sale. However, a tenant may exercise this right only once in any 12-month period (§55-243).

Landlord Right of Reentry

If a tenant's rent is in arrears or the tenant has breached the lease, the landlord may post a written eviction notice in a conspicuous location on the premises. The notice shall be in lieu of a demand and reentry; on proof to the court that the rent claimed was due and no sufficient distress was put upon the premises or that the terms of the lease were broken before the service of the eviction notice and that the landlord had power to reenter, the landlord will be due all rent in arrears and regain possession of the unit (§55-244).

Publication and recordation and certification of eviction proceedings shall be made by the sheriff to the appropriate court jurisdiction (§55-245).

■ VIRGINIA RESIDENTIAL LANDLORD AND TENANT ACT

Title §55, Chapter 13.2 of the Code of Virginia, the Residential Landlord and Tenant Act (VRLTA), became law in 1974. As stated in Article 1, the purposes of the act are to

- simplify, clarify, modernize and revise the law governing the rental of dwelling units and the rights and obligations of landlords and tenants;
- encourage landlords and tenants to maintain and improve the quality of housing; and
- establish a single body of law relating to landlord and tenant relations throughout the Commonwealth.

The VRLTA supersedes all local, county, or municipal ordinances or regulations concerning landlord and tenant relations and the leasing of residential property.

A full copy of VRLTA, effective July 1, 2011, is available at www.dhcd.virginia .gov/HomelessnesstoHomeownership/PDFs/Landlord_Tenant_Handbook.pdf.

The 2014 General Assembly enacted legislation that changed the applicability of VRLTA to owners of more than two rental properties plus their principal residence. The trigger number was formerly four rental properties in urban areas and a total of 10 statewide. This legislation also eliminated the payment of interest on security deposits to become effective in 2015. Originally, the interest rate allowed was subject to the Federal Reserve discount rate and had remained at zero since 2009.

Article 1 – General Provisions

Exemptions   As the title implies, the act concerns itself with residential property. However, not everyone or every residential property is subject to the act. The act does not apply to the following:

- Residence at a public or private institution if incidental to detention or the provision of medical, geriatric, educational, counseling, religious, or similar services
- Occupancy under a contract of sale of a dwelling unit by the purchaser of a property
- Occupancy by a member of a fraternal or social organization in a portion of a structure operated for the benefit of the organization
- Occupancy in a hotel, motel, or similar location for not more than a 90-day period if occupied continuously (changed from 30 days in 2013)
- Occupancy by an employee of a landlord whose right to occupancy is a requirement or benefit of employment (such as a property manager)
- Occupancy by an owner of a condominium unit or holder of a proprietary lease in a cooperative
- Occupancy under a rental agreement covering premises used primarily in connection with business, commercial, or agricultural purposes
- Occupancy in HUD-regulated housing, where regulation is inconsistent with the statute

- Occupancy by a tenant who pays no rent
- Property owners who do not rent more than two single-family residences or condominium units (§55-248.5)

Note that Virginia fair housing law applies to owners of three or more properties.

In Virginia, a Community Land Trust (CLT) is not considered to be a landlord as long as the CLT is non-profit, conveys property under long-term ground leases, transfers ownership of structural improvements to the lessee, and retains an option to purchase such improvements at a price determined to ensure that the improvement remains affordable to low- and moderate-income families (§55-221.1).

Application Fees   The landlord may require an application fee and a separate application deposit at the time the tenant applies to lease a dwelling. If the tenant does not rent the property, the landlord will refund all fees in excess of the landlord's expenses and damages (costs incurred for preparing the dwelling for occupancy, holding an unoccupied unit, etc.) within 20 days. If the application fees were made by cash, certified check, cashier's check, or money order, the refund will be made within 10 days of the applicant's failure to rent if such failure was due to the landlord's rejection of the application (§55-248.6:1).

An application deposit must be placed in an escrow account within five business days from approval of the tenant's application.

Terms and Conditions   Terms and conditions in a rental agreement may include rent, charges for late payment of rent, term of the agreement, automatic renewal of the agreement, requirements for notice of intent to vacate or terminate the agreement, and other provisions governing the rights and obligations of the parties. In the absence of a rental agreement, the tenant shall pay fair rental value. Legislation enacted in 2013 allows a landlord to include provisions for an early termination in the lease. Legislation in 2014 allows the landlord to use a mathematical formula to allocate energy service for tenants in a building as long as this provision is clearly stated in the rental agreement or lease.

Rent shall be payable without demand or notice at the place designated by the landlord. Periodic rent is payable at the beginning of any term of one month or less and otherwise in equal installments at the beginning of each month. A copy of the written agreement signed by both landlord and tenant shall be provided to the tenant within one month of the effective date of the agreement (§55-248.7).

A tenant may offer and a landlord may accept prepaid rent. A landlord who accepts prepaid rent must deposit the total amount in an escrow account and withdraw the monthly installments as they come due. **Prepaid rent** means rent paid more than one month in advance of the rent due date (§55-248.7:1).

Required Insurance   The landlord can require that the tenant pay the cost of premiums for both renter's insurance and damage insurance. In the case of damage insurance, the cost of premiums is not considered as a security deposit but rather as rent. The landlord cannot require that the tenant pay both security deposit and premiums if the amount exceeds two months' rent. Similarly, in the case of renter's insurance, the cost of premiums is considered rent, not a security deposit. If premiums are paid prior to the tenancy, the total of all payments for security deposits and renter's insurance as well as damage insurance shall not exceed two months' rent. Otherwise, the landlord may charge additional monthly rent to cover the costs. For both types of insurances, the tenant may elect to obtain separate policies (§55-248.7:2).

Unsigned or Undelivered Leases   If a written lease is not signed by either the lessor or the lessee but the agreed rent is paid and accepted, the rental agreement is binding on both parties. Similarly, even if a lease is never delivered but the rent payments are accepted, the lease remains binding. In such cases, if the term of the lease provides for a term longer than one year, it is only effective for one year (§55-248.8).

Prohibited Provisions   A rental agreement shall not contain provisions that the tenant will agree to waive or forego any rights or remedies covered in this chapter, will agree to pay landlord's attorney fees, or to any limitation of the landlord's liability. There shall be no provision that the tenant will agree to a limitation on lawful possession of a firearm or will pay more than two months for a combined security deposit and insurance premium. If a landlord brings a court action to enforce any of the prohibited provisions, the tenant may recover actual damages plus attorney fees (§55-248.9).

Confidentiality Exemptions   Section 55-248.9:1 covers the specific situations where a landlord or managing agent may release information about a tenant or prospective tenant to a third party, for example, where tenant has given prior consent, information is a matter of public record, is requested by a law enforcement official or information is requested by a lender for financing of the rental property or by the landlord's attorney (§55-248.9:1).

Article 2 – Landlord Obligations

Under VRLTA, landlords have specific obligations and responsibilities.

§55-248.11:1 Inspection of premises   Within five days of occupancy, a written report itemizing damages to the unit existing at the time of occupancy will be prepared by either the landlord, the tenant, or done jointly. Both the landlord and the tenant shall sign the written report and receive a copy.

§55-248.11:2 Disclosure of mold in dwelling units   The written report of the move-in inspection should disclose any evidence of mold. If there is visible mold evidence, the tenant has the option to terminate the tenancy. If the tenant agrees to take possession, the landlord shall promptly remediate the mold condition within five days.

§55-248.12 Disclosure of ownership   The landlord must disclose to the tenant the name and address of the property owner or anyone authorized to manage the property or otherwise act on behalf of the owner. The disclosure must be in writing and provided to the tenant prior to the beginning of the tenancy. If the property is sold, the tenant must be supplied with the name, address, and telephone number of the purchaser. If the property is being converted to a condominium or cooperative, or if the tenant will be displaced due to the demolition or rehabilitation of the property within the next six months, the tenant is entitled to written notice of the situation.

§55-248.12:1 Required disclosures for properties located adjacent to a military air installation; remedy for nondisclosure The landlord of property in any locality in which a military air installation is located, or any person authorized to enter into a rental agreement on the landlord's behalf, shall provide to a prospective tenant a written disclosure that the property is located in a noise zone or accident potential zone, or both, as designated by the locality on its official zoning map.

Disclosure shall be provided prior to the execution by the tenant of a written lease agreement, or in the case of an oral lease agreement, prior to occupancy by the tenant. The disclosure shall specify the noise zone or accident potential zone in which the property is located according to the official zoning map of the locality.

An inaccurate disclosure made regarding the location of the noise zone or accident potential zone shall be deemed as nondisclosure unless the inaccurate information is provided by an officer or employee of the locality in which the property is located.

Failure to disclose gives the tenant rights of termination in the first 30 days of occupancy.

§55-248.12:2 Required disclosures for properties with defective drywall; remedy for nondisclosure If the landlord has actual knowledge of the existence of defective drywall that has not been remediated, the landlord shall provide the tenant with a written disclosure prior to occupancy.

A tenant who is not provided the disclosure may terminate the lease agreement within 60 days of notice of discovery of the existence of defective drywall with written notice to the landlord.

As of July 1, 2014, any landlord who has actual knowledge that the property has been used for the manufacture of methamphetamine and has not been cleaned in accordance with Virginia Department of Health guidelines must provide a written disclosure when renting the property. A tenant may terminate the tenancy if the disclosure is not provided.

§55-248.13 Landlord to maintain fit premises The landlord shall

- comply with the requirements of applicable building and housing codes materially affecting health and safety;
- make all repairs and do whatever is necessary to put and keep the premises in a fit and habitable condition;
- keep all common areas shared by two or more dwelling units of the premises in a clean and structurally safe condition;
- maintain in good and safe working order and condition all electrical, plumbing, sanitary, heating, ventilating, air-conditioning, and other facilities and appliances, including elevators, supplied or required to be supplied by the landlord;
- maintain the premises in such a condition as to prevent the accumulation of moisture and the growth of mold and promptly respond to any written notices from a tenant;

- provide and maintain appropriate receptacles and conveniences, in common areas, for the collection, storage, and removal of ashes, garbage, rubbish, and other waste incidental to the occupancy of two or more dwelling units and arrange for the removal of same;
- supply running water and reasonable amounts of hot water at all times, reasonable air-conditioning if provided, and heat in season, except where the dwelling unit is so constructed that heat, air-conditioning, or hot water is generated by an installation within the exclusive control of the tenant or supplied by a direct public utility connection; and
- upon request in writing, install carbon monoxide alarms within 90 days of request (the tenant can be charged a reasonable fee for installation, but it is the landlord's responsibility to maintain the alarm once installed) (new requirement in 2014).

The landlord shall perform foregoing duties imposed in accordance with law; however, the landlord shall only be liable for the tenant's actual damages caused by the landlord's failure to exercise ordinary care.

Note that the landlord and tenant may agree in writing that the tenant will perform the landlord's duties specified above and also specified repairs, maintenance tasks, alterations and remodeling, but only if the transaction is entered into in good faith and not for the purpose of evading the obligations of the landlord and if the agreement does not diminish or affect the obligation of the landlord to other tenants in the premises.

§55-248.13:1 Landlord to provide locks and peepholes The governing body of any county, city, or town may require by ordinance that any landlord who rents five or more dwelling units in any one building must install the following to meet the requirements of the Uniform Statewide Building Code:

- Dead-bolt locks and peepholes in any exterior entrance door unless the door has a glass panel
- Manufacturer's locks and removable metal pins or Charlie bars on exterior sliding glass doors at any level
- Locking devices on all exterior windows

Any ordinance adopted pursuant to this law shall provide a reasonable time for the landlord to comply.

§55-248.13:2 Access of tenant to cable, satellite, and other television facilities The landlord may not demand or accept payment of any fee or charge from providers of television or modem service in exchange for granting the provider access to the landlord's tenants with the exception of a service agreement to provide marketing and other delivery services.

The landlord may not demand or accept payment from tenants for such service or discriminate in rental charges. Nothing prohibits a landlord from requiring the provider of the service and the tenant bear the entire cost of the installation, operation, or removal of the facilities.

§55-248.13:3 Notice to tenants for pesticide use The landlord shall give written notice to a tenant no less than 48 hours prior to an application of an insecticide or pesticide. If the tenant requests the application, the 48-hour notice is not required. The tenant shall prepare the dwelling unit for the application and follow any written instructions to eliminate the insects or pest.

The landlord shall post notice of all insecticide or pesticide applications in areas other than dwelling units at least 48 hours prior to application.

§55-248.14 Limitation of liability   A landlord who conveys premises that include a dwelling unit to a bona fide purchaser is relieved of liability under the rental agreement. Unless otherwise agreed, a managing agent is relieved of liability under the rental agreement as to events occurring after written notice of termination of management.

§55-248.15 Tenancy at will   A notice of change of any terms or provisions of a tenancy at will shall constitute a notice to vacate the premises.

§55-248.15:01 Notice to tenant in event of foreclosure   The landlord shall notify the tenant, by certified mail, of a mortgage default, notice of mortgage acceleration, or notice of foreclosure sale within 10 business days after the landlord receives written notice. Failure to provide this notice shall immediately terminate the rental agreement at the option of the tenant, with return of the security deposit with no deductions, within 10 days after termination of the tenancy. With a vacant unit, disclosure shall be made to any prospective tenant.

§55-248.15:1 Security deposits   The landlord may require that the tenant provide a security deposit at the time the property is leased. The **security deposit** is to protect the landlord against unpaid rents or damage—other than normal wear and tear—caused by tenants and/or pets during the lease period.

The security deposit may not exceed an amount equal to two months' rent. The deposit must be returned to the tenant within 45 days after the tenant vacates the property. If the landlord intends to withhold a portion of the security deposit to cover damages or losses, the tenant must be provided a written itemized list of such deductions. In certain circumstances, the landlord may withhold a reasonable amount of the security deposit to cover outstanding utility bills that were an obligation of the tenant as long as proper notice is given. The landlord is required to make a final inspection of the dwelling within 72 hours of the termination of the lease. The landlord must notify the tenant of the date and time of the inspection and the inspection must be at a reasonable time. The tenant has the right to be present during the landlord's inspection but must advise the landlord in writing of the intent to be present.

As of 2014, a landlord may charge an administrative fee for expedited return of the security deposit at the tenant's written request. If no forwarding address is given, the deposit is paid to the state treasury one year and 45 days following lease termination.

Article 3 – Tenant Obligations

Article 3 of the VRLTA specifies obligations of the tenant as follows.

§55-248.16 Tenant to maintain dwelling unit   In addition to provisions of the rental agreement, the tenant agrees to the following:

- Comply with all applicable building and housing codes that materially affect health and safety
- Keep the leased premises as clean and safe as conditions permit
- Keep the premises free from insects and pests and promptly notify landlord of the existence of any insects or pests
- Remove all ashes, garbage, rubbish, and other waste in the appropriate receptacles provided by the landlord
- Keep all plumbing fixtures as clean as their condition permits
- Use in a reasonable manner all electrical, plumbing, sanitary, heating, ventilating, and air-conditioning systems and equipment, including any elevators on the premises
- Not deliberately destroy, deface, damage, impair, or remove any part of the premises or permit anyone else to do so
- Not remove or tamper with smoke detectors or carbon monoxide detectors
- Use reasonable efforts to prevent accumulation of moisture and the growth of mold and promptly notify landlord if such conditions occur
- Not paint or disturb painted surfaces or make alterations in the unit without prior written approval of landlord in any unit built before 1978 that is subject to lead-based paint disclosure and regulations
- Be responsible for tenant's own conduct and conduct of other persons on the premises to insure that neighbors' peaceful enjoyment of the premises is not disturbed
- Abide by all reasonable rules and regulations imposed by the landlord

§55-248.17 Rules and regulations   A landlord, from time to time, may adopt rules or regulations concerning the tenants' use and occupancy of the premises. Such rules or regulations are only enforceable if the purpose is to promote the convenience, safety, or welfare of the tenants, to preserve the property from abusive use, or to make a fair distribution of services and facilities. The rules must apply to all tenants who must be provided with a written copy of the rules and regulations prior to entering into the rental agreement. Changes made after the tenant enters into the rental agreement must be given reasonable notice and not work a substantial modification of the original bargain.

Note that a change in swimming pool hours or a requirement that parking decals be shown on cars are appropriate house rule changes. A change in the number of persons allowed to reside in each unit is an alteration of the rental agreement.

§55-248.18 Access; consent   The tenant shall not unreasonably withhold consent to the landlord to enter the unit in order to inspect the premises, make necessary repairs, decorations, alterations, or improvements, or to exhibit the unit to prospective or actual purchasers, mortgagees, tenants, or workmen. The landlord may only enter the unit without consent in the case of emergency. The landlord shall give the tenant at least 24 hours' notice of routine maintenance. The law continues in §55-248.18 to outline procedures for any required temporary vacation of the property.

§55-248.18:1 Access following entry of certain court orders   A tenant who has obtained a court order excluding any co-tenants from occupancy may request that the landlord install new locks or security devices on exterior doors of the unit, or permit the tenant to do so as long as no permanent damage occurs, and the tenant is responsible for removing such devices upon termination of the lease.

§55-248.18:2 Relocation of tenant where mold remediation required
Where a mold condition in the unit materially affects the health or safety of any tenant, the landlord may require the tenant to temporarily vacate the unit in order for mold remediation to be performed. The landlord shall provide a comparable dwelling unit or hotel room at no cost to the tenant. The tenant remains responsible for rent.

§55-248.19 Use and occupancy by tenant
Unless otherwise agreed, the tenant shall occupy the unit only as a residence.

§55-248.20 Tenant to surrender possession of dwelling unit
At the termination of the tenancy, whether by expiration of the rental agreement or by reason of default by the tenant, the tenant shall promptly vacate the premises, removing all items of personal property and leaving the premises in good and clean order, reasonable wear and tear accepted. If the tenant fails to vacate, the landlord may bring an action for possession and damages, including reasonable attorney's fees.

Article 4 – Tenant Remedies
Article 4 and Article 5 of the VRLTA specify tenant and landlord remedies. These paragraphs are lengthy and cover legal issues that may require the assistance of legal counsel. The paragraphs, along with a brief summary, are listed here to be used as a reference tool.

§55-248.21 Noncompliance by landlord
If the landlord violates the lease agreement or is in violation of any provision affecting health and safety, the tenant may notify the landlord in writing of the violations and state that the lease agreement will terminate on a date not less than 30 days after the notice if the violations are not corrected in 21 days. If the landlord adequately corrects the violations, the lease agreement will not terminate. In certain situations, the tenant may be able to recover damages, reasonable attorney fees, injunctive relief, and security deposits.

§55-248.21:1 Early termination of rental agreement by military personnel
Any member of the armed forces of the United States and any member of the National Guard serving on full-time duty or as a civil service technician with the National Guard may, through the procedure detailed below, terminate his rental agreement if the member

- has received permanent change of station orders to depart 35 miles or more (radius) from the location of the dwelling unit;
- has received temporary duty orders in excess of three months' duration to depart 35 miles or more (radius) from the location of the dwelling unit;

- is discharged or released from active duty with the armed forces of the United States or from his full-time duty or technician status with the National Guard; or
- is ordered to report to government-supplied quarters resulting in the forfeiture of basic allowance for quarters.

Tenants who qualify to terminate a rental agreement under these circumstances must do so by giving the landlord a written notice of termination to be effective on a date stated in the notice. This date cannot be less than 30 days after the date on which the next rental payment (after the date on which the written notice is given) is due and payable. The termination date must be no more than 60 days prior to the date of departure required by the official orders or any supplemental instructions for interim training or duty prior to the transfer. Prior to the termination date, the tenant must furnish the landlord with a copy of the official notification of the orders or a signed letter, confirming the orders, from the tenant's commanding officer.

The landlord may not charge any liquidated damages.

Legislation in 2013 allows victims of domestic abuse or sexual assault to terminate a lease with 30 days' notice. The landlord should be provided with a copy of the court-ordered conviction. Other co-tenants remain responsible for their lease obligations. A landlord may terminate the lease and recover damages if the sole remaining tenant is the perpetrator of the crime.

§55-248.22 Failure to deliver possession   If the landlord fails to deliver possession of the unit, rent is abated, and the tenant can terminate the agreement or demand performance. If the failure to deliver possession is willful and not in good faith, the tenant may recover actual damages and reasonable attorney's fees.

§55-248.23 Wrongful failure to supply heat, water, hot water, or essential services   If the landlord willfully or negligently fails to supply heat, running water, hot water, electricity, gas, or other essential services, the tenant must serve notice specifying the breach and may recover damages based on the diminution in the fair rental value, or procure reasonable substitute housing, and is excused from paying rent for the period of the landlord's noncompliance.

§55-248.24 Fire or casualty damage   If the dwelling unit is damaged or destroyed by fire or casualty to an extent that the tenant's enjoyment of the unit is substantially impaired or if required repairs can only be accomplished if the tenant vacates the dwelling, either the tenant or the landlord may terminate the rental agreement. The tenant may vacate the premises and serve notice within 14 days to the landlord of the intent to terminate the agreement. The landlord may terminate the agreement by giving the tenant 30 days' notice with return of security deposit and any pre-paid rent.

§55-248.25 Landlord's noncompliance as defense to action for possession for nonpayment of rent   In an action for possession based on nonpayment of rent, the tenant may assert as a defense that there exists a condition which constitutes a fire hazard or serious threat to the life, health, or safety of occupants. This defense shall be conditioned on whether, prior to the commencement of the action for rent or possession, the landlord was served written notice of the aforesaid conditions and has refused to remedy them. The rent due is to be held by the court that is making a ruling.

§55-248.25:1 Rent escrow required for continuance of tenant's case
Where a landlord has filed an **unlawful detainer action** seeking possession of the premises, and the tenant seeks a continuance of the action, the court shall order the tenant to pay the rent into the court escrow account.

§55-248.26 Tenant's remedies for landlord's unlawful ouster, exclusion, or diminution of service
If the landlord unlawfully removes or excludes the tenant from the premises or willfully diminishes services, the tenant may recover possession or terminate the rental agreement and recover actual damages and reasonable attorney's fees.

§55-248.27 Tenant's assertion; rent escrow
The tenant may assert that there exists a condition which constitutes a material noncompliance by the landlord that, if not corrected, will constitute a fire hazard or threat to life, health, or safety of occupants. Prior to granting of any relief, the tenant must show that written notice was served to the landlord and that the landlord refused to remedy the condition. The rent has to have been paid into the court (many legal issues are covered in this paragraph, and legal counsel is recommended) (§55-226.12, 2011).

Article 5 – Landlord Remedies

§55-248.31 Noncompliance with rental agreement
If the tenant violates the terms of the lease or is in violation of the tenant's responsibility to maintain the dwelling so that it materially affects health and safety, the landlord may notify the tenant of the violation in writing and state that the rental agreement will terminate on a date not less than 30 days after notice is given, unless the tenant corrects the violation within 21 days. If the violation can be satisfied by repairs or by payment for damages and the tenant takes action to correct the violation, the leased agreement shall not be terminated. If the tenant fails to take action within 14 days, the landlord may enter the property, correct the problem, and charge the tenant for any costs incurred. In an emergency, the landlord may enter and correct the violation as promptly as necessary.

For tenant violations that cannot be corrected, the landlord will notify the tenant in writing of the violation and state that the rental agreement will terminate on a date not less than 30 days after notification. For violations that involve a criminal or willful act, cannot be corrected, and pose a threat to health and safety, the landlord may terminate the rental agreement immediately and proceed with actions to obtain possession. The court hearing for possession will be held within 15 calendar days from the date the tenant was notified. Any illegal drug activity shall constitute an immediate nonremediable violation, and the landlord may proceed to terminate the agreement without waiting for a court conviction. This section of the law also provides direction for procedures to be followed if the tenant is a victim of family abuse.

Nonpayment of Rent   If rent payments are not received when due, the landlord may take the following actions:

- *Five-day pay-or-quit notice.* The landlord may issue a written notice giving the tenant five days to pay the rent or vacate the property.
- *Unlawful detainer warrant.* The landlord may begin eviction proceedings immediately after issuing this warrant. The tenant remains obligated to pay the rent.
- *Eviction.* If full payment of rent is not received within five days, the landlord may file suit to have the tenant **evicted**. The landlord may not remove or exclude the tenant from the property or deny essential services until such time as the court takes eviction action. As of 2013, during an eviction, the landlord may remove the tenant's personal property from the dwelling, the premises, or any on-site storage area.

The unlawful detainer process now requires an initial hearing within 21 days, and the execution of the writ of possession by the sheriff should occur within 15 calendar days from the date received. Legislation in 2014 now allows for additional rent that is due from the time of the filing and the date of the hearing to be added to the amount due.

As of 2013, failed electronic rent payments are subject to the same civil action as a bad check. This legislation also allows the landlord's attorney or agent to present affidavits in court proceedings listing outstanding rent, fees, and damages owed and receive a judgment if the defendant does not appear. The unlawful detainer tenant redemption remedy may only be used once in any 12-month period.

§55-248.31:01 Barring guest or invitee of tenants   A guest or invitee of a tenant may be barred from the premises upon written notice served personally on the guest or invitee for conduct that violates the terms and conditions of the rental agreement, a local ordinance, or a state or federal law.

§55-248.31:1 Sheriffs authorized to serve certain notices; fees therefore   The sheriff of any county or city, upon request, may deliver any notice to a tenant on behalf of a landlord for a fee not to exceed $12.

§55-248.32 Remedy by repair, etc.; emergencies   If there is a violation affecting health and safety that can be remedied by repair, replacement of a damaged item, or cleaning, the landlord shall send written notice to the tenant specifying the breach and stating that the landlord will enter the unit and perform the work necessary and then submit an itemized bill to the tenant due with the next rent payment.

§55-248.33 Remedies for absence, nonuse, and abandonment   During any absence of the tenant in excess of seven days, the landlord may enter the property for the purpose of protecting it. If the terms of the lease require tenant notification of extended absences and if the tenant fails to advise the landlord, the tenant may be responsible for any damage that occurs during the absence.

§55-248.34:1 Landlord's acceptance of rent with reservation   Provided the landlord has given written notice to the tenant that the rent will be accepted with reservation, the landlord may accept full payment of all rent and receive an order of possession from a court of competent jurisdiction pursuant to an unlawful detainer action. The landlord must include this written notice in the termination notice given to the tenant or in a separate written notice given to the tenant within five business days of receiving the rent. The landlord shall continue to accept the rent with reservation until the alleged violation has been remedied or the matter has been adjudicated in a court of competent jurisdiction.

§55-248.35 Remedy after termination   If the rental agreement is terminated, the landlord may have a claim for possession and rent, plus a separate claim for actual damages for breach of the rental agreement. Actual damages may include a claim for rent that would have accrued until the expiration of the term.

§55-248.36 Recovery of possession limited   A landlord may not recover or take possession of the dwelling unit by willful diminution of services or by refusal to permit the tenant access unless pursuant to a court order.

§55-248.37 Periodic tenancy; holdover remedies   The landlord or tenant may terminate a week-to-week tenancy by serving written notice at least seven days prior to the next rent due date. A month-to-month tenancy requires 30 days' notice.

§55-248.38:1 Disposal of property abandoned by tenants   If any items of personal property are left in the premises or any storage area after the rental agreement has terminated and delivery of possession has occurred, the landlord may consider such property to be abandoned. The landlord may dispose of the property provided a termination notice has been given to the tenant that includes a statement that any items of personal property left in the premises is disposed of within a 24-hour period after termination. The tenant has the right to remove the property within that 24-hour period.

Any funds received from the sale of the abandoned property may be used to offset debts owed by the tenant, including the cost of moving and storing the property.

§55-248.38:2 Authority of sheriffs to store and sell personal property removed from residential premises; recovery of possession by owner; disposition or sale   When personal property is removed from a dwelling unit pursuant to an action of unlawful detainer or ejectment, the sheriff shall oversee the removal of such personal property to be placed into the public way. The tenant shall have the right to remove personal property during the 24-period after eviction. After expiration of the 24-hour period, the landlord shall remove or dispose of any such personal property remaining in the public way.

§55-248.38:3 Disposal of property of deceased tenants   If a tenant, who is the sole occupant of the dwelling unit, dies and there is no person authorized by order of the circuit court to handle probate matters for the deceased tenant, the landlord may dispose of the personal property left in the premises, or in a storage area provided by the landlord, provided the landlord has given at least 10 days' written notice to

1. the person identified in the rental application, lease agreement, or other landlord document as the authorized person to contact in the event of the death of the tenant; or
2. the tenant if no such person is identified in the rental application, lease agreement, or other landlord document as the authorized contact person.

The notice given under clause (1) or (2) shall include a statement that any items of personal property left in the premises is treated as abandoned property and disposed of, if not claimed within 30 days.

Note that while the second option above might appear nonsensical, the possibility exists that a person unknown to the landlord has been duly authorized by the tenant and could act on behalf of the tenant's estate upon receiving the notice among the pieces of mail sent to the tenant's address.

Article 6 – Retaliatory Action

§55-248.39 Retaliatory conduct prohibited   A landlord may not retaliate against a tenant who sues or otherwise seeks to enforce her legal rights or rights under the lease. Rent increases, a decrease in service, or termination of the lease are all barred retaliatory actions. The tenant is protected from retaliation if the landlord has notice of any of the following:

- The tenant has complained to the government about building code violations or conditions dangerous to health or safety
- The tenant has made a complaint to or filed suit against the landlord for violation of any provision of the VRLTA
- The tenant has organized or has become a member of a tenants' organization
- The tenant has testified against the landlord in court
- The tenant has complained about possible fair housing law violations

If the landlord acts in violation of this section, the tenant is entitled to recovery of actual damages and may assert such retaliation as a defense in any action for possession. The burden of proving retaliatory intent shall be on the tenant.

§55-248.40 Actions to enforce chapter   Any person adversely affected by an act or omission prohibited under this chapter may institute an action for injunction and damages against the person responsible.

■ MANAGEMENT RESPONSIBILITY

A property manager shares the owner's responsibility for ensuring that landlord–tenant relations comply with the VRLTA. As the owner's agent, a property manager could be liable for any violations, especially fair housing and tenants' rights issues.

Property managers often take on the responsibility for making or contracting for repairs on behalf of the landlord. Care should especially be taken when dealing with issues like mold or remediating a meth lab. The owner must remain liable and the rental agent is under no obligation to lease the property until such repairs are complete.

The specific duties of a licensee engaged to manage real estate are listed under the Law of Agency covered in Chapter 2.

CHAPTER 9 QUIZ

1. A licensee, who lives in Virginia, is acting as resident agent for the owner of an apartment building in Alexandria. The owner lives in Los Angeles. When a tenant is injured on the premises and decides to sue the owner, the resident agent is on an extended vacation and cannot be located. Official notices should be served to

   a. the sheriff.
   b. the president of the tenants' association.
   c. the owner.
   d. the secretary of the Commonwealth.

2. The owner of an apartment complex that has fallen into disrepair decides to repair and renovate the buildings and convert them to condominiums. The number of days' notice required to terminate the tenants' month-to-month leases is

   a. 30 days.
   b. 60 days.
   c. 90 days.
   d. 120 days.

3. A tenant rents farmland, a barn, and a house. The buildings are destroyed by a fire caused by lightning. Must the tenant still pay rent and abide by all the terms of the lease?

   a. Yes, based on common law principles governing ground leases, the tenant must still pay rent.
   b. Yes, any damage to or destruction of the leased premises is the tenant's responsibility.
   c. No, destruction of the improvements terminates a ground lease.
   d. No, if the tenant is not at fault, she is entitled to release from the lease or a reduction in rent until her use of the land is restored.

4. A one-year lease period begins on April 1, 2015. The tenant stops paying rent on July 1, the notice to quit is received on August 1, and the landlord's lien is recorded on December 15. The landlord's lien attaches to the tenant's property on

   a. April 1, 2015.
   b. July 1, 2015.
   c. August 1, 2015.
   d. December 15, 2015.

5. A prospective tenant applies for a lease in an apartment building and pays the mandatory $125 application fee. If the tenant decides *NOT* to sign a lease, the application fee

   a. may be kept by the landlord.
   b. must be returned to the prospective tenant within 20 days.
   c. must be returned to the prospective tenant, less a 10% charge to cover paperwork.
   d. must be returned minus any actual expenses incurred by the landlord.

6. A landlord, who is subject to the VRLTA, charges $750 per month for an apartment. The maximum amount the landlord can require as a security deposit is

   a. $750.
   b. $1,000.
   c. $1,500.
   d. $2,250.

7. Which of the following is *NOT* subject to the requirements of the Virginia Residential Landlord Tenant Act (VRLTA)?

   a. Someone who owns two rental properties
   b. Someone who owns 10 rental properties in rural counties
   c. Someone who owns three rental properties
   d. Someone who owns four rental properties in an urban area

8. A tenant decides to install a burglar alarm in a rented house. Does the tenant need to inform the landlord?

   a. No, the tenant has full right of possession during the lease.
   b. No, only tenants in multiunit apartment buildings are required to inform a landlord about a security system.
   c. Yes, the tenant must also give the landlord instructions and passwords.
   d. Yes, the tenant must inform the landlord, but the cost of the system may be deducted from the rent.

9. An Air Force sergeant rented an apartment four months ago. He has now been reassigned to a different airbase with orders to move in 30 days. His landlord may charge him for damages of

   a. one month's rent.
   b. seven months' rent.
   c. one-half of one month's rent.
   d. nothing because he is military.

10. A landlord must disclose in writing the existence of any visible evidence of mold in the dwelling

   a. within three days of occupancy.
   b. within 48 hours of occupancy.
   c. when the lease is signed.
   d. within five days of occupancy.

11. The tenant, after having received a notice from the landlord regarding abandonment, must give written notice to the landlord that the tenant intends to remain in occupancy of the dwelling unit within

   a. 5 days.
   b. 7 days.
   c. 10 days.
   d. 14 days.

12. The landlord can require a tenant to pay the premium for

   a. only renter's insurance.
   b. only damage insurance.
   c. neither renter's nor damage insurance.
   d. both renter's and damage insurance.

13. A woman living in Fairfax County, Virginia, just won the Virginia Lottery. She intends to purchase outright four homes for members of her family and allow them to live rent-free. Additionally, she is purchasing outright two condominium units for investment, which she intends to rent. All of the properties are in Fairfax County. The woman's properties will NOT be subject to the VRLTA because

   a. the VRLTA does not apply to properties that have no mortgages.
   b. only two of the woman's properties will be subject to a lease.
   c. she owns fewer than 10 properties in Virginia.
   d. the VRLTA does not cover properties purchased for family use.

14. Which of the following lease provisions are prohibited under Virginia law?

   a. Two months' rent security deposit required
   b. Prohibition against pets
   c. Restriction against lawful possession of a firearm
   d. Tenant's responsibility for the conduct of guests

15. Article 6 of the Virginia Residential Landlord Tenant Act deals with

   a. general leasing principles.
   b. obligations of the landlord.
   c. obligations of the tenant.
   d. retaliatory action.

CHAPTER 10

Virginia Fair Housing Law

■ **LEARNING OBJECTIVES**   *After successfully completing this chapter, you will be able to*

- ■ **describe** the makeup and responsibilities of the Virginia Fair Housing Office and Virginia Fair Housing Board,
- ■ **list** and define exemptions under Virginia Fair Housing Law,
- ■ **identify** unlawful discriminatory housing practices, and
- ■ **explain** the procedure for enforcement of the Virginia Fair Housing Law.

■ **KEY TERMS**

civil action	elderliness	respondent
complainant	familial status	service animal
conciliation	handicap	
dwelling	hoarding	

The Virginia Fair Housing Law falls under Title 36, Chapter 5.1 (§§36-96.1 through 36.96.23) of the Code of Virginia. The law states that it is the policy of the Commonwealth of Virginia to provide for fair housing throughout the Commonwealth for all its citizens, regardless of race, color, religion, national origin, sex, elderliness, familial status, or handicap and that all discriminatory practices in residential housing transactions are prohibited. The law applies to property managers, owners, landlords, real estate agents, banks, savings institutions, credit unions, insurance companies, mortgage lenders, and appraisers.

Fair housing in Virginia is also covered by the Virginia Administrative Code, 18 VAC 135-50-10 through 135.50-550, as published in the Real Estate Board Fair Housing Regulations, effective September 22, 2007.

Title 54.1 Chapter 23.2, §§54.1-2343 and 54.1-2344, relates to the Department of Professional and Occupational Regulation (DPOR) and the creation of the Fair Housing Board. The Virginia Fair Housing Office also falls under the auspices of the DPOR and serves as the investigative arm of both the Fair Housing Board and the Real Estate Board.

■ VIRGINIA FAIR HOUSING OFFICE

The Virginia Fair Housing Office (VFHO) is the investigative arm for both the Fair Housing Board and the Real Estate Board. It consists of an administrator, who has overall responsibility for the office; an investigative supervisor, who oversees all investigations; a program conciliator, who attempts to resolve complaints through informal negotiation; and four field investigators and two administrative investigators. The VFHO has two mandates: investigation and training.

Investigation Mandate

After the investigator has completed interviews with the complainant, respondent, and witnesses and reviewed pertinent documents and records, a final report is prepared and submitted to the appropriate board. During the investigative process, the program conciliator attempts to resolve the complaint through conciliation—a voluntary process where the parties attempt to resolve the complaint by agreeing to mutually acceptable terms. If conciliation is not successful, the investigation continues.

Training Mandate

Each year, staff from the VFHO travel throughout Virginia providing training to housing providers, consumers, and local and state officials. Presentations range from handouts to PowerPoint presentations, are interactive, and are offered at no cost to participants.

The VFHO can be reached by phone at 804-367-8530 or 888-551-3247 or by email at fairhousing@dpor.virginia.gov.

■ FAIR HOUSING BOARD

The Fair Housing Board was created at DPOR in 2003 to administer and enforce the provisions of both state and federal fair housing law. The Fair Housing Board also oversees an education-based certification program for individuals involved in selling or renting dwellings. Both the Real Estate Board and the Fair Housing Board have the power to initiate and receive complaints, conduct investigations, attempt resolution of complaints by conference or conciliation, and issue a charge to be referred to the attorney general for action. The Real Estate Board is responsible for the administration and enforcement of the fair housing law with respect to real estate licensees or their employees. The Fair Housing Board is responsible for all others who violate the fair housing law. A case that involves both licensees and a member of the general public will be heard by the Real Estate Board.

The Fair Housing Board is composed of 12 members, appointed by the governor for four-year terms, as follows:

- One representative of local government
- One architect licensed in accordance with Chapter 4 (§54.1-400 et seq.) of this title
- One representative of the mortgage lending industry
- One representative of the property and casualty insurance industry
- Two representatives of the residential property management industry not licensed in accordance with Chapter 21 (§54.1-2100 et seq.) of this title
- One contractor licensed in accordance with Chapter 11 (§54.1-1100 et seq.) of this title
- One representative of the disability community
- One representative of the residential land lease industry subject to Chapter 13.3 (§55-248.41 et seq.) of Title 55
- Three citizen members selected in accordance with §54.1-107

The Fair Housing Board can be reached by phone at 804-367-0115 or by email at fhcertification@dpor.virginia.gov.

Protected Classes in Virginia

The Virginia Fair Housing Law prohibits discrimination in housing and real estate activities on the basis of

- race,
- color,
- religion,
- national origin,
- sex,
- elderliness,
- familial status, or
- handicap.

Virginia added the additional protected class of elderliness to the seven federal protected classes.

Important Definitions

Certain terms in the fair housing law have specific legal definitions. A few of the most relevant ones are:

Complainant   A **complainant** is a person who files a fair housing complaint.

Conciliation   **Conciliation** is the attempted resolution of issues raised by a complainant through informal negotiations involving the aggrieved person, the respondent, their respective authorized representatives, and the Fair Housing Board.

Dwelling   A **dwelling** is all or part of any building or structure designated or intended for use as a residence by one or more families. The term also includes vacant land offered for sale or lease for the construction or location of any residential building or structure.

Elderliness   For purposes of the fair housing law, **elderliness** refers to any individual who has attained her 55th birthday.

Familial Status   The **familial status** class protects individuals under the age of 18 who live with either

■ a parent or other person having legal custody, or
■ the designee of a parent or other person having custody with the written permission of the parent or other person.

The definition also includes pregnant women and people who are in the process of securing legal custody of a minor.

IN PRACTICE   Three related adults, including one 19-year-old, have applied to rent a one-bedroom apartment and have been turned down by the landlord based on a reasonable occupancy standard. Regardless of the reasonable occupancy standard, they then claim that they are a family under *familial status* and are entitled to rent the unit as a family regardless of the occupancy standard.

The fair housing law protects *individuals*, not *families*, and does not apply in this situation. However, if one party was a minor, the law could apply under familial status.

Handicap   A person is considered **handicapped** if that person suffers from a physical or mental impairment that substantially limits one or more major life activities. Having a record of such impairment, or being regarded as having such an impairment, also constitutes a handicap under the fair housing law. The law does apply to individuals in a recognized drug treatment program. The term does not apply to current, illegal use of or addiction to a controlled substance as defined by law. Transvestites are specifically excluded from the definition of handicap.

Hoarding is now classified by the Diagnostic Manual of Mental Disabilities as a disability. A reasonable accommodation must be allowed to enable remedying any adverse effects created by the hoarding.

Respondent   A **respondent** is the person or entity alleged to have violated the provisions of the fair housing law.

■ EXEMPTIONS

As with the federal law, there are some exemptions in Virginia, as follows:

■ A single-family residence sold or rented by the owner is exempt from the statute, as long as the owner owns no more than three such homes at the time. In the case of a sale where the owner was not residing in the home at the time of the sale or was not the resident of the home prior to the sale, the exemption applies to only one sale within any one 24-month period. The sale or rental of any such single-family dwelling shall be exempt only if the property is sold or rented without the use of any real estate broker or broker facilities and without the use of any advertisement that is in violation of fair housing law.

- Rooms or units in one- to four-family structures are exempt if the owner occupies one of the units and does not use discriminatory advertising.
- Religious organizations, institutions, associations, or societies may limit the sale or rental of property they own or operate for other than commercial purposes to persons of the same religion. Such organizations may give preference to their members, as long as membership in the organization is not restricted on the basis of race, color, national origin, sex, elderliness, familial status, or handicap.
- Private, state-owned, or state-supported educational institutions, hospitals, nursing homes, religious organizations, and correctional institutions may, for personal privacy reasons, require single-sex occupancy of its owned and operated single-family residences, rooms, and units. Single-sex restrooms in such dwellings or buildings are not illegal.
- Private membership clubs not open to the public that provide lodging that they own or operate for other than commercial purposes may give preference to their members.
- An individual who intends to share living quarters with another may advertise on the basis of sex, but only on the basis of sex. For example, an ad could say, "Females only need apply," but it could not say, "Christian females" or "white females."
- Certain restrictive covenants and zoning laws exist that restrict housing in an area to single-family housing. According to the Virginia Fair Housing Law, a family care home, foster home, or group home in which persons reside who are physically handicapped, mentally ill, mentally retarded, or developmentally disabled, together with resident counselors or staff, is considered single-family occupancy for zoning purposes. For purposes of restrictive covenants, there is no maximum number of residents.
- Condominium unit owners' association may, if permitted by the bylaws, restrict the number of occupants in any unit, as long as the limitation is reasonable and not more restrictive than the local zoning ordinance.
- It is legal to discriminate on the basis of age to permit housing for elderly persons. Housing is exempt from the familial status protection if it is provided under a state or federal program designed to assist the elderly, or if it is intended for and solely occupied by persons at least 62 years of age, or if it has at least one person 55 years of age or older in 80% of the occupied units. Qualified housing in this second category must provide the elderly with important housing opportunities and adhere to published policies and procedures that demonstrate the intent to provide such housing.

Criminal Background

People who have been convicted of the illegal manufacture or distribution of controlled substances are not protected by the fair housing law.

Rental applications may require the disclosure of any criminal convictions, and applicants may be required to consent to and to pay for a criminal background check. A building manager or property owner may refuse to rent a dwelling to an individual who has a record of prior criminal convictions involving harm to persons or property, and whose presence would pose a threat to the health or safety of others. Consistently applying a criminal background check means that the policy must be in writing, must have the applicant's permission, and must be applied to all applicants.

Similarly, the law's protections do not make it unlawful for an owner to deny or limit residential rentals to persons who pose a clear and present threat of substantial harm to others or the premises.

IN PRACTICE   Local counties, cities, and towns may enforce legislation adopted prior to 1991 that is *more restrictive* (protective of more classes) than either the state or the federal law. Any amendments to the local legislation, however, must conform to the state's law. Because licensees often practice in more than one jurisdiction within the state, they must be aware of all local legislation that differs from federal and state laws.

Liability for Licensees

It is illegal for real estate licensees to be involved in discriminatory housing practices in any way. While licensees should be aware of the exemptions in order to fully comply with the law when acting in the best interests of client, it is of more vital importance that they personally comply with the law's nondiscriminatory intent. The law (§36.96.2A) states, "this exemption shall not apply to or inure to the benefit of any licensee of the Real Estate Board or regulant of the Fair Housing Board, regardless of whether the licensee is acting in his personal or professional capacity."

In other words, there are no exemptions from fair housing law for real estate licensees in Virginia.

■ UNLAWFUL DISCRIMINATORY HOUSING PRACTICES

In Virginia, it is illegal for anyone to commit any of the following discriminatory acts on the basis of a person's race, color, religion, national origin, sex, elderliness, familial status, or handicap:

- Refusing to sell or rent a dwelling to any person who has made a bona fide offer to do so or refusing to negotiate the sale or rental of a dwelling
- Discriminating against any person in the terms, condition, or privileges of the sale or rental of a dwelling or in providing services or facilities
- Making, printing, or publishing any notice, statement, or advertisement with respect to the sale or rental of a dwelling that indicates an actual or intended preference, limitation, or discrimination
- Falsely representing that a dwelling is not available for inspection, sale, or rental
- Denying membership or participation in a multiple-listing service (MLS), real estate brokers' organization, or any other service, organization, or facility related to the business of selling or renting dwellings
- Including any discriminatory restrictive covenant in the transfer, sale, rental, or lease of housing or honoring any discriminatory restriction
- Inducing or attempting to induce the sale or rental of a dwelling by representations regarding the entry or prospective entry into the neighborhood of protected persons

- Refusing to sell, rent, or negotiate with anyone on the basis of their own handicap, that of anyone who will be residing in the dwelling, or that of anyone associated with them
- Discriminating in the terms, conditions, or privileges of the sale or rental of a dwelling or in its services or facilities on the basis of an individual's handicap or that of anyone associated with the individual

Additional Prohibited Actions

Virginia Fair Housing Regulations list the following additional actions that are prohibited:

- Failing or delaying maintenance or repairs of sales or rental dwellings
- Limiting the use of privileges, services, or facilities associated with a dwelling
- Discouraging the purchase or rental of a dwelling by exaggerating drawbacks or failing to inform of desirable features
- Communicating to a prospective purchaser or renter that they would not be comfortable or compatible with existing residents of a community
- Assigning any one to a particular section of a community or particular floor or section of a building
- Denying or limiting services or facilities because a person failed or refused to provide sexual favors

Discriminatory Advertising

The law applies to all written or oral notices or statements, including applications, flyers, brochures, deeds, signs, banners, posters, billboards, or documents.

The use of words or symbols associated with a particular religion, national origin, sex, or race is considered prima facie evidence of an illegal preference. The use of such words or symbols may not be overcome by a general disclaimer that no discrimination is intended.

An ad with directions to a rental property that included "turn left at St. Matthew's Cathedral" or "three blocks past the new mosque" might be considered to be steering people of a certain religion to a property.

The selective use of language, geography, or human models should always reflect the true demographic makeup of a community.

The HUD-approved fair housing poster should be displayed at all places of business that sell or rent dwellings. All advertising of residential real estate for sale, rent, or financing should contain an equal housing opportunity logotype, statement, or slogan.

Special Rules for Handicapped Persons

Persons with disabilities must be permitted to make reasonable modifications, at their own expense, of existing premises to make the premises fully accessible to the individual. A landlord may make modification of rented premises conditional on the tenant's agreement to restore the premises to their original condition (reasonable wear and tear accepted) if it affects the value of the property.

It is unlawful to refuse to make reasonable accommodations in rules, practices, policies, or services in order to afford handicapped individuals equal opportunities to use and enjoy a dwelling. For example, a no-pets policy should be flexible enough to accommodate **service animals**, such as a guide dog or an assistance monkey.

Hoarding is now classified as a mental disability. A reasonable accommodation is allowing time for the tenant or someone assisting the tenant to correct lease violations, such as odor, pest infestation, blocked exits, or fire hazards. Any imminent threats should be addressed immediately.

New multifamily dwellings, that is, those with four or more units, must be designed and constructed in such a way that the public use and common areas are readily accessible to handicapped persons. All ground-floor units must have doors that allow passage by persons in wheelchairs plus light switches, electrical outlets, thermostats, and environmental controls that are accessible by persons in wheelchairs. Kitchens and bathrooms must be designed for full maneuverability with reinforced bathroom walls to allow later installation of grab bars. In four or more unit buildings with elevators, all units must meet the accessibility requirements.

The Americans with Disabilities Act (ADA) prohibits discrimination against people with disabilities in employment, transportation, public accommodations, communications, and governmental activities. The Architectural and Transportation Barriers Compliance Board (also called the Access Board) issues guidelines to ensure that buildings, facilities, and transit vehicles are accessible and usable by people with disabilities. Although ADA standards do not apply to all residential dwellings, they do apply to any area that has public access, such as common use areas or any real estate or rental management office.

Fair Housing Application for Lending Institutions

The fair housing law also applies to lending institutions and other businesses involved in residential real estate transactions. It is unlawful to discriminate in the availability, terms, or conditions of real estate financing on the basis of race, color, religion, national origin, sex, elderliness, familial status, or handicap. It is not unlawful for any person or business engaging in residential real estate transactions to require any applicant to qualify financially. If any lending institution is found to be engaging in unlawful discriminatory practices, the fair housing law forbids state, county, city, or municipal treasurers or other government officials to deposit public funds in the institution. Existing deposits of public funds must be withdrawn from offending lenders although the action may be deferred for one year to avoid financial loss to the state, county, city, or agency. If the lender corrects its practices, there is no prohibition against the deposit of public funds.

The Virginia Fair Housing Law also applies to those who are involved indirectly in the sale or rental of real property, such as newspapers and other publications. Appraisers cannot include any discriminatory information in appraisal reports.

ENFORCEMENT OF THE FAIR HOUSING LAW

Persons who feel that their rights under the fair housing law have been violated may take action against the party alleged to have discriminated. Complaints involving persons licensed by the Real Estate Board (REB) must be filed with the REB, which is empowered to initiate and receive complaints against licensees, investigate alleged violations, and resolve conflicts either by conference and conciliation or by issuing a charge and referring the matter to the attorney general for action. Complaints against non-licensees may be made to the Fair Housing Board (FHB) at fairhousing@dpor.virginia.gov. The procedures to be followed are the same for both the FHB and the REB. Effective July 1, 2013, the Real Estate Board has the authority to hear fair housing violations with multiple respondents, at least one of whom is a licensee.

A complaint must be filed in writing with the Board within one year of the occurrence or termination of the alleged discriminatory practice.

In any action brought under the Virginia Fair Housing Law, the burden of proof is upon the complainant. The Board must acknowledge receipt of the complaint and advise the claimant of time limits and choices of forums for hearing the complaint.

Accused persons must be notified of the allegation and of their legal rights within 10 days. Proceedings must commence within 30 days after receiving the complaint. The investigation should be completed within 100 days. If the Board is unable to complete the investigation within 100 days, both the complainant and the respondent shall be notified in writing of the reasons for not doing so.

The REB may issue subpoenas, interview witnesses, and request the production of documents in the course of its investigation. During the investigative period, it is possible for the complainant and respondent to enter into a conciliation agreement, subject to REB approval. A conciliation agreement may provide for binding arbitration and may award appropriate relief, including monetary relief.

If reasonable cause exists to believe that a discriminatory housing practice has occurred or is about to occur, the REB must seek resolution by conciliation or forward the charge to the attorney general for **civil action**. If no reasonable cause exists, the case will be dismissed. If the Board determines that a discriminatory housing practice involving the legality of any local zoning or land use ordinance has occurred, the complaint shall be immediately referred to the attorney general for civil action.

Penalties

If the case results in civil action by the attorney general, the court may

- award preventive relief by temporary or permanent injunction, restraining order, or other necessary order;
- assess a civil penalty of up to $50,000 for a first violation and up to $100,000 for any subsequent violation; and
- award the prevailing party reasonable attorney's fees and costs.

Whether or not a complaint has been filed with the REB, a civil action may also be initiated by an injured person in a U.S. district court or state court within two years after the occurrence or termination of an alleged discriminatory housing practice. If a civil action is filed at the same time a complaint is filed with the REB, the REB will delay action until the court rules. If a conciliation agreement is breached, a civil action may be filed within two years of the breach.

If any real estate licensee is found guilty of violating the fair housing law, the REB will take appropriate steps to consider suspension or revocation of the license or to take other disciplinary action.

Additional information about the Virginia Fair Housing Law is available at http://leg1.state.va.us/cgi-bin/legp504.exe?000+cod+54.1-2344.

CHAPTER 10 QUIZ

1. Which of the following is protected by the Virginia Fair Housing Law?

   a. Marital status
   b. Familial status
   c. Source of income
   d. Dietary restriction

2. All of the following are protected by the Virginia Fair Housing Law's provisions for the handicapped or elderly *EXCEPT*

   a. a 55-year-old recovered heroin addict.
   b. a 62-year-old currently using cocaine.
   c. a paralyzed veteran.
   d. a person who is a hoarder.

3. Which of the following is *NOT* exempt under Virginia Fair Housing Law?

   a. Single-family residence rented by an owner who owns no more than three homes
   b. Presbyterian Home for the Aged
   c. Single-sex occupancy of a state-supported nursing home
   d. Owner-occupied four-unit building advertising as "singles only"

4. A single woman placed the following advertisement in the local paper: "Share lovely town house. Large wooded lot, near transp, shops, and recreation. $650 per mo. Female only." Which of the following is *TRUE*?

   a. The ad is a violation of the fair housing law because it discriminates against males.
   b. The ad violates the fair housing law's prohibition against sexual discrimination.
   c. The ad is legal because she is sharing her own home.
   d. The newspaper is now subject to a civil action for publishing a discriminatory ad.

5. A building manager receives a lease application from a prospective tenant. The application disclosed that he served time in prison for income tax evasion but now has regular income from a manufacturing job. Can the building manager lawfully refuse to rent an apartment to him?

   a. No, the fair housing law prohibits discrimination on the basis of prior criminal record.
   b. No, his criminal conviction did not involve harm to persons or property.
   c. Yes, the fair housing law permits a building manager to refuse to rent to any convicted criminal.
   d. Yes, the fair housing law does not apply to actions by building managers.

6. When a young couple recently emigrating from El Salvador attempted to rent an apartment, they were told that no units were available, when in fact there were at least four available at that time. The rental company was guilty of

   a. nothing; it has the right to say what it pleases.
   b. nothing; it has the right to limit rentals to U.S. citizens.
   c. unlawful discriminatory housing practice of false representation.
   d. discrimination based on age.

7. Housing projects for the elderly are exempt from the familial status category of fair housing law as long as

   a. all occupants are at least 60 years old.
   b. 75% of occupants are at least 60 years old.
   c. all occupants of 80% of the units are at least 55 years old.
   d. at least one of the occupants in 80% of the units is 55 years old.

8. Two people apply for a mortgage loan. One is a 65-year-old blind male with no income or savings, and the other is a 35-year-old black female with no debts and a six-figure income from her law practice. Based on these facts alone, if both applicants are turned down, the lender has MOST likely committed unlawful discrimination against

   a. the 65-year old blind male.
   b. the 35-year old black female.
   c. both applicants.
   d. neither applicant.

9. Investigations of fair housing complaints should be completed within

   a. 30 days.
   b. 60 days.
   c. 100 days.
   d. 1 year.

10. A civil action brought by the attorney general for a first violation of the Virginia Fair Housing Law could subject a guilty party to a monetary civil penalty of

   a. up to $10,000 for a first offense.
   b. up to $25,000 for a first offense.
   c. up to $50,000 for a first offense.
   d. actual damages and legal fees only.

11. A licensee with a realty firm in Prince William County is charged with a violation of the Virginia Fair Housing Law. Her case will be heard before

   a. the Real Estate Board.
   b. the Fair Housing Board.
   c. the local real estate association board.
   d. the County Fair Housing Board.

12. The Fair Housing Board consists of 12 members. How many citizen members are appointed to the board?

   a. One
   b. Two
   c. Three
   d. Five

13. All of the following are discriminatory acts according to Virginia Fair Housing Law EXCEPT

   a. falsely representing that a dwelling is not available for sale or rental.
   b. denying membership in a multiple listing service.
   c. inducing the sale or rental of a dwelling by representation regarding the prospective entry into the neighborhood of protected persons.
   d. requiring a handicapped tenant to pay for installation of an access ramp.

14. Under the fair housing law, what symbol or logo is deemed discriminatory if printed on a licensee's business card?

   a. HUD's Equal Housing symbol
   b. The REALTOR® logo/symbol
   c. A local MLS's logo/symbol
   d. A religious cross or symbol

15. A landlord (who is not a real estate licensee) refuses to rent an apartment to an elderly man who has a guide dog, stating that his advertisement clearly states "no pets." If the man wishes to file a fair housing complaint, he should contact the Virginia

   a. Real Estate Board.
   b. Fair Housing Office.
   c. Fair Housing Board.
   d. Attorney General's Office.

Exclusive Right to Sell Listing Agreement

Exclusive Right to Sell Listing Agreement

EXCLUSIVE RIGHT TO SELL LISTING AGREEMENT

This Exclusive Right to Sell Listing Agreement ("Agreement") is made on _____ ("Date") by and between _____("Seller") and (Insert Firm Name) _____("Broker").

1. **APPOINTMENT OF BROKER.** In consideration of the services provided by Broker and described in this Agreement, Seller hereby appoints Broker as Seller's sole and exclusive listing agent and grants Broker the exclusive right to sell the real property described below ("Property").

2. **PROPERTY.**

   Street Address _____ Unit # _____

   City_____, Virginia Zip Code _____

   TAX Map/ID # _____

   Parking Space #_____   Storage Unit # _____   Mailbox #_____

   Historic District Designation _____

   Legal Description:

   ☐ Lot/Block/Subdivision:

       Lot(s) _____ Block/Square _____ Section_____ Phase _____

       Subdivision or Condominium _____

       County/Municipality _____ Deed Book/Page # _____

   ☐ Metes/Bounds: see attached description or survey.

3. **NOTICES.** All notifications and amendments under this Agreement shall be in writing and shall be delivered using the contact information below.

   Seller

   Mailing Address: _____

   City, State, and Zip Code:_____

   Phone: (H) _____ (W) _____   (Cell) _____

   Email: _____   Fax: _____

   Broker (Firm)

   Mailing Address: _____

   City, State, and Zip Code: _____

   Phone: (W) _____   (Cell) _____

   Email: _____   Fax: _____

4. **TERM OF AGREEMENT.** This Agreement shall run for the period commencing after signature by all parties and expiring at 11:59 p.m. on _____ ("Listing Period"). If a sales contract for Property is ratified during Listing Period which provides for a settlement date beyond Listing Period, this Agreement shall be extended automatically until final disposition of the sales contract.

5. **LISTING PRICE.** Seller instructs Broker to offer Property for sale at a selling price of $_____, or such other price as later agreed upon by Seller, which price includes Broker's compensation. (Note: Broker does not guarantee that Property will appraise or sell at the price stated hereunder, nor does Broker guarantee any net amount Seller might realize from the sale of Property).

Exclusive Right to Sell Listing Agreement (cont.)

6. **CONVEYANCES.**

A. **Personal Property and Fixtures.** Property includes the following personal property and fixtures, if existing: built-in heating and central air conditioning equipment, plumbing and lighting fixtures, sump pump, attic and exhaust fans, storm windows, storm doors, screens, installed wall-to-wall carpeting, window shades, blinds, window treatment hardware, smoke and heat detectors, TV antennas, exterior trees and shrubs. Unless otherwise agreed to in writing, all surface or wall mounted electronic components/devices **DO NOT** convey.

If more than one of an item convey, the number of items is noted. The items marked YES below are currently installed or offered:

Yes	No	#	Items	Yes	No	#	Items	Yes	No	#	Items
☐	☐	___	Alarm System	☐	☐	___	Freezer	☐	☐	___	Satellite Dish
☐	☐	___	Built-in Microwave	☐	☐	___	Furnace Humidifier	☐	☐	___	Storage Shed
☐	☐	___	Ceiling Fan	☐	☐	___	Garage Opener	☐	☐	___	Stove or Range
☐	☐	___	Central Vacuum	☐	☐	___	w/ remote	☐	☐	___	Trash Compactor
☐	☐	___	Clothes Dryer	☐	☐	___	Gas Log	☐	☐	___	Wall Oven
☐	☐	___	Clothes Washer	☐	☐	___	Hot Tub, Equip & Cover	☐	☐	___	Water Treatment System
☐	☐	___	Cooktop	☐	☐	___	Intercom	☐	☐	___	Window A/C Unit
☐	☐	___	Dishwasher	☐	☐	___	Playground Equipment	☐	☐	___	Window Fan
☐	☐	___	Disposer	☐	☐	___	Pool, Equip, & Cover	☐	☐	___	Window Treatments
☐	☐	___	Electronic Air Filter	☐	☐	___	Refrigerator	☐	☐	___	Wood Stove
☐	☐	___	Fireplace Screen/Door	☐	☐	___	w/ ice maker				

Other: _____

_____

B. **As-Is Items.** Seller will not warrant the condition or working order of the following items and/or systems: _____

_____

C. **As-Is Marketing.** Seller ☐ does **OR** ☐ does not authorize Broker to offer the entire Property in "As-Is" condition.

D. **Leased Items, Systems, And/Or Service Contracts.** Any leased items, systems, or service contracts (including, but not limited to, termite or pest control, home warranty, fuel tanks, water treatment systems, lawn contracts, security system monitoring, and satellite contracts) DO NOT CONVEY absent an express written agreement by purchaser and Seller. The following is a list of the leased items within Property:

_____

_____

_____

7. **HOMEOWNER WARRANTY.** Seller has the option to purchase a homeowner warranty, which can be in effect during the Listing Period and will transfer to the buyer upon settlement. Seller should review the scope of coverage, exclusions and limitations.

Cost not to exceed $_____ Warranty provider to be _____

8. **UTILITIES.** (Check all that apply)

Hot Water: ☐ Oil ☐ Gas ☐ Electric ☐ Other _____ Number of Gallons _____

Air Conditioning: ☐ Oil ☐ Gas ☐ Electric ☐ Heat Pump ☐ Other _____ ☐ Zones ____

Heating: ☐ Oil ☐ Gas ☐ Electric ☐ Heat Pump ☐ Other _____ ☐ Zones ____

Water Supply: ☐ Public ☐ Private Well ☐ Community Well

Sewage Disposal: ☐ Public ☐ Septic Approved for _____ Bedrooms

FIGURE A.1

Exclusive Right to Sell Listing Agreement (cont.)

Type of Septic System: ☐ Community ☐ Conventional ☐ Alternative ☐ Experimental

*Section 32.1-164:1 of the Code of Virginia requires Seller to disclose whether the onsite septic system serving Property is operating under a waiver of repair and/or maintenance requirements imposed by the State Board of Health. If the septic system is operating pursuant to a waiver, then Seller must provide the buyer with the "Disclosure Regarding Validity of Septic System Permit" prior to contract ratification. Such waiver is not transferable to the buyer.

Seller represents that the septic system ☐ is **OR** ☐ is not operating under a waiver from the State Board of Health.

9. **BROKER DUTIES.** Broker shall perform, and Seller hereby authorizes Broker to perform, the following duties. In performing these duties, Broker shall exercise ordinary care, comply with all applicable laws and regulations and treat all parties honestly.

   A. Broker shall protect and promote the interests of Seller and shall provide Seller with services consistent with the standards of practice and competence that are reasonably expected of licensees engaged in the business of real estate brokerage. Seller acknowledges that Broker is bound by the bylaws, policies and procedures, and rules and regulations governing the MLS, the Code of Ethics of the National Association of REALTORS®, and the Regional Rules and Regulations for the electronic lockbox system.

   B. Broker shall use reasonable efforts and act diligently to seek buyers for Property at the price and terms stated herein or otherwise acceptable to Seller, to negotiate on behalf of Seller and to assist in the consummation of the sale of Property.

   C. Broker shall market Property, at Broker's discretion, including without limitation, description, interior and exterior photographs in appropriate advertising media, such as publications, mailings, brochures and internet sites; provided, however, Broker shall not be obligated to continue to market Property after Seller has accepted an offer.

   D. Broker shall present all written offers or counteroffers to and from Seller, in a timely manner, even if Property is already subject to a ratified contract of sale, unless otherwise instructed by Seller in writing.

   E. Broker shall account, in a timely manner, for all money and property received in trust by Broker, in which Seller has or may have an interest.

   F. Broker shall show Property during reasonable hours to prospective buyers and shall accompany or accommodate, as needed, other real estate licensees, their prospective buyers, inspectors, appraisers, exterminators and other parties necessary for showings and inspections of Property, to facilitate and/or consummate the sale of Property. Broker ☐ shall **OR** ☐ shall not install an electronic lockbox on Property to allow access and showings by persons who are authorized to access Property.

   G. Broker ☐ shall **OR** ☐ shall not install "For Sale" signs on Property, as permitted. Seller is responsible for clearly marking the location of underground utilities, equipment or other items that may be damaged by the placement of the sign.

10. **MARKETING/MLS/INTERNET ADVERTISING.**

   A. Broker shall make a blanket unilateral offer of cooperation and compensation to other brokers in any multiple listing service ("MLS") that Broker deems appropriate. Broker shall disseminate information regarding Property, including the entry date, listing price(s), final price and all terms, and expired or withdrawn status, by printed form and/or electronic computer service, which may include internet advertising, during and after the expiration of this Agreement.

Exclusive Right to Sell Listing Agreement (cont.)

Broker shall enter the listing information into the MLS database:

☐ Within 48 hours (excluding weekends and holidays) of commencement of the Listing Period **OR** ☐ on or before: _____

B. The parties agree and understand that internet advertising includes:

1) Broker's internet website;

2) The internet websites of licensed real estate salespersons or associate real estate brokers affiliated with Broker;

3) Any other internet website in accordance with applicable MLS rules and regulations;

4) Printed media; and/or

5) Any available MLS program(s) that enable participants to display aggregated MLS active listing information on other such participants' and authorized users' public websites.

C. Seller agrees and understands that Broker has provided an opportunity to Seller to opt-out of any of the following four provisions which govern the display of information on Virtual Office Websites (VOW) and that Broker is thus hereby authorized by Seller to submit and market Property as follows.

PART I:

☐ Seller authorizes **OR** ☐ Seller does not authorize Broker to submit and market Property by and through the display on any internet websites.

If Seller selects the second option, consumers who conduct searches for listings on the internet will not see the corresponding information about Property in response to a search.

PART II:

☐ Seller authorizes **OR** ☐ Seller does not authorize the display of Property address on any internet website.

PART III:

☐ Seller authorizes **OR** ☐ Seller does not authorize the display of unedited comments or reviews of Property (or display a hyperlink to such comments or reviews) on MLS participants' internet websites.

PART IV:

☐ Seller authorizes **OR** ☐ Seller does not authorize the display of an automated estimate of the market value of Property (or a hyperlink to such estimate) on MLS participants' internet websites.

D. During the term of this Agreement, Seller may, by written notice to Broker, authorize Broker to enable or disable use of any feature as described in 10.C. above. Broker agrees to update the MLS database accordingly.

11. TYPES OF REAL ESTATE REPRESENTATION - DISCLOSURE AND INFORMED CONSENT.

Seller representation occurs by virtue of this Agreement with Seller's contract to use Broker's services and may also include any cooperating brokers who act on behalf of Seller as subagent of Broker. (Note: Broker may assist a buyer or prospective buyer by performing ministerial acts that are not inconsistent with Broker's duties as Seller's listing agent under this Agreement.)

Buyer representation occurs when buyers contract to use the services of their own broker (known as a buyer representative) to act on their behalf.

FIGURE A.1

Exclusive Right to Sell Listing Agreement (cont.)

Designated representation occurs when a buyer and seller in one transaction are represented by different sales associate(s) affiliated with the same broker. Each of these sales associates, known as a designated representative, represents fully the interests of a different client in the same transaction. Designated representatives are not dual representatives if each represents only the buyer or only the seller in a specific real estate transaction. In the event of designated representatives, each representative shall be bound by client confidentiality requirements, set forth in the CONFIDENTIAL INFORMATION paragraph. The broker remains a dual representative.

☐ Seller does not consent to designated representation and does not allow Property to be shown to a buyer represented by this Broker through another designated representative associated with the firm. **OR**

☐ Seller consents to designated representation and allows Property to be shown to a buyer represented by this Broker through another designated representative associated with the firm.

Dual representation occurs when the same broker and the same sales associate represent both the buyer and seller in one transaction. In the event of dual representation, the broker shall be bound by confidentiality requirements for each client, set forth in the CONFIDENTIAL INFORMATION paragraph.

☐ Seller does not consent to dual representation and Seller does not allow Property to be shown to a buyer represented by this Broker through the same sales associate. **OR**

☐ Seller consents to dual representation and allows Property to be shown to a buyer represented by this Broker through the same sales associate.

An additional disclosure is required before designated or dual representation is to occur for a specific transaction.

Broker will notify other real estate licensees via the MLS whether Seller consents to designated or dual representation.

Non-Agency occurs when the real estate licensee does not represent either party to the real estate transaction and acts to facilitate the transaction by assisting one or both of the parties to reach an agreement, as an independent contractor and without being an advocate for the interest of either party. In the event of non-agency, the real estate licensee would not owe traditional duties to either party, but would still owe the parties duties imposed on all licensees by the Commonwealth of Virginia.

12. **BROKER COMPENSATION.**

A. **Payment.** Seller shall pay Broker in cash total compensation of _____ _____ ("Compensation") if, during the term of this Agreement, anyone produces a buyer ready, willing and able to buy Property.

Compensation is also earned if, within _____ days after the expiration or termination of this Agreement, a contract is ratified with a ready, willing, and able buyer to whom Property had been shown during the term of this Agreement; provided, however, that Compensation need not be paid if a contract is ratified on Property while Property is listed with another real estate company.

B. **Selling Broker.** Broker shall offer a portion of Compensation to the selling broker as indicated:

Buyer Agency Compensation: _____   **OR**

Sub-Agency Compensation: _____   **OR**

Non-Agency Compensation: _____

Exclusive Right to Sell Listing Agreement (cont.)

Note: Compensation may be shown by a percentage of the gross selling price, a definite dollar amount or "N" for no compensation.

Broker's compensation and the sharing of compensation between brokers are not fixed, controlled, recommended or suggested by any multiple listing service or Association of REALTORS®.

C. **Retainer Fee.** Broker acknowledges receipt of a retainer fee in the amount of _____ which ☐ shall **OR** ☐ shall not be subtracted from Compensation. The retainer fee is non-refundable and is earned when paid.

D. **Early Termination.** In the event Seller wishes to terminate this Agreement prior to the end of Listing Period, without good cause, Seller shall pay Broker _____ before Broker's execution of a written release.

13. **CONFIDENTIAL INFORMATION.** Broker shall maintain the confidentiality of all personal and financial information and other matters identified as confidential by the client which were obtained by Broker during the brokerage relationship, unless the client consents in writing to the release of such information or as otherwise provided by law. The obligation of Broker to preserve confidential information continues after termination of the brokerage relationship. Information concerning material defects about Property is not considered confidential information.

14. **AUTHORIZATION TO DISCLOSE OTHER OFFERS.** In response to inquiries from buyers or cooperating brokers, Broker may not disclose, without Seller's authorization, the existence of other written offers on Property. If Seller does give such authorization, Seller acknowledges that Broker and sales associate(s) must disclose whether the offers were obtained by the listing agent, another member of the listing Broker's firm, or by a cooperating broker.

Seller ☐ does **OR** ☐ does not authorize Broker and sales associate(s) to disclose such information to buyers or cooperating brokers.

15. **COMPLIANCE WITH FAIR HOUSING LAWS.** Property shall be shown and made available without regard to race, color, religion, sex, handicap, familial status or national origin as well as all classes protected by the laws of the United States, the Commonwealth of Virginia and applicable local jurisdictions, or by the REALTOR® Code of Ethics.

16. **EMPLOYEE RELOCATION PROGRAM.** Seller is participating in any type of employee relocation program: ☐ Yes **OR** ☐ No.

If "Yes": (a) the program is named: _____
Contact Name _____ Contact Information_____
and (b) terms of the program are: _____
_____

If: "No" or if Seller has failed to list a specific employee relocation program, then Broker shall have no obligation to cooperate with or compensate any undisclosed program.

17. **CONDOMINIUM ASSOCIATION.** Seller represents that Property ☐ is **OR** ☐ is not located within a development which is a Condominium or Cooperative. Condominiums or Cooperatives being offered for sale are subject to the receipt by buyers of the required disclosures, and Seller is responsible for payment of appropriate fees and for providing these disclosure documents to prospective buyers as prescribed in the Condominium Act, Section 55-79.39 et seq., and the Cooperative Act, Section 55-424, et seq., of the Code of Virginia.

The Condominium or Cooperative dues are $ _____ per _____ (frequency of payment).

Special Assessment $ _____ for _____

NVAR – K1336 – rev. 01/13   Page 6 of 10   Seller: _____/_____ Broker: _____/_____

F I G U R E   A.1

Exclusive Right to Sell Listing Agreement (cont.)

Condominium or Cooperative Association Name: _____

Management Company: _____ Phone #: _____

Seller represents that Seller ☐ is **OR** ☐ is not current on all condo association dues and/or special assessments.

18. **PROPERTY OWNER'S ASSOCIATION.** Seller represents that Property ☐ is **OR** ☐ is not located within a development(s) which is subject to the Virginia Property Owners' Association Act, Sections 55-508 through 55-516 of the Code of Virginia. If Property is within such a development, Seller is responsible for payment of the appropriate fees and for providing these disclosure documents to the buyers.

The Property Owners Association dues are $ _____ per _____ (frequency of payment).

Special Assessment $ _____ for _____

Property Owners Association Name: _____

Management Company: _____ Phone #: _____

Seller represents that Seller ☐ is **OR** ☐ is not current on all property owners association dues and/or special assessments.

19. **PROPERTY CONDITION.** Seller acknowledges that Broker has informed Seller of Seller's rights and obligations under the Virginia Residential Property Disclosure Act. Property ☐ is **OR** ☐ is not exempt from the Act. If not exempt, Seller has completed and provided to Broker a Residential Property Disclosure Statement.

Seller acknowledges Broker is required to disclose to prospective buyers all material adverse facts pertaining to the physical condition of Property actually known by Broker. Broker shall not, however, be obligated to discover latent defects in Property or to advise on property condition matters outside the scope of Broker's real estate license. Seller shall indemnify, save, and hold Broker harmless from all claims, complaints, disputes, litigation, judgments and attorney's fees arising from any incorrect information supplied by Seller or from Seller's failure to disclose any material adverse facts.

20. **LEAD-BASED PAINT DISCLOSURE.** Seller represents that the residential dwelling(s) at Property ☐ were **OR** ☐ were not constructed before 1978. If the dwelling(s) were constructed before 1978, Seller is subject to Federal law concerning disclosure of the possible presence of lead-based paint at Property, and Seller acknowledges that Broker has informed Seller of Seller's obligations under the law. If the dwelling(s) were constructed before 1978, unless exempt under 42 U.S.C. 4852(d), Seller has completed and provided to Broker the form, "Sale: Disclosure And Acknowledgment Of Information On Lead-Based Paint And/Or Lead-Based Paint Hazards" or equivalent form.

21. **CURRENT LIENS.** Seller represents to Broker that the below information is true and complete to the best of Seller's information, knowledge and belief:

A. Property is security for a first mortgage or deed of trust loan held by (Lender Name): _____ Account # _____
with an approximate balance of $_____. Lender Phone: _____

B. Property is security for a second mortgage or deed of trust loan held by (Lender Name): _____ Account # _____
with an approximate balance of $_____. Lender Phone: _____

C. Property is security for a line of credit or home equity line of credit held by (Lender Name): _____ Account # _____
with an approximate balance of $_____. Lender Phone: _____

NVAR – K1336 – rev. 01/13   Page 7 of 10   Seller: _____/_____   Broker: _____/_____

Exclusive Right to Sell Listing Agreement (cont.)

Check all that are applicable:

D. ☐ Property is not encumbered by any mortgage or deed of trust.

E. ☐ Seller is current on all payments for the loans identified in items A, B, and C above.

F. ☐ Seller is not in default and has not received any notice(s) from the holder(s) of any loan identified in items A, B, and C above, or from any other lien holder of any kind, regarding a default under any loan, threatened foreclosure, notice of foreclosure, or the filing of foreclosure.

G. ☐ There are no liens secured against Property for Federal, State or local income taxes; unpaid real property taxes; or unpaid condominium or homeowners' association fees.

H. ☐ There are no judgments against Seller (including each owner for jointly held property). Seller has no knowledge of any matter that might result in a judgment that may potentially affect Property.

I. ☐ Seller has not filed for bankruptcy protection under Federal law and is not contemplating doing so during the term of this Agreement.

During the term of this Agreement, should any change occur with respect to answers A through I above, Seller shall immediately notify Broker and sales associate/listing agent, in writing, of such change.

22. SELLER FINANCING. Seller ☐ does **OR** ☐ does not agree to offer seller financing by providing a _____ deed of trust loan in the amount of $_____ with further terms to be negotiated.

23. CLOSING COSTS. Fees for the preparation of the deed of conveyance, that portion of the settlement agent's fee billed to Seller, costs of releasing existing encumbrances, Seller's legal fees, Grantor's Tax, and any other proper charges assessed to Seller will be paid by Seller unless provided otherwise in the sales contract.

The "Seller's Estimated Cost of Settlement" form ☐ is **OR** ☐ is not attached. These estimates are for informational purposes only and will change based upon the terms and conditions of the purchase offer.

> **Seller's Proceeds:** The Seller acknowledges that Seller's proceeds may not be available at the time of settlement. The receipt of proceeds may be subject to the **Virginia Wet Settlement Act**, and may be subject to other laws, rules and regulations (e.g. Virginia estate statutes and the **Foreign Investment Real Property Tax Act - FIRPTA**).
>
> **Seller is advised to seek legal and/or financial advice concerning these matters.**

24. IRS/FIRPTA. Section 1445 of the Internal Revenue Service (IRS) Code may require the settlement agent to report the gross sales price, Seller's federal tax identification number and other required information to the IRS. Seller will provide to the settlement agent such information upon request. In certain situations, the IRS requires a percentage (currently 10%) of the sales price to be withheld from Seller's proceeds if Seller is a foreign person for purposes of U.S. income taxation. A foreign person includes, but is not limited to, non-resident aliens, foreign corporations, foreign partnerships, foreign trusts or foreign estates.

Seller represents that Seller ☐ is **OR** ☐ is not, a foreign person for purposes of U.S. income taxation.

25. MISCELLANEOUS PROVISIONS.

A. Seller Representations and Warranties.

Seller is aware that Seller may be responsible for failing to disclose information and/or misrepresenting the condition of Property. Seller warrants that:

FIGURE A.1

Exclusive Right to Sell Listing Agreement (cont.)

1) Seller has capacity to convey good and marketable title to Property by general warranty deed and represents that Property is insurable by a licensed title insurance company with no additional risk premium.

2) Seller is not a party to a listing agreement with another broker for the sale, exchange or lease of Property.

3) No person or entity has the right to purchase, lease or acquire Property, by virtue of an option, right of first refusal or otherwise.

4) Seller ☐ is **OR** ☐ is not a licensed (active/inactive) real estate agent/broker.

5) Seller ☐ has **OR** ☐ has no knowledge of the existence, removal or abandonment of any underground storage tank on Property.

6) Property ☐ is **OR** ☐ is not tenant-occupied.

B. Access to Property. Seller shall provide keys to Broker for access to Property to facilitate Broker's duties under this Agreement. If Property is currently tenant-occupied, Seller shall provide Broker with any current lease documents and contact information for current tenant, and shall use best efforts to obtain the full cooperation of current tenants, in connection with showings and inspections of Property.

C. Seller Assumption of Risk.

1) Seller retains full responsibility for Property, including all utilities, maintenance, physical security and liability until title to Property is transferred to purchaser. Seller is advised to take all precautions for safekeeping of valuables and to maintain appropriate property and liability insurance through Seller's own insurance company.

Broker is not responsible for the security of Property or for inspecting Property on any periodic basis. If Property is or becomes vacant during the Listing Period, Seller is advised to notify Seller's home owner's insurance company and request a "Vacancy Clause" to cover Property.

2) In consideration of the use of Broker's services and facilities and of the facilities of any Multiple Listing Service, Seller and Seller's heirs and assigns hereby release Broker, Broker's designated agents, sub-agents, sales associates and employees, any Multiple Listing Service and the Directors, Officers and employees thereof, including officials of any parent Association of REALTORS®, except for malfeasance on the part of such parties, from any liability to Seller for vandalism, theft or damage of any nature whatsoever to Property or its contents that occurs during the Listing Period. Seller waives any and all rights, claims and causes of actions against them and holds them harmless for any property damage or personal injury arising from the use or access to Property by any persons during the Listing Period.

D. Appropriate Professional Advice. Broker can counsel on real estate matters, but if Seller desires legal advice, Seller is advised to seek legal counsel. Seller is advised further to seek appropriate professional advice concerning, but not limited to, property or tax and insurance matters.

E. Subsequent Offers After Contract Acceptance. After a sales contract has been ratified on Property, Broker recommends Seller obtain the advice of legal counsel prior to acceptance of any subsequent offer.

F. Governing Law. The laws of Virginia shall govern the validity, interpretation and enforcement of this Agreement.

G. Binding Agreement. This Agreement will be binding upon the parties, and each of their respective heirs, executors, administrators, successors and permitted assigns. The provisions hereof will survive the sale of Property and will not be merged therein. This

FIGURE A.1

Exclusive Right to Sell Listing Agreement (cont.)

Agreement, unless amended in writing by the parties, contains the final and entire agreement and the parties will not be bound by any terms, conditions, oral statements, warranties or representations not herein contained.

26. **ATTORNEY'S FEES.** If any Party breaches this Agreement and a non-breaching Party retains legal counsel to enforce its rights hereunder, the non-breaching Party shall be entitled to recover against the breaching Party, in addition to any other damages recoverable against any breaching Party, all of its reasonable Legal Expenses incurred in enforcing its right under this Agreement, whether or not suit is filed, and in obtaining, enforcing and/or defending any judgment related thereto. Should any tribunal of competent jurisdiction determine that more than one Party to the dispute has breached this Agreement, then all such breaching Parties shall bear their own costs, unless the tribunal determines that one or more of the Parties is a "Substantially Prevailing Party", in which case any such Substantially Prevailing Party shall be entitled to recover from any of the breaching Parties, in addition to any other damages recoverable against any breaching Party, all of its reasonable Legal Expenses incurred in enforcing its rights under this Agreement, whether or not suit is filed, and in obtaining, enforcing and/or defending any judgment related thereto. "Party" as used in this paragraph includes any third party beneficiary identified herein. "Legal Expenses" as used in this paragraph includes attorney fees, court costs, and litigation expenses, if any, including, but not limited to, expert witness fees and court reporter fees.

27. **ADDITIONAL TERMS.** _____

_____
_____
_____
_____
_____

_____/_____   _____/_____
Date   Seller   Date   Broker/Sales Manager

_____/_____
Date   Seller

_____/_____
Date   Seller

_____/_____
Date   Seller

****

Sales Associate Contact Information

Sales Associate (Listing Agent): _____

Phone: (W) _____ (Cell) _____

Email: _____ Fax: _____

2013 Northern Virginia Association of REALTORS®, Inc. ©

B

Exclusive Right to Represent Purchaser Agreement

FIGURE B.1

Exclusive Right to Represent Purchaser Agreement

EXCLUSIVE RIGHT TO REPRESENT PURCHASER AGREEMENT

This Exclusive Right to Represent Purchaser Agreement ("Agreement") is made on_____
_____ (Date) by and between _____ ("Purchaser")
and (Insert Firm Name) _____("Broker").

1. **APPOINTMENT OF BROKER.** In consideration of services and facilities, Broker is
   hereby granted the right to represent Purchaser in the acquisition of real property.

2. **PURCHASER'S REPRESENTATIONS.** Purchaser represents that as of the
   commencement date of this Agreement, Purchaser is not a party to a purchaser representation
   agreement with any other brokerage firm. Purchaser further represents that Purchaser has
   disclosed to Broker information about any properties that Purchaser has previously visited at
   any new homes communities or resale open houses, or that Purchaser has been shown by any
   other real estate sales associate(s) in any area where Purchaser seeks to acquire property
   under this Agreement.

3. **NOTICES.** All notifications and amendments under this Agreement shall be in writing and
   shall be delivered using the contact information below.

   Purchaser
   Mailing Address:_____
   City, State, and Zip Code:_____
   Phone: (H)_____ (W) _____ (Cell)_____
   Email: _____ Fax: _____
   Broker (Firm)
   Mailing Address:_____
   City, State, and Zip Code:_____
   Phone: (W) _____(Cell)_____
   Email: _____ Fax: _____

4. **TERM.** This Agreement commences when signed and, subject to the COMPENSATION
   paragraph, expires at 11:59 p.m. on _____.

5. **RETAINER FEE.** Broker acknowledges receipt of a retainer fee in the amount of
   _____, which ☐ shall **OR** ☐ shall not be subtracted from any compensation due
   Broker under this Agreement. The retainer fee is non-refundable and is earned when paid.

6. **BROKER'S DUTIES.** Broker shall promote the interests of Purchaser by: (a) performing
   the terms of the brokerage agreement; (b) seeking a property at a price and terms acceptable
   to Purchaser; (c) presenting in a timely manner all written offers or counteroffers to and from
   Purchaser; (d) disclosing to Purchaser all material facts related to the property or concerning
   the transaction of which they have actual knowledge; (e) accounting for in a timely manner
   all money and property received in which Purchaser has or may have an interest. Unless
   otherwise provided by law or Purchaser consents in writing to the release of the information,
   Broker shall maintain the confidentiality of all personal and financial information and other
   matters identified as confidential by Purchaser, if that information is received from Purchaser
   during the brokerage relationship. In satisfying these duties, Broker shall exercise ordinary
   care, comply with all applicable laws and regulations, treat all prospective sellers honestly
   and not knowingly give them false information. In addition, Broker may: show the same
   property to other purchasers; represent other purchasers on the same or different properties;
   represent sellers relative to other properties; or provide assistance to a seller or prospective
   seller by performing ministerial acts that are not inconsistent with Broker's duties under this
   Agreement.

FIGURE B.1

Exclusive Right to Represent Purchaser Agreement (cont.)

7. **PURCHASER'S DUTIES**. Purchaser shall: (a) work exclusively with Broker during the term of this Agreement; (b) pay Broker, directly or indirectly, the compensation set forth below; (c) comply with the reasonable requests of Broker to supply any pertinent financial or personal data needed to fulfill the terms of this Agreement; (d) be available during Broker's regular working hours to view properties.

8. **PURPOSE**. Purchaser is retaining Broker to acquire the following type of property: _____
_____

9. **COMPENSATION**. In consideration of the time and effort expended by Broker on behalf of Purchaser, and in further consideration of the advice and counsel provided to Purchaser, Purchaser shall pay compensation ("Broker's Fee") to Broker as described below. Broker's Fee, less the retainer fee if so indicated in the RETAINER FEE paragraph above, shall be earned, due and payable under any of these circumstances whether the transaction is consummated through the services of Broker or otherwise:

   A. If Purchaser enters into a contract to acquire real property during the term of this Agreement and goes to settlement on that contract any time thereafter; **OR**

   B. If, within _____ days after expiration or termination of this Agreement, Purchaser enters into a contract to acquire real property that has been described to or shown to Purchaser by Broker during the term of this Agreement, unless Purchaser has entered into a subsequent Purchaser Broker Agreement agreement with another real estate broker; **OR**

   C. If, having entered into an enforceable contract to acquire real property during the term of this Agreement, Purchaser defaults under the terms of that contract.

   Broker's Fee shall be _____. If the seller or the seller's representative offers compensation to Broker, then Purchaser authorizes Broker to receive such compensation and the amount of such compensation shall be credited against Purchaser's obligation to pay Broker's Fee. Broker may retain any additional compensation offered by the seller or seller's representative, even if this causes the compensation paid to Broker to exceed the fees specified above. In no case shall Compensation be less than the fees specified above.

   Any obligation incurred under this Agreement on the part of Purchaser to pay Broker's Fee shall survive the term of this Agreement.

10. **EMPLOYEE RELOCATION PROGRAM.** Purchaser is participating in any type of employee relocation program ☐ Yes **OR** ☐ No.

    If "Yes": (a) the program is named: _____,
    Contact Name: _____ Contact Information: _____
    and (b) terms of the program are: _____
    _____

    If "No" or Purchaser has failed to list a specific employee relocation program, then Broker shall have no obligation to cooperate with or compensate any undisclosed program.

11. **TYPES OF REAL ESTATE REPRESENTATION - DISCLOSURE AND INFORMED CONSENT.**

    Seller representation occurs when sellers contract to use the services of their own broker (known as a listing agent) to act on their behalf.

FIGURE B.1

Exclusive Right to Represent Purchaser Agreement (cont.)

Purchaser representation occurs by virtue of this Agreement. (Note: Broker may assist a seller or prospective seller by performing ministerial acts that are not inconsistent with Broker's duties as Purchaser's agent under this Agreement.)

Designated representation occurs when a purchaser and seller in one transaction are represented by different sales associate(s) affiliated with the same broker. Each of these sales associates, known as a designated representative, represents fully the interests of a different client in the same transaction. Designated representatives are not dual representatives if each represents only the purchaser or only the seller in a specific real estate transaction. In the event of designated representatives, each representative shall be bound by client confidentiality requirements, set forth in the BROKER'S DUTIES paragraph. The broker remains a dual representative.

☐ Purchaser does not consent to designated representation thus Purchaser does not allow Broker to show properties owned by a seller represented by this Broker through another designated representative associated with the firm **OR**

☐ Purchaser consents to designated representation and the Purchaser allows Broker to show properties owned by a seller represented by this Broker through another designated representative associated with the firm.

Dual representation occurs when the same Broker and the same sales associate represent both the purchaser and seller in one transaction. In the event of dual representation, Broker shall be bound by confidentiality requirements for each client, set forth in the BROKER'S DUTIES paragraph.

☐ Purchaser does not consent to dual representation thus Purchaser does not allow Broker to show properties owned by a seller represented by this Broker through the same representative **OR**

☐ Purchaser consents to dual representation and thus Purchaser allows Broker to show properties owned by a seller represented by this Broker through the same representative.

An additional disclosure is required before designated or dual representation is to occur for a specific transaction.

Non-Agency occurs when the real estate licensee does not represent either party to the real estate transaction and acts to facilitate the transaction by assisting one or both parties to reach an agreement, as an independent contractor and without being an advocate for the interest of either party. In the event of non-agency, the real estate licensee would not owe traditional duties to either party, but would still owe the parties duties imposed on all licensees by the Commonwealth of Virginia.

12. **DISCLAIMER.** Purchaser acknowledges that Broker is being retained solely as a real estate agent and not as an attorney, tax advisor, lender, appraiser, surveyor, structural engineer, mold or air quality expert, home inspector or other professional service provider. Purchaser is advised to seek professional advice concerning the condition of the property or concerning legal and tax matters. Purchaser should exercise whatever due diligence Purchaser deems necessary with respect to information on any sexual offenders registered under Chapter 9 of Title 9.1 of the Code of Virginia. Such information may be obtained by contacting your local police department or the Department of State Police, Central Criminal Records Exchange, at (804)674-2000 or http://sex-offender.vsp.virginia.gov/sor/.

13. **COMPLIANCE WITH FAIR HOUSING LAWS.** Property shall be shown and made available without regard to race, color, religion, sex, handicap, familial status or national origin as well as all classes protected by the laws of the United States, the Commonwealth of Virginia and applicable local jurisdictions, or by the REALTOR® Code of Ethics.

14. **OTHER PROVISIONS.** _____

_____

F I G U R E   B.1

Exclusive Right to Represent Purchaser Agreement (cont.)

_____

_____

15. **MISCELLANEOUS.** This Agreement, any exhibits and any addenda signed by the parties constitute the entire agreement between the parties and supersedes any other written or oral agreements between the parties. This Agreement can only be modified in writing when signed by both parties. The laws of Virginia shall govern the validity, interpretation and enforcement of the Agreement.

16. **ATTORNEY'S FEES.** If any Party breaches this Agreement and a non-breaching Party retains legal counsel to enforce its rights hereunder, the non-breaching Party shall be entitled to recover against the breaching Party, in addition to any other damages recoverable against any breaching Party, all of its reasonable Legal Expenses incurred in enforcing its right under this Agreement, whether or not suit is filed, and in obtaining, enforcing and/or defending any judgment related thereto. Should any tribunal of competent jurisdiction determine that more than one Party to the dispute has breached this Agreement, then all such breaching Parties shall bear their own costs, unless the tribunal determines that one or more of the Parties is a "Substantially Prevailing Party", in which case any such Substantially Prevailing Party shall be entitled to recover from any of the breaching Parties, in addition to any other damages recoverable against any breaching Party, all of its reasonable Legal Expenses incurred in enforcing its rights under this Agreement, whether or not suit is filed, and in obtaining, enforcing and/or defending any judgment related thereto. "Party" as used in this paragraph includes any third party beneficiary identified herein. "Legal Expenses" as used in this paragraph includes attorney fees, court costs, and litigation expenses, if any, including, but not limited to, expert witness fees and court reporter fees.

The Buyer ☐ does **OR** ☐ does not hold an active or inactive Virginia real estate license.

(NOTE: Purchaser should consult with Sales Associate before visiting any resale or new homes or contacting any other Real Estate Associates representing sellers, to avoid the possibility of confusion over the brokerage relationship and misunderstandings about liability for compensation.)

_____/_____   _____/_____
Date   Purchaser   Date   Broker/Sales Manager
_____/_____
Date   Purchaser
_____/_____
Date   Purchaser
_____/_____
Date   Purchaser

****

Sales Associate Contact Information

Sales Associate (Purchaser's Agent): _____

Phone: (W) _____   (Cell) _____

Email: _____   Fax: _____

REALTOR®

© 2013 Northern Virginia Association of REALTORS®, Inc.

EQUAL HOUSING OPPORTUNITY

NVAR – K1338 – rev. 01/13   Page 4 of 4   Purchaser: _____/_____   Broker: _____

Information Sources

Common Interest Community (CIC) Board
9960 Mayland Drive, Suite 400
Richmond, VA 23233-1485
804-367-0362
www.dpor.virginia.gov/Boards/CIC-Board/

Department of Professional and Occupational Regulation (DPOR)
9960 Mayland Drive, Suite 400
Richmond, VA 23233-1485
804-367-8500
www.dpor.virginia.gov

Virginia Association of REALTORS® (VAR)
10231 Telegraph Road
Glen Allen, VA 23059
804-264-5033
www.varealtor.com

Virginia Department of Taxation
Office of Consumer Service
P.O. Box 1115
Richmond, VA 23218-1115
804-367-8031
www.tax.virginia.gov

Virginia Fair Housing Office
9960 Mayland Drive, Suite 400
Richmond, VA 23233-1463
804-367-8530 or 888-551-3247
fairhousing@dpor.virginia.gov
www.dpor.virginia.gov/FairHousing/

Virginia Housing Development Authority (VHDA)
601 S. Belvidere Street
Richmond, VA 23220
804-782-1986 or 877-834-2123
www.vhda.com

Virginia Real Estate Board (REB)
9960 Mayland Drive, Suite 400
Richmond, VA 23233-1485
804-367-8552
www.dpor.virginia.gov/Boards/Real-Estate/

Virginia State Bar
1111 East Main Street, Suite 700
Richmond, VA 23219-3565
804-775-0500
www.vsb.org

Virginia State Police—Sex Offender and Crimes Against Minors Registry
http://sex-offender.vsp.virginia.gov/sor/

U.S. Department of Housing and Urban Development
451 7th St. SW
Washington, D.C. 20410
202-708-1112
www.hud.gov

U.S. Environmental Protection Agency—Lead
www2.epa.gov/lead/

PRACTICE EXAMINATION

1. Two salespersons work for the same broker. One represents the seller and the other represents the buyer in the same transaction. In this situation, each of the salespersons will be assigned as
   a. an associate broker.
   b. a subagent.
   c. a single agent.
   d. a designated agent.

2. Which of the following must hold a real estate license in Virginia?
   a. An attorney preparing an abstract of title
   b. A local multiple-listing service company
   c. An officer of a limited liability company who specializes in listing commercial property
   d. A business executive selling her company's surplus acreage

3. The duties that an agent owes to his client are established by
   a. statute.
   b. common law.
   c. the agent's broker.
   d. the agent's client.

4. All of the following are ways to terminate a brokerage relationship *EXCEPT*
   a. default by either party.
   b. death of the salesperson.
   c. expiration of the agreement.
   d. mutual agreement by the parties to terminate.

5. The residential property disclosure statement that contains notice to purchasers regarding seller's representations regarding the property is now found
   a. in the Code of Virginia.
   b. in the REB Rules and Regulations.
   c. on the REB website.
   d. in the Virginia Administrative Code.

6. If the buyer receives the required residential property disclosure statement three days after the contract is signed, when can the buyer terminate the contract?
   a. Within 15 days of date sent, if emailed
   b. Within 10 days, if hand-delivered
   c. Within 5 days of postmark, if mailed
   d. Under the doctrine of caveat emptor, cannot terminate the contract

7. If a married woman with three children dies intestate, how will her property be distributed?
   a. To her husband under laws of dower and curtesy
   b. One-third to her husband, the remaining two-thirds to her children equally
   c. One-half to her husband, the other half to her children equally
   d. Two-thirds to her husband, the remaining third to her children equally

8. What is the total maximum value of an unmarried homeowner's homestead exemption on a $475,000 property?
   a. $4,750
   b. $5,000
   c. $237,500
   d. $475,000

9. A man died, leaving his wife $10,000 and all of the rest of his property to his two children. The wife renounced the will in order to claim her elective share of his augmented estate. She will now be entitled to
   a. all of his estate.
   b. one-half of his estate.
   c. one-third of his estate.
   d. none of his estate, but she may continue to live there.

10. Doctors A, B, and C purchased an office building as joint tenants. Doctor A sells his tenancy to doctor D. Which of the following is *TRUE* of this situation?

    a. Doctors B, C, and D are now joint tenants.

    b. Doctors B, C, and D are now tenants in common.

    c. Doctors B and C are tenants in common with a joint tenancy with doctor D.

    d. Doctors B and C are joint tenants with a tenancy in common with doctor D.

11. Two individuals own property as tenants in common. When one dies intestate, his interest passes to

    a. his heirs.

    b. the other party as a sole owner.

    c. his heirs with the other party as a joint tenant.

    d. his heirs if the property is sold.

12. The owner of an individual unit in a condominium building wants to sell it. All of the following documents must be included in the Disclosure Packet *EXCEPT*

    a. a statement of all assets and fees currently imposed.

    b. a copy of the current budget.

    c. a copy of the current bylaws and rules and regulations.

    d. a plat map indicating the location of the condominium building.

13. A couple has recently signed a contract to purchase a town house in a development governed by a Property Owner's Association. They will be able to cancel this contract if they

    a. change their minds.

    b. cancel any time prior to closing.

    c. cancel within 3 days of receiving the POA disclosure packet.

    d. cancel within 14 days of receiving the POA disclosure packet.

14. The following is what kind of legal description? *All those certain lots, pieces or parcels of land, situated in the city of Roanoke, Virginia, known, numbered and designated on the Plat of Hampton Square and recorded in the clerk's office of the Circuit Court of the City of Roanoke, Virginia, in Map Book 26, page 7, as Lots No. 9 and 10.*

    a. Metes and bounds

    b. Rectangular survey

    c. Government survey

    d. Lot and block

15. The *MOST* common description of real estate in Virginia is a combination of

    a. metes and bounds and government survey.

    b. metes and bounds and lot and block.

    c. lot and block and government survey.

    d. rectangular survey and government survey.

16. If a contractor records a mechanic's memorandum of lien on September 15, 2014, he must file a suit to enforce it by

    a. October 15, 2014.

    b. December 31, 2014.

    c. March 15, 2015.

    d. September 15, 2015.

17. If all of the following liens are recorded against a property and the bank forecloses, the first to be paid will be the

    a. real estate tax lien.

    b. mechanic's lien.

    c. deed of trust lien.

    d. vendor's lien.

18. A man owns a house in severalty and wishes to sell it. His broker tells him that his wife will need to sign the contract even though she does not own the property because the wife is required to

    a. sign the contract under the Statute of Frauds.

    b. sign the contract to convert the equitable title into legal title.

    c. sign the contract so that the title is marketable.

    d. release any future interest in the property she might hold.

19. An implied warranty against structural defects on new construction continues for
    a. six months after the date of transfer of title or the buyer's taking possession.
    b. one year after the date of transfer of title or the buyer's taking possession.
    c. two years after the date of transfer of title or the buyer's taking possession.
    d. five years after the date of transfer of title or the buyer's taking possession.

20. All of the following are requirements for a valid deed EXCEPT
    a. the signature of the grantee.
    b. consideration.
    c. accurate legal description of the property.
    d. delivery and acceptance of the deed.

21. Establishing title to a property through adverse possession requires
    a. use of the property with the knowledge of the owner.
    b. 20 years of possession.
    c. tacking over a 15-year period.
    d. hostile and continuous use of the property.

22. An elderly lady was very careful to execute a will leaving her beachfront condominium to her favorite niece. The niece will receive title to the property
    a. after the will has gone through probate court.
    b. anytime she wants to file with the clerk's office.
    c. immediately after the will is read.
    d. as soon as she pays the next month's condo fee.

23. The Virginia requirement that a deed of trust be recorded and all settlement proceeds be distributed within two days of the date of settlement is covered under
    a. the Fair Lending Act.
    b. the Residential Deed of Trust Act.
    c. the Statute of Frauds.
    d. the Wet Settlement Act.

24. All of the following information is found on a title report EXCEPT
    a. easements and covenants.
    b. buyer's full legal name.
    c. status of taxes.
    d. existing lenders.

25. A gap in the chain of title could be caused by any of the following EXCEPT
    a. a deed for one transfer of the property was never recorded.
    b. the seller was divorced in a foreign country.
    c. the name of the party on the deed was changed but never recorded.
    d. the property was sold to a relative for $1 with a recorded deed.

26. Under Virginia Real Estate License Law, an independent contractor is
    a. anyone practicing real estate in Virginia.
    b. a salesperson who must pay federal taxes on an estimated quarterly basis.
    c. a licensee representing a client according to a written agreement and not as a standard agent.
    d. a person contracted with to add a deck to the property.

27. The members of the Real Estate Board are
    a. elected by the public.
    b. selected by the Virginia Association of REALTORS®.
    c. appointed by the governor.
    d. volunteers from real estate community.

28. A young man completes his real estate salesperson course on June 20, 2011. He then takes and passes the Virginia licensing exam on July 15, 2014. To avoid having to retake the exam, he must apply for his license by
    a. December 20, 2014.
    b. January 15, 2015.
    c. June 20, 2015.
    d. July 14, 2015.

29. If a licensee is found guilty of a violation of the license law or rules and regulations, the Real Estate Board may take all of the following disciplinary actions *EXCEPT*
    a. impose a prison sentence of no more than one year.
    b. levy fines.
    c. deny license renewal.
    d. suspend or revoke a license.

30. The Real Estate Board's activities include which of the following?
    a. Arbitrate disputes between salespersons and brokers
    b. Issue real estate licenses
    c. Recommend commission rates and commission splits
    d. Approve standardized listing agreements and sales contracts

31. A licensee's license is about to expire, so she signs up for some continuing education classes. She takes two hours of Virginia real estate laws and regulations, three hours of ethics and standards of conduct, two hours of real estate taxes, and two hours of escrow requirements. Assuming she successfully completes these courses, will she have met her renewal education requirements?
    a. Yes, because she has completed at least eight hours of continuing education
    b. No, because she has failed to take a course on federal real estate laws
    c. No, because she has failed to take a course on the Americans with Disabilities Act
    d. No, because she has failed to take the mandatory 8 hours, which includes a course on fair housing laws, and she has not completed a total of 16 hours of continuing education

32. A licensee accidentally let his salesperson's license expire, but two months later is ready to renew it. He will need to send the Real Estate Board the current annual fee for
    a. a salesperson renewal.
    b. reinstatement.
    c. renewal plus the current fee for reinstatement.
    d. renewal plus reinstatement plus $100 fine.

33. As of July 2009, the requirement for licensure is that all applicants must
    a. have a college degree.
    b. submit a set of fingerprints.
    c. be at least 21 years old.
    d. achieve a grade of 90% or better on the required education course.

34. A salesperson decides to leave one brokerage firm and work at another firm. She will need to
    a. file a Change of Brokerage form with the REB.
    b. give her license to her new broker.
    c. fill out the application for the change, obtain the new broker's signature, and send with appropriate fee to the REB.
    d. file a Termination of Brokerage form with the REB.

35. A licensee is currently holding her salesperson's license in inactive status. She decides to sell her home with the help of a local brokerage firm. Should she disclose her license status to potential buyers?
    a. Yes, because disclosure is required regardless of an inactive license status
    b. No, because the local brokerage firm will be earning the commission from the sale
    c. No, because disclosure is not required when a licensee sells her own home
    d. No, because disclosure is not required when a license is inactive

36. A salesperson finds a buyer for a home he has listed. The buyer gives him an earnest money cashier's check for $2,000. When a sales contract is ratified, what should the salesperson do with the check?
    a. Keep it until closing
    b. Deposit it in his escrow account within three business banking days
    c. Deposit it in his escrow account within five business banking days
    d. Immediately give it to his broker

37. The name of the broker must appear in all advertising *EXCEPT*

    a. an open house ad placed by a salesperson in the local newspaper.

    b. a For Rent ad placed on a grocery store bulletin board by a salesperson.

    c. a cable TV ad paid for by a salesperson.

    d. a salesperson selling own home as a For Sale By Owner with disclosure that owner is licensed.

38. If the Real Estate Transaction Recovery Fund falls below $400,000, how much money may the Real Estate Board assess each licensee?

    a. $20 from each salesperson; $40 from each broker

    b. $20 from each inactive licensee; $40 from each active licensee

    c. $20 from each salesperson and broker, inactive or active

    d. $40 from each salesperson and broker, inactive or active

39. All of the following actions are considered improper delivery of instruments *EXCEPT*

    a. failing to promptly deliver complete and legible copies of any written contracts to each party in a transaction.

    b. failing to maintain all signed documents for a period of three years.

    c. failing to deliver a complete and accurate statement of money received and disbursed by a licensee.

    d. failing to provide timely, written notice of any material change in the transaction to all parties.

40. Which of the following statements is *TRUE* regarding institutional financing in Virginia?

    a. Mortgage loans, rather than deeds of trust, are the instruments primarily used in residential sales transactions.

    b. VA and FHA notes require notarization to be valid.

    c. Late charges on a loan may not exceed 3% of the installment due.

    d. Due-on-sale clauses are prohibited in Virginia.

41. One of the primary functions of the Virginia Housing Development Authority (VHDA) is to

    a. build housing for low/moderate-income people.

    b. research new methods of housing development.

    c. provide housing financing for low- and moderate-income residents of Virginia.

    d. enforce Fair Housing and RESPA regulations.

42. A foreclosure of a deed of trust could be achieved without court action or sale of the property through which of the following?

    a. Strict foreclosure

    b. Deed in lieu of foreclosure

    c. Trustee sale

    d. Equitable foreclosure

43. A landlord has just purchased a rental property that has four months to go on the current lease. The present tenants now have the right to

    a. continue their lease under current terms.

    b. move out immediately.

    c. sue the former owner for breaking the terms of their lease.

    d. demand repainting and new carpet by the new owner.

44. A tenant entered into a one-year lease on October 1, 2014, with the right to continue on a month-to-month basis after the lease expires. He gave the landlord a security deposit. In accordance with the terms of the lease, the tenant gives proper notice and vacates the property on December 31, 2015. How much interest will accrue on the security deposit?

    a. None

    b. 2 months' interest

    c. 12 months' interest

    d. 15 months' interest

45. The Virginia Residential Landlord and Tenant Act protects the rights of both landlords and tenants and applies to

    a. all properties advertised for rent.

    b. hotels offering two-week rentals.

    c. all apartment building rentals.

    d. occupancy by a property manager employed by the landlord.

46. If a tenant leaves one couch and two chairs in his apartment after the lease has ended, is the landlord allowed to sell them?

    a. Yes, provided the tenant is given 10 days' written notice, the landlord may sell them.

    b. Yes, within one week of the lease's termination date, the landlord may sell them.

    c. No, Virginia includes a nonabandoned property clause in all leases.

    d. No, the furniture remains the property of the tenant.

47. Which one of the following is protected by Virginia's Fair Housing Law?

    a. A 58-year-old AIDS victim

    b. A 45-year-old homosexual

    c. A 35-year-old transvestite

    d. A 51-year-old veteran

48. A landlord will be in violation of the Virginia Fair Housing Law if he refuses to rent his two-bedroom apartment for any of the following reasons EXCEPT

    a. the couple applying are from Nigeria.

    b. the couple has two small children.

    c. the applicant is 65 years old.

    d. the applicants do not have adequate income.

49. All of the following apartment building accommodations for handicapped persons are considered reasonable requests EXCEPT

    a. allowing a blind person to have an assistance monkey in a no pets building.

    b. allowing a paralyzed person to install railings in her bathroom.

    c. removing walls along a corridor of a common area to make the hallway wide enough for wheelchair access.

    d. giving parking preferences to a wheelchair-bound person.

50. If an alleged fair housing discriminatory act has taken place, the injured party must file a complaint with the REB within

    a. three months.

    b. six months.

    c. nine months.

    d. one year.

51. An important change in agency law that took place as of July 1, 2012, is that

    a. dual agency will no longer be allowed.

    b. all brokerage agreements must be in writing.

    c. disclosure of limited service representation will no longer require a list of duties to be performed.

    d. designated agency will be assumed and not require written disclosure.

52. An agent is holding an open house on her new listing and is approached by a potential buyer. She is able to proceed with the transaction under all of the following circumstances EXCEPT

    a. disclose her brokerage relationship to the seller and treat the buyer as a customer.

    b. explain disclosed dual agency to both the potential buyer and the seller and proceed if written permission is received.

    c. request her broker to designate another agent to represent the buyer.

    d. proceed with the sale working in the best interests of both parties.

53. A salesperson has recently completed the education requirements and passed the state broker's exam. She will now have continuing education requirements of

    a. 30 hours new licensee training.

    b. 16 hours (8 required, 8 elective).

    c. 24 hours (8 required, 8 elective, 8 related to broker supervision and management).

    d. 40 hours (16 required, 24 broker supervision and management).

54. A man and a woman recently married. It is a second marriage for the wife, and they have agreed that she should be allowed to will her share of the property to her grandchildren upon her demise. They should take title as

    a. tenancy by the entirety.

    b. tenants in common.

    c. joint tenants.

    d. community property.

55. A landlord has a house for rent and placed the following ad on the supermarket bulletin board: "SF house for rent, $2,200 per month, no children, no smokers, no old folks." If the landlord is found guilty of discrimination, he could be fined

a. $25,000.
b. $50,000.
c. $75,000.
d. $100,000.

56. VHDA funding comes from

a. Fannie Mae.
b. the U.S. government.
c. the Virginia General Fund.
d. bonds sold through the private sector.

57. A landlord has lived in Virginia since moving here from Pennsylvania 30 years ago and has amassed a portfolio of 20 rental properties. He is now returning to Pennsylvania and will manage his holdings from there. Virginia will require him to

a. leave a forwarding address.
b. sell all of his properties.
c. place his properties with a nonresident trust management firm.
d. appoint a resident agent.

58. The Virginia Residential Landlord Tenant Act (VRLTA) now applies to any landlord who has

a. two rental properties.
b. more than two rental properties.
c. four rental properties.
d. 10 rental properties.

59. A landlord asks for two months' security deposit on all rentals and requires all tenants to pay the cost of renters and damage insurance (premiums) available from the landlord. If the premiums total $100 per year per unit and all units rent for $995 per month, what is the maximum the landlord can receive as a security deposit?

a. $1,790
b. $1,890
c. $1,990
d. $2,090

60. A landlord could safely decline renting to

a. a wheelchair-bound person wishing to live on the top floor of a three-story walkup.
b. a handicapped person requiring major modifications at the landlord's expense for living and accessibility.
c. an ex-drug user currently in a rehab program.
d. a blind veteran with no guide dog.

61. The Virginia Fair Housing Board is empowered to do all of the following EXCEPT

a. initiate and receive complaints.
b. conduct investigations.
c. refer charges to the attorney general.
d. discipline real estate licensees.

62. A small company wants to hire a licensed agent to help them find a specific property, but it does NOT want to establish an agency relationship with him. The licensed agent will probably work for the company as

a. a buyer agent.
b. a dual agent.
c. a standard agent.
d. an independent contractor according to a written contract between the company and the agent.

63. A young college graduate is thinking about getting a real estate license. His plan is to affiliate with a broker and use the marketing skills of his unlicensed wife to expand his practice. The unlicensed wife will be able to

a. show properties when the agent is available.
b. show properties when the agent is not available.
c. assist one of the agent's buyers in filling out a contract.
d. design and mail brochures for the agent.

64. An individual wants to sell his house himself and is NOT licensed. He will be required to

a. make full disclosure that he is not licensed.
b. obtain a temporary license to sell his own house.
c. hire a licensed agent to sell his own house.
d. avoid any discriminatory advertising.

65. A licensee wants to sell her house herself. She must
    a. disclose that she is licensed.
    b. obtain a special license to sell her own house.
    c. hire a licensed agent to sell her house.
    d. obtain her broker's permission.

66. A landlord is also a licensee and has had a fair housing complaint filed against him. His hearing will be held before
    a. the 9-member Real Estate Board.
    b. the 11-member Fair Housing Board.
    c. the 8-member Real Estate Board.
    d. a combined session of both the Fair Housing and Real Estate Boards.

67. ADA standards must be met in all of the following EXCEPT
    a. the entry lobby to a condominium.
    b. a common area swimming pool.
    c. a second floor residence in a building without an elevator.
    d. a real estate office.

68. At foreclosure, a tax lien has priority over all other liens EXCEPT
    a. the deed of trust.
    b. court costs.
    c. a mechanic's lien.
    d. a landlord's lien for rent.

69. A young handicapped woman needs the skills of her service spider monkey. With rent of $1,550, her landlord can charge a pet deposit of
    a. $55.
    b. $310.
    c. $1,550.
    d. none of these.

70. Fannie Mae and Freddie Mac are regulated by
    a. FHA.
    b. FHFA.
    c. VHDA.
    d. USDA.

71. All of the following transfers of property are exempt from the Virginia Residential Property Disclosure Act EXCEPT
    a. a transfer made pursuant to a court order.
    b. a transfer made between two co-owners.
    c. a transfer made without the assistance of a real estate broker.
    d. a transfer made to or from a government entity.

72. The Common Interest Community (CIC) Board is a separate agency under
    a. the Code of Virginia.
    b. the VAC.
    c. the REB.
    d. the DPOR.

73. All of the following aspects of Virginia's law of agency are true EXCEPT
    a. all brokerage agreements must be in writing.
    b. a licensee may represent both parties in the same transaction.
    c. acting as a dual agent or representative terminates any prior or future relationship.
    d. a broker may assign two agents in the firm to work on the same transaction as designated agents.

74. A limited service agent is required to
    a. have a brokerage agreement in writing.
    b. provide a list of services to be provided.
    c. provide a list of services of a standard agent that will not be provided.
    d. have a signed independent contractor agreement.

75. Property management agreements must be in writing and include all of the following EXCEPT
    a. a definite termination date.
    b. the amount of management fees and how they will be paid.
    c. the services to be rendered.
    d. a proposed operational budget.

ANSWER KEY

Chapter 1: Virginia Real Estate Law

1. **(d)** The principal is the client with whom the broker has an established brokerage relationship.
2. **(c)** By Virginia statutory definition, a salesperson may perform all of the functions listed except serve as a managing broker.
3. **(c)** Since there can only be one principal broker, all others are associate brokers whether or not they are in a managerial or supervisory position.
4. **(c)** When a licensee acts as an independent contractor and not as a standard agent, a written agreement governs the relationship between the licensee and the client, not the statute.
5. **(a)** An individual who wants to sell her own house does not need a real estate license.
6. **(d)** The branch office license must be displayed in the branch office.
7. **(c)** Every officer of a firm who actively participates in real estate brokerage must be licensed.
8. **(c)** The Virginia Real Estate Transaction Recovery Fund was established to protect consumers from suffering monetary loss due to the misconduct of a licensee.
9. **(b)** A balance of $400,000 must be maintained in the Transaction Recovery Fund.
10. **(a)** The maximum amount that any single claimant may receive is $20,000.
11. **(c)** The REB regulations are found in the Virginia Administrative Code with references to the Code of Virginia.
12. **(d)** The Residential Property Disclosure Act is still regulated by the Real Estate Board.
13. **(d)** The requirements for Common Interest Community managers do not include mandatory training for 100% of all employees.
14. **(b)** The Residential Property Disclosure Act also applies to transfers made without the assistance of a licensed real estate broker.
15. **(c)** The list of seller representations is found on the Real Estate Board website.
16. **(c)** The contract may be terminated within three days from hand delivery, five days from postmark, or prior to settlement.
17. **(a)** Federal Emergency Management Agency (FEMA) flood maps indicate that flood insurance is required in order to obtain approval for a mortgage loan.
18. **(b)** The exemption to the National Do Not Call Registry is within three months of a consumer inquiry.
19. **(d)** Selection of the settlement agent is not part of the office policy or procedures of a brokerage firm.
20. **(a)** FACTA does not require that client records be returned to the client, but does specify how such records must be disposed of.

Chapter 2: Brokerage Relationships and Agency

1. **(d)** An agency relationship could best be described as one in which a licensee acts for or represents another person in a real estate transaction.
2. **(c)** Routine services that do not create an agency relationship are called *ministerial acts*.
3. **(a)** A brokerage relationship can be terminated by any of the reasons listed except one party unilaterally firing the other party.
4. **(c)** The seller is not liable for misrepresentations made by a licensee.
5. **(d)** When both buyer and seller are represented by agents from different firms, no agency disclosure is required.
6. **(d)** In this scenario, both seller and buyer are (potential) clients of the broker. The broker has the option to make designated agents of both salespersons; the broker remains the dual agent.
7. **(d)** The listing agent doesn't have to make an agency disclosure to the prospective buyer because she is already in an agency relationship with another agent. (A reminder that the listing agent solely represents the seller is still a good idea.)
8. **(d)** Because no specific property was discussed, no disclosure was required.

9. **(c)** A licensee is not required to always be obedient to the client's demands.

10. **(a)** Only sellers and landlords would require marketing of their property.

11. **(c)** "Physical condition of the property" is confined to the limits of the lot and property being sold.

12. **(d)** Disclosing any confidential information is a violation of the duty to a client.

13. **(a)** This listing must be declined because it violates REB regulations, which state that net listings are prohibited.

14. **(b)** July 1, 2008, is the correct way to enter the termination date on a listing form.

15. **(d)** Oral agreements are legal in Virginia, but not enforceable based on the Statute of Frauds, which requires the sale of property to be in writing.

Chapter 3: Interests and Forms of Ownership

1. **(c)** A change in a county ordinance does not constitute the exercise of eminent domain by the process of condemnation.

2. **(d)** A 52-foot sailboat purchased during the marriage cannot be excluded from an augmented estate.

3. **(d)** The householder is entitled to keep the $5,000 exemption in addition to the family bible, wedding rings, and burial plots.

4. **(d)** Inconvenience is not a basis for an easement by necessity.

5. **(d)** The couple owned the real property as tenants by entirety survivorship. The husband's creditors have no claim on the property.

6. **(d)** Virginia is not a community property state.

7. **(a)** Tenants by the entirety is reserved strictly for married couples.

8. **(b)** Contracts for the initial purchase of a condominium may be rescinded without penalty 10 days after the later of contract ratification or receipt of the POS (Public Offering Statement).

9. **(a)** If a condominium unit owner fails to pay the owners' association's assessment against his unit, the owners' association may place a lien against the unit.

10. **(a)** After hand-delivery of the documents, buyer B will have three days to cancel the contract.

11. **(b)** When the owner's interest in a time-share includes either a freehold interest or an estate for years, it is a time-share estate.

12. **(c)** If he decides to make an offer on the property, he will have seven days after ratification of the contract to cancel the contract without penalty.

13. **(c)** The couple can cancel the contract within three days after receiving the POA disclosure packet.

14. **(a)** Both the Condominium Act and the Property Owner Association Act have a set limit of $150 for two hard copies, $25 for an additional copy, and $50 for an expedite fee.

15. **(b)** The Common Interest Community Board (CIC) is charged with the administration of the Virginia Property Owners' Association Act.

Chapter 4: Real Estate Taxes and Other Liens

1. **(a)** Tax rates and assessments must be uniformly applied to similar properties.

2. **(b)** For real estate tax purposes, they will be classified differently, according to use.

3. **(a)** A non-profit burial ground is exempt, but not a for-profit cemetery.

4. **(d)** Taxes on new construction are not based on comparable values in an area.

5. **(a)** In Virginia, the buyer owns a property (for real estate tax purposes) on the date of sale (not true in all states).

6. **(c)** Property tax liens have first priority.

7. **(c)** A mechanic may wait no more than 90 days after the work was done before filing a mechanic's lien.

8. **(b)** A mechanic has six months to enforce a lien by filing suit.

9. **(a)** Specific language must be included in all sales contracts.

10. **(d)** A creditor on a judgment must enforce the judgment within 20 years once it is rendered.

11. **(d)** A lien against the property of a resident decedent remains enforceable for 10 years.

12. **(c)** The name of a prospective purchaser is not necessary for a lis pendens.

Chapter 5: Real Estate Contracts

1. **(d)** The description does not enclose a parcel of land.
2. **(d)** The fact that Block F has only six lots and the street address is Lot 5 is enough correct information to permit identification. The deed is valid.
3. **(a)** A lender may use the services of either licensed or exempt surveyors, but the lender cannot require that a particular surveyor conduct the survey.
4. **(d)** A survey that shows the location of the house, the garage, the fence, utility lines, and the children's playhouse in the backyard is most likely an as-built survey.
5. **(d)** The Statute of Frauds requires a written contract to be enforceable, but the parties are free to comply with its terms.
6. **(c)** There is no set standard form for a sales contract.
7. **(c)** The age of the parties is immaterial to the contract unless one is a minor.
8. **(c)** A contingency for a well and septic inspection would depend on the property.
9. **(c)** Any property built before 1978 may have lead-based paint and requires disclosure of the hazards.
10. **(c)** A contingency for a home inspection is always a good idea but is not required by law.
11. **(c)** Virginia law states that the buyer is responsible, but most contracts provide that the seller remains responsible.
12. **(c)** The builder is subject to an implied warranty against foundation defects for 5 to 10 years.
13. **(c)** *Marketable* and *insurable* are not synonymous. Insurable title may list exceptions that will not be covered.
14. **(a)** The builder implied warranty covers the dwelling and its fixtures for one year.
15. **(d)** Because the spouse might make a later claim, the buyer would have to accept a deed that remains subject to that interest.

Chapter 6: Real Estate Financing

1. **(c)** When borrowers sign a note and deed of trust, they give the lender the right to initiate a non-judicial (no court) foreclosure in case of default.
2. **(c)** The lender has the responsibility for preparing the note and deed of trust involved in a closing.
3. **(a)** CFPB was created to protect the interests of the consumer.
4. **(b)** The maximum late charge of 5% may be assessed on a mortgage loan payment.
5. **(b)** If a payment is made on June 18, the lender can legally impose a late charge, but no more than $77.25 (5% of ¹⁄₁₂ of $18,540).
6. **(d)** A HELOC (Home Equity Line of Credit) permits the borrower to receive advances from time to time up to a maximum amount secured by real property.
7. **(d)** Nothing in the new CFPB rules requires a lender to grant any moratorium on payments.
8. **(b)** The primary purpose of the Virginia Housing Development Authority is to make housing more affordable for low-income and moderate-income buyers.
9. **(c)** VHDA funding is derived from the sale of bonds in the private sector.
10. **(a)** VHDA does not provide funding for schools.
11. **(b)** The Virginia Residential Landlord and Tenant Act is covered under the Code of Virginia.
12. **(a)** The expenses of executing the trust, including a commission to the trustee, must be paid first.
13. **(d)** A bankruptcy sale is not a method of foreclosure.
14. **(b)** Sale must be no earlier than 8 days after first advertisement, and no later than 30 days after last advertisement.
15. **(d)** The HAMP program was created in 2009 and has helped some consumers avoid foreclosure.

Chapter 7: Transfer of Title

1. **(c)** Failure of all grantors to sign would most likely invalidate a deed.
2. **(d)** The heir will not win because a person is presumed competent unless a court has ruled otherwise.
3. **(a)** Any affidavits or sworn statements the seller is required to deliver at the closing must be signed by the seller.

4. **(c)** The seller is expected to pay grantor tax of $0.50 per $500 of purchase price.

5. **(c)** Entering an orchard and taking apples every October would not constitute *possession* of the property.

6. **(b)** The witnesses signed the will; therefore, the will is valid.

7. **(d)** The seller of real property is required to have marketable title at closing.

8. **(b)** Because the seller has a reasonable time to correct defects, the contract is still in effect.

9. **(b)** According to Real Estate Settlement Agents (RESA) law, the selection of a settlement agent is made by the buyer.

10. **(d)** The listing agent is not required to determine whether a seller has marketable title at the time a property is held out for sale.

11. **(c)** A full title search goes back 60 years.

12. **(a)** A change from a fee simple to a life estate may not be accomplished by using a correction deed.

13. **(b)** In cases where title must be cleared by having correction deeds signed, the seller is responsible for locating the parties who must sign.

14. **(c)** The buyer should be worried because judgment liens remain against the property.

15. **(b)** Discovery that an unreleased deed of trust still shows on the county records is most likely because the lender neglected to have a deed of release signed and recorded.

Chapter 8: Virginia's Real Estate License Law

1. **(d)** The Real Estate Board consists of nine members: seven licensees and two consumers.

2. **(d)** The Virginia Property Owners Association Act is administered by the Common Interest Community (CIC) Board.

3. **(c)** A limited service agent must list the duties that will be done and those duties expected of a standard agent that will not be done.

4. **(c)** If she wants to remain licensed, she must apply for reinstatement of her license and pay the current reinstatement fee.

5. **(d)** Real estate licenses are renewed in Virginia biennially, on the last day of the month in which issued.

6. **(b)** An active licensed broker who has been licensed in Virginia since 1975 is not exempt from the continuing education requirements on the basis of having been licensed for more than 15 years.

7. **(a)** If a broker establishes an account to hold money belonging to others, all checks, deposit slips, and bank statements must include the word *escrow* as part of the account name.

8. **(c)** Earnest money deposits may not be distributed from the broker's escrow account when requested by one party's attorney.

9. **(c)** The broker may not borrow money from the escrow account of one of the other properties to make the repairs.

10. **(d)** The name of the broker/firm must appear on all For Sale signs placed on property by a broker.

11. **(d)** Online disclosure requirements require that she include on each page her name, her firm's name and address, and the jurisdiction in which her firm is licensed.

12. **(b)** Based on these facts, both the conviction and the broker's failure to notify the REB within 30 days violate REB regulations.

13. **(d)** In this situation, accepting the money is a violation of REB regulations because monies must be paid through the broker.

14. **(b)** This is not a violation of the license law if the fee is disclosed in writing to the parties to the contract but may be considered a violation under RESPA and should be avoided.

15. **(d)** Non-licensed persons cannot be paid for a referral.

16. **(d)** When a sole proprietor has her license suspended for two years, all licenses affiliated with the proprietor must be returned to the REB.

17. **(a)** When a salesperson is alleged to have violated the license law, possibly resulting in disciplinary action, an investigation will be conducted by the REB.

18. **(b)** All incoming fees must be paid to the broker.

19. **(b)** Bait and switch advertising is prohibited under the REB Rules and Regulations as misrepresentation.

20. **(a)** The maximum monetary penalty imposed by the REB is $2,500.

Chapter 9: Leasing Real Estate in Virginia

1. **(d)** The secretary of the Commonwealth will receive these notices.
2. **(d)** 120 days' notice is required to terminate the tenants' month-to-month leases.
3. **(d)** No, because the tenant is not at fault. She is entitled to release from the lease or a reduction in rent until her use of the land is restored.
4. **(a)** The landlord's lien attaches to the tenant's property on April 1, 2015.
5. **(d)** If the tenant decides not to sign a lease, all sums in excess of the landlord's actual expenses must be returned to the prospective tenant.
6. **(c)** The maximum amount the landlord can require as a security deposit is $1,500 (two months' security).
7. **(a)** Legislation in 2014 made the "trigger" for application of VRLTA two rental properties in addition to a personal residence, effective throughout Virginia. Formerly, the number was four rental properties in an urban area and 10 statewide.
8. **(c)** The tenant needs to inform the landlord, and the tenant must also give the landlord instructions and passwords.
9. **(d)** Nothing because he is in the military.
10. **(d)** Within five days of occupancy, the landlord must disclose in writing the existence of any visible evidence of mold in the dwelling.
11. **(b)** The tenant has seven days to give written notice to the landlord.
12. **(d)** The landlord can require that a tenant pay damage and renter's insurance premiums.
13. **(b)** The woman's properties are not subject to the VRLTA because only two of her properties will be subject to a lease.
14. **(c)** A landlord may not prohibit the lawful possession of a firearm.
15. **(d)** Article 6 of the VRLTA deals with retaliatory action.

Chapter 10: Virginia Fair Housing Law

1. **(b)** Familial status is protected by the Virginia Fair Housing Law. Age is not a protected category but elderliness is.
2. **(b)** A 62-year-old cocaine user is not protected by the Virginia Fair Housing Law's provisions.
3. **(d)** Even though it is an owner-occupied four-unit building, the owner may not discriminate in advertising against any protected class.
4. **(c)** Male or female can be specified when sharing one's own home.
5. **(b)** The building manager cannot lawfully refuse to rent an apartment to him because his criminal conviction did not involve harm to persons or property.
6. **(c)** The rental company was guilty of the unlawful discriminatory housing practice of false representation.
7. **(d)** Senior housing where at least one occupant of 80% of the dwellings is 55 years old is exempt from the familial status category.
8. **(b)** Based on these facts alone, if both applicants are turned down, the lender has most likely committed unlawful discrimination against the 35-year-old black female only.
9. **(c)** Investigations of fair housing complaints must be completed within 100 days after a complaint is filed.
10. **(c)** A first violation of the Virginia Fair Housing Law could subject a guilty party to a monetary civil penalty of up to $50,000 for a first offense.
11. **(a)** The licensee's case will be heard before the Real Estate Board because she is a Virginia licensee.
12. **(c)** The Fair Housing Board consists of 12 members with 3 citizen members.
13. **(d)** A landlord is required to allow a handicapped tenant to make alterations to the property, but the tenant must pay for the changes and restore them at the end of the lease.
14. **(d)** Under the fair housing law, a religious cross or symbol is deemed discriminatory if printed on a licensee's business card.
15. **(c)** The Fair Housing Board is the recipient for fair housing complaints for non-licensees. The REB receives complaints for Virginia licensees.

Practice Examination

1. **(d)** In this situation, each of the salespersons will be a designated agent.
2. **(c)** Any officer of a firm that specializes in listing commercial property must hold a real estate license in Virginia.

3. **(a)** The duties that an agent owes to his client are established by Virginia's agency statute.

4. **(b)** The death of the salesperson is not a way to terminate a brokerage relationship. The relationship is established between the broker and the client.

5. **(c)** As of July 2011, the Residential Property Disclosure Statement is provided on the REB website in order to be sure that the most current form is used.

6. **(c)** If the buyer receives the required Residential Property Disclosure Statement three days after the contract is signed, the buyer can terminate the contract within five days of postmark, if mailed.

7. **(b)** If a married woman with three children dies intestate, her property will be distributed one-third to her husband, and the remaining two-thirds equally to her children.

8. **(b)** The Virginia homestead exemption is $5,000, regardless of the value of any property owned.

9. **(c)** If a wife renounces the will to claim her elective share, she will now be entitled to one-third of his estate.

10. **(d)** When one joint tenant sells his interest, the remaining owners continue to be joint tenants but are tenants in common with the new purchaser.

11. **(a)** Any interest as a tenant in common passes to the heirs whether by will or the law of descent and distribution.

12. **(d)** A plat showing the building location is not required in the Condominium Disclosure Packet.

13. **(c)** They will be able to cancel this contract if they cancel within three days of receiving the POA disclosure packet by hand or electronic delivery or five days from postmark.

14. **(d)** The example is a lot-and-block kind of legal description.

15. **(b)** A combination of the metes-and-bounds and lot-and-block methods is the most common description of real estate in Virginia.

16. **(c)** If a contractor records a mechanic's memorandum of lien on September 15, 2014, he will have six months to file a suit to enforce it.

17. **(a)** The real estate tax lien will be paid first.

18. **(d)** The wife is required to release any future interest in the property she might hold.

19. **(b)** An implied warranty against structural defects on new construction continues for one year after the date of transfer of title or the buyer's taking possession.

20. **(a)** The signature of the grantee is not a requirement for a valid deed.

21. **(d)** Adverse possession requires unauthorized, hostile, and continuous use over a period of 15 years. Tacking is not permitted.

22. **(a)** The niece will receive title to the property after the will has gone through probate court.

23. **(d)** Under the Wet Settlement Act, Virginia requires that a deed of trust be recorded, and all settlement proceeds be distributed within two days of the date of settlement.

24. **(b)** The buyer's full legal name is not found on a title report.

25. **(d)** The sale of a property to a relative for $1 with a recorded deed could cause a gap in the chain of title.

26. **(c)** An independent contractor is a licensee representing a client according to a written agreement and does not have the duties of a standard agent.

27. **(c)** The Real Estate Board members are appointed by the governor.

28. **(d)** An applicant has to apply for a license within one year of passing the Virginia licensing exam before being required to retake the exam.

29. **(a)** The Real Estate Board may not impose a prison sentence on a licensee.

30. **(b)** The activities of the Real Estate Board include the issuance of real estate licenses.

31. **(d)** She will not have met her renewal education requirements because she has failed to take the 8-hour mandatory course, which includes 2 hours of fair housing law, and meet the requirement for a total of 16 continuing education hours.

32. **(b)** He will need to send the Real Estate Board the current annual fee for reinstatement for his renewal fee.

33. **(b)** All applicants must submit a set of fingerprints along with their license examination.

34. **(c)** A salesperson may change brokerage firms by filling out the application, obtaining the new broker's signature, and sending the form with appropriate fee to the REB.

35. **(a)** She should disclose her license status because disclosure is required regardless of an inactive license status.

36. **(d)** He should immediately give the check to his broker. The broker is responsible for placing the check in an escrow account.

37. **(d)** A salesperson selling as For Sale By Owner with disclosure that the owner is licensed is not required to include the name of the broker in all advertising.

38. **(c)** If the Real Estate Transaction Recovery Fund falls below $400,000, the Real Estate Board can assess $20 from each salesperson and broker, inactive or active.

39. **(b)** Failing to maintain all signed documents for a period of three years is not considered improper delivery of instruments. It is, however, a violation of the REB regarding the retention of records.

40. **(b)** In Virginia, VA and FHA notes require notarization to be valid.

41. **(c)** One of the primary functions of the Virginia Housing Development Authority (VHDA) is to provide housing financing for low- and moderate-income residents of Virginia.

42. **(b)** A foreclosure of a deed of trust could be achieved without court action or sale of the property through a deed in lieu of foreclosure where the lender accepts the deed and forgives the debt.

43. **(a)** The present tenants have the right to continue their lease under current terms.

44. **(a)** Interest is not accrued on security deposits as of 2015. No interest has been required since 2009.

45. **(c)** The Virginia Residential Landlord and Tenant Act applies to all apartment building rentals.

46. **(a)** If a tenant leaves one couch and two chairs in his apartment after the lease has ended, the landlord is allowed to sell them if the tenant is given 10 days' written notice.

47. **(a)** A 58-year-old AIDS victim is protected by Virginia's Fair Housing Law. While age, per

se, is not protected, disability and elderliness (55 years or older) are.

48. **(d)** A landlord will not be in violation of the Virginia Fair Housing Law if he refuses to rent his two-bedroom apartment to applicants who do not have adequate income.

49. **(c)** Removing walls along a corridor of a common area to make the hallway wide enough for wheelchair access in an apartment building is not considered a reasonable request.

50. **(d)** An injured party has one year to file a complaint with the REB if an alleged fair housing discriminatory act has taken place.

51. **(b)** As of July 1, 2012, all brokerage agreements with either seller or buyer must be in writing.

52. **(d)** Proceeding with the sale without full disclosure to both seller and buyer is undisclosed dual agency, which is prohibited.

53. **(c)** Continuing education requirement for brokers is 24 hours (8 required, 8 elective, and 8 on broker supervision and management).

54. **(b)** Tenants in common will give the wife the ability to will her interest in the property to her grandchildren.

55. **(d)** If the landlord is found guilty of discrimination, the maximum amount he could be fined is $100,000 for two violations ($50,000 each). Familial status and the elderly are both protected.

56. **(d)** VHDA funding comes from bonds sold through the private sector.

57. **(d)** A nonresident landlord with properties subject to the VRLTA must appoint a resident agent.

58. **(d)** After 13 months, a landlord must pay interest on a security deposit.

59. **(c)** In no case may the landlord receive more than two months' rent as a security deposit. All units rent for $995 per month. The maximum the landlord can receive as a security deposit is $1,990; $995 × 2 = $1,990. Insurance is not part of the security deposit.

60. **(b)** A landlord could safely decline to rent to a handicapped person who requires major modifications for living and accessibility and wants the landlord to pay for it.

61. **(d)** The Fair Housing Board only deals with non-licensees. Licensees are disciplined under the Real Estate Board.
62. **(d)** The agent will probably work for the company as an independent contractor according to a written contract.
63. **(d)** The unlicensed wife will only be able to design and mail brochures for the agent; all of the other activities will require licensure.
64. **(d)** An owner can sell his house himself; a license is not required, but he must not advertise in a discriminatory way.
65. **(a)** She must disclose that she is licensed.
66. **(a)** His hearing will be held before the Real Estate Board because he is a licensee.
67. **(c)** ADA standards only apply to areas of public use or according to standards for new construction; they are only required in first floor units in buildings without an elevator.
68. **(b)** Court costs must always be paid first.
69. **(d)** The landlord may not charge a pet deposit when the animal is a service animal and not a pet.
70. **(b)** As a result of the financial crisis starting in 2007, Fannie Mae and Freddie Mac were placed under the regulation of the Federal Housing Finance Agency.
71. **(c)** Except for a few states' exemptions, all transfers of residential property are subject to the Residential Property Disclosure Act whether sold with the assistance of a real estate broker or not.
72. **(d)** The Common Interest Community Board falls under the authority of the Department of Professional and Occupational Regulation as does the Real Estate Board.
73. **(c)** Acting as a dual agent or representative does not terminate any prior or future relationship with either party to the transaction.
74. **(d)** A limited service agent is still a form of agency and does not require an independent contractor agreement.
75. **(d)** The proposed operational budget would not be included in the property management agreement itself.

Index

Notes

Notes

Notes

Notes

Notes